THE AUTHOR
Adventure

ENDORSEMENTS

"As someone who has helped dozens of authors write their books, I can confidently say *The Author Adventure* is what any new author needs to get the job done. Jaime Fleres does a tremendous job addressing the common hurdles every first-time author faces and laying out a clear path forward, full of encouragement, introspection, and inspiration. This book is like having a book coach in your back pocket. A must-read for any author embarking on the challenging yet supremely rewarding journey of writing that first book."

—AMANDA JOHNSON

author of *Becoming Enough* and *Becoming Free*, book doula, and founder of Awaken Village Press

"*The Author Adventure* by Jaime Fleres is a comprehensive body of work deeply grounded in the body of the writer. As we breathe in the essence of a book idea, we embody the skin of our story, tapping into our own inner genius, unleashing our unique self-expression. Fleres generously pours everything she has into this important foundation, sharing the tools, insight, and strategies you need to create, publish, and market your book."

—STANLEY DANKOSKI

ghostwriter, book mentor, editor, and founder of The Grounded Writer

"I love Jaime's no-nonsense approach to writing and publishing a book. She nails it with this essential guide, providing actionable content in a fashion that allows authors to hit the ground running. At the same time, she covers her topic broadly enough to give writers the perspective they need to create a great manuscript and then get it published. As a bonus, she has packed her knowledge in a delightful layout that any author would be proud to emulate. I highly recommend this book!"

—EVERETT O'KEEFE

WSJ and USAToday Bestselling Author, Founder of Ignite Press

"As someone who has firsthand experience working with Jaime to bring my publishing dreams to life, I can say working with her was one of the most magnificent collaborations I've ever experienced. Jaime truly understands the deep and holistic work involved to bring one's writing creations into their most impeccable and beautiful fulfillment. I am so joyous that she's offering her mastery in this field in her stunning book *The Author Adventure*, which now allows the wider world to engage her genius in the convenience and awesomeness of this incredible book. Herein, authors will find so much encouragement, skillful guidance, inspiring wisdom, and so much more to give them all-encompassing know-how to bring their books to life with success and grace. Jaime's writing is so sagacious and playfully insightful, making it captivatingly engaging. This is a true masterclass and a gift to all authors out there looking to further empower their writing and publishing skills!"

—DARREN AUSTIN HALL, Author of *Love's Revolution*

WRITE, EDIT, AND PUBLISH A BOOK
THAT TRANSFORMS LIVES

THE
AUTHOR
Adventure

JAIME FLERES

WHALE SONG

Whale Song Press
Asheville, North Carolina
www.whalesongcreative.com

Copyright © by Jaime Fleres

All rights reserved. No part of this book may be shared, reproduced or utilized in any form or by any means, electronic, or mechanical, including photocopying, recording, or by any information storage and retrieval system, without permission in writing from the author. No part of this book may be used or reproduced to train artificial intelligence technologies or systems.

ISBN: 978-0-9991637-0-2 (print)
ISBN: 978-0-9991637-1-9 (eBook)

Proofread by Jennifer Jas
Design and layout by The Book Designers

To order bulk copies of this book for use in your own programs and offerings, please contact Jaime via her website: JaimeFleres.com. You can also direct other inquiries there, via the contact page. Thank you.

I dedicate this book to every writer I've been blessed to work with—from the freshmen students in my first semester teaching college writing at San Diego State University, to the teams I've led in the professional writing world, to the hundreds of amazing authors I've served as a book coach, editor, and publishing guide through my work as Whale Song's founder and chief steward.

You inspire me daily with your courage and creativity, and I am so grateful for you. I love seeing my bookcase lined with all the books we created together and knowing I get to add many more to the shelves. Thank you for trusting me to accompany you on your author adventure.

To the creatives, change-makers, visionaries, intuitives, and healers I am blessed to companion on their journeys—this book is in your honor.

CONTENTS

Introduction 1

SECTION ONE: AUTHOR ACTIVATION 7

1.1 Inner Author Support 9
Chapter 1: Creative Manifesto 11
Chapter 2: The Creative Life Cycle 15
Chapter 3: Working with the Inner Critic 19
Chapter 4: Activating Your Inner Genius 29

1.2 Essential Groundwork 37
Chapter 5: Anchoring in Your Why 39
Chapter 6: Audience Focus 49
Chapter 7: Your Book Concept 61
Chapter 8: Back-of-Book Visioning 67

1.3 Structural Support 77
Chapter 9: Structural Framework Overview 79
Chapter 10: Frameworks for Nonfiction 83
Chapter 11: Frameworks for Memoir 91
Chapter 12: Story-Based Frameworks 97

1.4 Organizing and Outlining 107
Chapter 13: Organizing Your Ideas 109
Chapter 14: Outline or Working Table of Contents 115

1.5 Action Plan 119
Chapter 15: Fitting a Book Into Your Life 121
Chapter 16: Rhythms and Rituals of Writing 137

SECTION TWO: ROCK YOUR FIRST DRAFT 145

Chapter 17: First Draft Best Practices 147
Chapter 18: Principles of Composition 153
Chapter 19: Chapter Structure 157
Chapter 20: Book Introductions 163
Chapter 21: Stylistic and Linguistic Choices 169
Chapter 22: Persuasive Writing Strategies 173
Chapter 23: Summarizing, Quoting, and Transitions 183
Chapter 24: Scenes and Summaries in Stories 189
Chapter 25: Layers of a Story 195
Chapter 26: Dialogue and Beats 205

SECTION THREE: SELF-EDITING SUPERSTAR 211

Chapter 27: Overview of Self-Editing 213
Chapter 28: Self-Editing Best Practices 217
Chapter 29: Review and Appreciate 223
Chapter 30: Revision 227
Chapter 31: Beta Readers 237
Chapter 32: Refinement 241
Chapter 33: Final Polishing 247
Chapter 34: Comma Police 251
Chapter 35: Professional Editing 259
Chapter 36: Anatomy of a Book 263

SECTION FOUR: CHOOSE YOUR PUBLISHING PATH 269

Chapter 37: Explore Your Publishing Options 271
Chapter 38: Publishing: Key Factors to Consider 281
Chapter 39: Traditional Publishing Path........................289
Chapter 40: Book Proposals 297
Chapter 41: Indie Publishing Path 309
Chapter 42: Book Marketing and Promotion 317

Conclusion 323

APPENDICES 325
Appendix A: Audience Consideration 327
Appendix B: Sketchy First Drafts 333
Appendix C: Research...337
Appendix D: Fair Use and Permissions 347
Appendix E: How to Get Endorsements 349

Acknowledgments 355
About the Author 357
Notes..359
Invitation for Writing Support.................................365

INTRODUCTION

Welcome to *The Author Adventure*, a practical and experientially-based travel guide for the adventurous and courageous creative—designed to meet and support you on the journey of writing your transformational nonfiction book. I often say that writing a book is much more like a wilderness adventure than a neat subway jaunt across town, and this book is meant to be your map, your compass, and your sherpa, all in one.

In my years of experience working with authors, one thing I find time and again is that writing a book is a personal journey of transformation—*first* for the author, then for their readers. Writing a book takes us on a profound journey—where we are invited to revisit the wisdom we pour onto the page to receive it again ourselves, come face-to-face with some of our biggest fears and working growth edges, dare to step deeper into our unique medicine, and become more of who we are.

If you have felt the call to write a nonfiction book or memoir and have no idea how to get started or what to do next, you are in the right place. If you've done this before but know you could use more support to vastly improve your process, you are in the right place.

In my professional work as a book coach, editor and publishing partner, I work closely with healers, coaches, therapists, entrepreneurs, visionaries and change agents seeking to write nonfiction and memoir books in the realms of self-help, personal growth, spirituality, relationships, healing, and navigating the Wilds of human life. These folks are my primary audience for this book, and their work is what I mean by *transformational* nonfiction. If you're here to change lives, your own and others', with a story or message your soul seeks to share beyond the confines of your own heart and mind, you've come to the right place.

What is Unique About *The Author Adventure*?

This book is different from others on the market because it will get you into action and move you along the journey of authorship in the order that you will likely need this material. It is a reference guide you can reach for when you need specific, actionable guidance on the next leg of your journey. It is not fluffy or particularly hand-holding, and though I am a book coach who offers heaps of warm attunement and soul-level accompaniment to clients, that is not the tone of this book. This is a straight-to-business, nuts-and-bolts compilation of the resources I use to guide every client we work with at Whale Song. It is the yang to my coaching yin. It is here to provide the tools and information you need to write a strong book and find your way through your author adventure.

I originally designed this book as a manual to help my author-clients via private book coaching, small-group immersions, and author retreats. I will continue to use this resource for those purposes (in fact, it may be why you are reading these words right now!), but I also wanted to make it available to a broader audience of writers seeking guidance. Learning the ins and outs of writing a book is something most of us have never encountered before, and there is much to learn and explore. This book is your map of the terrain. And I am grateful to be your guide.

How This Work is Informed

This work is born out of my twenty-plus years helping writers professionally—as a professional writer, copywriting department manager, university writing professor, book coach, and guide to wise and wild creatives. I began birthing this body of work in my early years as the founder of Whale Song, a creative agency that helps folks like you write, edit, and publish their books. I've been refining and tinkering ever since. That you are reading this means I finally let it go, however imperfect or incomplete, and let it make its way into your hands—and that thrills me.

The guidance contained herein is deeply informed by the advanced post-baccalaureate academic studies I completed in the art of communication (called *rhetoric*, though the layperson doesn't use this term as do word-nerds in a master's program). After earning my master's in Teaching Writing (yes, that is a thing), I was a college professor at three universities in California and Minnesota. This experience not only taught me how to think about and develop writing skills in myself and others, but it also forged me in the fires of how to actually help people improve their writing. I have loved bringing the expertise I developed as a college professor into this work. You will get value from this book that you won't find elsewhere, given my extensive academic background in the art of persuasive writing.

This work is also informed by my lifelong love of personal growth and healing practices. I am a certified Integrative Somatic Trauma Practitioner, international facilitator of embodied movement (dance/Qoya, yoga, and somatic healing), trained Shamanic practitioner, astrologer, sound healer, and soul guide. I am devoted to the path of personal and collective wholeness and well-being. Given this aspect of who I am and my teaching style, you will see meditations, movement practices, art activities, rhythms and rituals, and other practice invitations woven into this book to support your authorship experience.

How This Book is Organized

The book is divided into four sections that explore how to PLAN for your book, WRITE your book, EDIT your book, and PUBLISH your book.

SECTION ONE: Author Activation is intended to help you lay a strong foundation for your writing. Many authors want to skip this stage, but the work done here *is* what will set you up for success in all subsequent stages of your writing adventure. If you are ritual or ceremonially minded, think of this as the essential preparation you do before a ceremony. It's the most important part! If you are not so inclined, think of this work as akin to the preparation you'd do before giving a talk in your area of expertise. A little extra time here will yield benefits; just don't make the work of this section a substitute for actually moving into the *writing*. This section covers crucial Inner Author groundwork, your audience, your concept, how to organize your book ideas, how to develop a working Table of Contents or outline, and how to fit writing into your busy life in a way that is feasible and feels good.

SECTION TWO: **Rock Your First Draft** is designed to help you during the first-draft writing process. It explores best practices for this phase of your journey and gives you practical and valuable tips on making your writing clear, strong, and effective and avoiding major pitfalls. Its topics include how to build authority in your writing, use storytelling (all authors need this), appeal to your reader's emotions, effectively bring in the ideas and words of others, and structure your chapters and introduction.

SECTION THREE: **Self-Editing Superstar** is a behind-the-scenes look at the process that professional editors use to strengthen and refine a manuscript. This work is valuable to engage in after you've written your first draft and before you hand it off to your editor. Your preliminary polishing will make all the difference in how much value you can get out of the professional editorial process. This section also covers beta readers and what to include in your book beyond the "meat" of it.

SECTION FOUR: **Choose Your Publishing Path** is designed to help you decide whether you will traditionally or independently publish your book and give you high-level insight into what these processes entail. Why did I place this section *after* the foundational writing and editing sections? Because many of the authors we work with are interested in developing their manuscript first, before deciding on how they will publish it. That said, some authors seek a publisher before they complete their manuscript. (You'll still need much of the material in Sections One, Two, and Three to be able to write a strong book proposal.) You're welcome to skip to this section if publishing is top of mind. We dispel myths and talk truth about your publishing options, discuss how to find agents and publishers, review the self-publishing process, and get acquainted with book proposals.

How to Work with This Book (Read This Part!)

Here's the deal: the author's adventure is *full* of potential off-ramps and reasons to feel overwhelmed. Writing a book is like having a child—there is never a perfect time, and the amount of energy and resources required to nurture this being into its maturity is substantial. It's not a logical decision (even if you are writing a book connected to your business, and it makes sense from a strategy perspective). Books require a lot of energy and effort. I remember those pregnancy and new-mother books I read when pregnant with my daughter. They contained so much information about *all* the stages of this massive transformational journey into motherhood. To take it all in at once was overwhelming. I was only ready to take one bite at a time, appropriate to the stage of the journey I was in.

This book is similar. This adventure guide is packed with information you'll need on your journey—but not all at once. I strongly suggest you take one bite of this book at a time and just the next bite that you need. Don't try to read this thing all at once (I mean, you can—*free will*, after all—but it might not serve you). This is not a binge-worthy book (no offense to myself) like the one you might write. It's meant for you to dip in, get what you need, and then get back to your writing process.

Make this book work for you. If you find yourself feeling daunted or overwhelmed, put the book down and do something you love. Then come back when you're ready to take the next tolerable right step. If you get stuck, check out Chapters 3 and 4. Do the practices. Do the meditations and connect to your Inner Author and your book's consciousness. You might also head to Chapters 15 and 16 to create an actionable plan that will support you in this process. Slow down if it serves you, down to a crawl if needed, but keep going. Take one step at a time, and I promise you can make this entire journey.

This book is much like a travel guide book—you don't need to go to all the places, but for the places you need to go, this book has the essential information you need to get there. Take what feels nourishing and interesting for your unique author adventure, and leave the rest. I find that most authors need most of the resources in this book, but some don't—because they have passed a particular stage or because certain materials just don't apply (such as the research materials if your book has no research, or the memoir tips for those not writing a memoir).

This Book Does Not Take the Place of Real Human Support

While this book is packed with valuable information, insight, and invitations to engage in experiences that will support your writing, it doesn't take the place of working with a coach or mentor while you write your book. Working with a coach—someone who provides you with accountability, champions you and believes in your work, and knows how to support you along your *specific* journey—is an absolute essential for most authors we know. This support is often the difference between a dejected draft collecting proverbial dust on your laptop, and an actual book that has made its way fully into creation and is out making magic in the world on your behalf. For more about coaching options with Whale Song Creative, please visit JaimeFleres.com.

Well Wishes on Your Author Adventure!

Wherever you are in your journey, I hope *The Author Adventure* provides a fresh and unique set of valuable resources for your creative quest. You'll find offerings here that you won't find anywhere else. I hope you find what you need and more. Without further ado, let's get you *Author Activated*!

1.1 INNER AUTHOR SUPPORT

CHAPTER 1

CREATIVE MANIFESTO

Let's kick off this adventure with a few supportive mantras and perspectives to help us get into the right mindset for the journey ahead. May these support you as is, or stimulate your own inner creative to come up with the mantras that serve you best.

 I CONSISTENTLY SHOW UP

I know that showing up for my creative project is 90 percent of the battle. I'm willing to consistently show up for myself and this work, no matter what. I trust that power and inspiration gather around me when I simply show up and say "yes." I know that creating is in *action*, not in *thinking*.

 I AM COMMITTED FOR THE LONG HAUL

I know that writing a book is a long-term commitment that requires stamina and perseverance. It's not a one-hundred-yard dash; it is the Iditarod. Like any massive creation, it takes tremendous time and energy. I pace myself and conserve my energy so I can complete the full journey. I know that breaks and rest are a crucial part of the creative life cycle.

 I PRACTICE HUMILITY AND HUMOR

"Be the weirdo who dares to enjoy." —ELIZABETH GILBERT, *Big Magic: Creative Living Beyond Fear*

I have a sense of humor and lightness about my failures and mistakes. I know it's part of the territory. I walk that fine line between self-validation and preciousness. I also know that creating can be fun and feel good. I look for ways to "let out the pressure" in the system so I can enjoy my art.

I REMEMBER THE CRITIC'S ROLE

"It is not the critic who counts; not the (wo)man who points out how the strong (wo)man stumbles or where the doer of deeds could have done it better. The credit belongs to the (wo)man who is actually in the arena, whose face is marred by dust and sweat and blood … who at the best knows in the end the triumph of high achievement, and who at worst, if (s)he fails, at least fails while daring greatly."

— THEODORE ROOSEVELT, *"The Man in the Arena"*

I know my Inner Critic is the most ruthless of all critics I may encounter on my creative journey. I know its strategies are crazy clever. I also know that when I dare to show up authentically and creatively, I may be exposed to judgment from others. I maintain my sovereignty and keep my focus even in the face of challenges, never allowing criticism from any source to trump my faith in myself and my work. I do not allow criticism to stop me—I may listen as a way to learn and grow, or I may ignore it altogether. I am not interested in the feedback of those in the "cheap seats." To the critics, inner and outer, I say: "I see you, I hear you, and I am going to show up and do this anyway."

 ## I DON'T FIGHT FEAR, AND I DON'T LET IT STOP ME

I know that fear is not something to eliminate or overcome in order for me to write this book. I know that the Inner Critic is along for the ride and will find creative ways to keep me away from the risk of creativity—because creating is the source of both our power and our vulnerability. I remember that fear is in my mind, not in my actions. I know that when I can get into the action of writing, the fear will recede. I prepare for the changing ways that self-sabotage may arise and commit to finding healthy ways to coexist with it.

 ## I AM IN RIGHT RELATIONSHIP WITH MY ART

"There is a vitality, a life force, an energy, a quickening that is translated through you into action, and there is only one of you in all time, this expression is unique, and if you block it, it will never exist through any other medium; and be lost."

— MARTHA GRAHAM

I want to make things that didn't exist until I made them, things that can only come through me. I love my work and am invested wholeheartedly in my creative projects. I remember that my creative work and I are two separate creative beings: my work is not me. Just as one's children are not their own, my creative projects come through me but don't belong to me.

I know that being overly invested and over-identified in my work can create paralysis and impede my creative process. It's my job to work courageously with creativity and be a clear channel for the life that wants to come through me. Thus, I am more committed to the process than attached to the outcome.

 I VALUE ORGANIZATION AS A CONTAINER FOR CREATIVITY

I seek order and eliminate chaos from my inner and outer worlds so that I may not be distracted from my creative work. I also recognize that this is not a linear or straightforward path I walk—that there will come meanderings off the trail, double-backs, moments of seeming lostness, sprints or leaps into new territory, and so much more. I remember that my creativity is an untamable wild force. And yet, I understand how to apply order and organization in a way that serves my creative flame, the way a woodstove creates a contained and concentrated place for fire's warmth.

 I KNOW I DON'T CREATE IN ISOLATION

I remember to reach out for support, inspiration, and guidance. I learn from the masters, writers I adore, and those who have gone before me. I identify and stay connected to those I know are champions for me and my creations. I seek support from other writers, creatives, coaches, allies, and professionals.

What would you add to this manifesto for your own author adventure?

CHAPTER 2

THE CREATIVE LIFE CYCLE

Now that we have built the first draft of our creative manifesto together, let's get clear about the cyclical nature of creativity. Because we live in a time and place where linear, outward productivity is held on a pedestal, we need reminders of what the *organic* creative process looks like. Nature herself is governed by these laws, and so are our creative cycles.

Just like the seasons in nature, there are four cycling seasons to our creative processes. I find this helpful to remember since not every day will feel like the outwardly productive ideal (summer day) we strive to make the norm.

These cycles manifest at different levels and intervals. For example, an entire book project from beginning to end will roughly follow this cycle. And you will also experience many smaller revolutions through the cycle within a project—perhaps with each draft or each chapter. You may traverse all phases within a week or even a single day.

The creative cycle is circular and spiral-like, not linear or hierarchical—no one season is better than another. We often begin a creative cycle in the Fertile Darkness phase but may not notice we are in the cycle until we hit the Bud phase. We often complete a project during the Harvest phase. It's crucial to remember that we need all four phases of the cycle. They are integral to our creations. Note that only one of these seasons, Bloom, involves the writing or creating, as we often consider them.

Use this exploration of the phases or seasons of creativity to locate yourself within your current creative cycle. This will help you recognize, accept, and honor where you are and act in ways that serve yourself and the creative process rather than fighting against it.

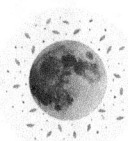

FERTILE DARKNESS PHASE
(Winter | New Moon | Preconception)

This is the phase before a creation has been conceived or before the next step or idea in a project becomes known or manifest.

It's a time to incubate your visions, meditate, enjoy solitude, reflect, attend to your dreams, journal, surrender the desire to always *do* and *produce*, and allow Not Knowing and Not Doing to exist. If you're in the middle of a project and find the next part isn't clear or known, put it down and go do something else. Trust the void. The fertile darkness is potent, offers space of great possibility, and *is* the place from which everything is created.

This could also be called the Soil phase, where you've planted the seeds, but it still looks like dirt so far. Trust what's unfolding that you cannot fully see yet.

You may feel quiet, calm, still, humble, open, trusting, or dreamy/visionary. You may also feel uncertain, uncomfortable, unclear, concerned, unsettled, frustrated, scared, sensitive, discouraged, and the like—particularly if you are viewing this phase as a problem rather than as a natural part of the cycle.

BUD PHASE
(Spring | Waxing Moon | Conception)

During this phase, you are full of ideas and creativity.

This is when fresh new insights, connections, and ideas come in, and you have the energy to plan, strategize, brainstorm, research, and begin new elements of your creative project. This is a time of exploration and new beginnings. This can be a time of many ideas, and it can feel like Grand Central Station in your mind. In this phase, you may not be actively writing or creating, but you are making important preparations.

You may feel energetic, enthusiastic, engaged, and encouraged. You may also feel full and perhaps even a bit scattered or overwhelmed by the energy of this phase.

BLOOM PHASE
(Summer | Full Moon | Pregnancy)

During this phase, the initial intensity of the Bud phase has worn off, but you are burning a steady blue flame of creativity that feels sustainable, and you're making steady progress forward on your book or an element of your process. You maintain a consistent writing practice, daily if not many times a week, and things feel like they are moving forward.

In this phase, **you may feel** capable, steady, centered, focused, engrossed, determined, and clear.

HARVEST PHASE
(Fall | Waning Moon | Birth)

You've completed all, or a significant portion, of your project, or you've reached a major milestone.

You may begin to slow down and reflect on the efforts you've made in the Bud and Bloom phases.

You may celebrate your successes and reflect on what you've learned from what didn't work. This is a time for organizing, editing, or reaching out for support from editors or your coach, for example.

In this phase, **you may feel** reflective, introspective, proud, grateful, accomplished, valuable, and content.

TAKE ACTION

On the next page, please write a paragraph or two about what season of the creative cycle you are in right now.

Are you in:
- Fertile Darkness: visioning/dreaming and incubating; not doing
- Bud phase: full of ideas, insights, and energy to begin; planning, strategizing, researching, getting started
- Bloom phase: steady creative fuel; sustained, committed consistent action
- Harvest phase: slowing down to take stock, reflect, review, revise, and reconsider

What phase of the creative cycle are you in? How do you feel in this phase, and what are the best actions to take or refrain from at this time? What feels most aligned with the energy of this phase?

CHAPTER 3

Working with the Inner Critic

"No one can wrestle the pencil out of your hand.
You get to keep going in absolute defiance."
— AMANDA HAPPÉ

We all have an Inner Critic who feeds us messages that impede our confidence and ability to create. In his book *The War of Art*,[1] Steven Pressfield calls the Inner Critic "Resistance" and identifies it as the shadow of our genius. Sara Avant Stover, in *The Book of She*,[2] similarly differentiates between our Demons—our inner darkness—and our Daemons—the goddess within, the inner deity, our guiding spirit, or Higher Self. Hal and Sidra Stone, pioneers of an inner parts work process called "Voice Dialogue," wrote a book about the Inner Critic. A mentor of mine calls it "Bitchety Cricket" sitting on your shoulder, chirping into your ear. Internal Family Systems (also known as Parts Work) has also put the Inner Critic on the map.

We *all* have an Inner Critic. Our Inner Critic will absolutely show up to the party when we say yes to a massive creative undertaking such as writing a book. Therefore, we need to understand our Inner Critic, how it shows up, and how to work with it if we want to successfully coexist with this energy as we write our book.

A Few Key Universal Facts About the Inner Critic

Let's orient ourselves to the energy we are working with. The Inner Critic is an inner voice that is critical of ourselves. (The Inner Judge is the one who points the proverbial finger outward toward others critically.)

The Inner Critic was born in our childhoods (regardless of our upbringing). It was created in an attempt to protect us from vulnerability and keep us safe. Its original function was to spare us from shame and pain. It desperately wants us to be accepted and liked by others. If it fears we are at risk in those areas, it will pipe up loudly (or stealthily).

This voice is not you. It's like a radio station you were programmed to tune in to a long time ago. And it's been running the same tired show ever since. This voice has the potential to slow or stop your personal growth and block your ability to live a creative life.

No matter how much you try, you cannot please the Inner Critic. It doesn't matter how much personal work you've done, how smart you are, or anything else.

The thing is, the harder you try to battle it, the stronger it becomes. So, we need a different approach.

HOW THE INNER CRITIC SHOWS UP

Our Inner Critic is pretty savvy and can show up in any number of ways throughout our book-writing journey. It may show up as any of the following. Which ones do you relate to? Check all that apply.

- ☐ An internal voice that argues why you shouldn't/couldn't write, now or ever
- ☐ Logical reasons why you can't create/write today/right now
- ☐ A lot more thinking/overthinking about creating rather than actually creating
- ☐ Big feelings like fear, discouragement, confusion, doubt, anxiety, and self-belittlement
- ☐ Procrastination
- ☐ Busyness
- ☐ Distraction and being scattered
- ☐ Numbness
- ☐ Boredom, restlessness
- ☐ Self-sabotage
- ☐ An inability to commit; half-heartedness
- ☐ Others in our lives who don't support us or are critical of us
- ☐ Overly judgmental of others' work—inner perfectionism-turned-outward-judge
- ☐ Drama in other areas of our lives
- ☐ Disorder, disorganization, and chaos

How does your Inner Critic show up in your creative process?

_____
_____
_____
_____
_____
_____
_____

WHAT THE INNER CRITIC SAYS

While the Inner Critic can be powerfully persuasive, it is not particularly creative or original in terms of its messaging. It is universal: a program operating in our psyches, designed with intelligence and meant to help us survive our childhoods. But ultimately, it limits our creative adult selves when its messages halt our creativity. Most of us can identify with some version of the following statements, which come from the Inner Critic—check all those you've heard inside your own head.

- ☐ You have nothing meaningful to say; nobody cares
- ☐ You are going to fail and embarrass yourself
- ☐ Others are better than you
- ☐ What you want to do or say has been done before
- ☐ You are not _____ enough
  (good, smart, strong, rich, interesting—fill in the blank)
- ☐ You are a terrible writer
- ☐ It's too hard to write a book—you don't have what it takes
- ☐ You don't have enough time
- ☐ You should just start tomorrow/later
- ☐ Who do you think you are, anyway?

What does your Inner Critic say to you?

_____
_____
_____
_____
_____
_____

How to Manage the Inner Critic

> *"The more important a call or action is to our soul's evolution, the more Resistance we will feel toward pursuing it."*
> —STEVEN PRESSFIELD

The thing about this Inner Critic (or outer critic) is that we can't eliminate it. Rather, we must work with it. Believe it or not, the critic serves a purpose. Like a well-meaning protector who loves you and wants to keep you safe—but perhaps isn't effective in their actions—this part of you desires to protect the vulnerable parts of your being. Sometimes, the more fiercely fired up its protective response, the more we know we are onto something big and important in our lives.

If we have an energy inside of us that we need to transform, we need to take care of it rather than battle with it, or it will certainly destroy us.

So, this part of us exists. And it affects our writing process. What can we do? We can give it a seat at the table but not allow it to call the shots. We need to find ways not to battle it but to dance with it. Trying to fight it or prove it wrong only intensifies its power by activating a ceaseless quest for improvement (totally the realm of the Inner Critic!).

We must shift its voice from being an authority in our lives to an annoyance, at minimum, or, at best, a source of creative fuel. We must find ways to practice bearing witness to this voice inside, to see it for what it is without judgment, and to offer it empathy so it can be seen and cared for enough to no longer command us from a position in our unconscious.

In *Embracing Your Inner Critic*, Hal and Sidra Stone[3] explain that we need to call upon our adult *Aware Ego*, or what is called *Self Energy* in Parts work, that has access to the opposing messages inside of us and has real agency about what we do in our lives. The Aware Ego allows you to discover the complexity of your feelings and the richness of the selves inhabiting your psyche, and it lets you reclaim the human being you were born to be. We'll talk about this Aware Ego and its close cousin, the Inner Genius, in the next chapter.

But first, here's how to work with your Inner Critic when it shows up on the scene in your psyche and threatens to thwart your creative progress.

> *"Dearest Fear: Creativity and I are about to go on a road trip together. I understand you'll be joining us, because you always do. I acknowledge that you believe you have an important job to do in my life, and that you take your job seriously. Apparently, your job is to induce complete panic whenever I'm about to do anything interesting [...]. So by all means, keep doing your job, if you feel you must. But I will also be doing my job on this road trip, which is to work hard and stay focused. And creativity will be doing its job, which is to remain stimulating and inspiring. [...] Understand this: Creativity and I are the only ones who will be making any decisions along the way."*
>
> —ELIZABETH GILBERT

INNER CRITIC PRACTICES

The Inner Critic will show up on our journeys in some form or another, and we need a plan to work with it. Here are ten ways to manage your Inner Critic; I encourage you to find others. Some of these early ways invite us to unblend from and differentiate ourselves from our Inner Critic in some way. It is so imperative to realize that the Inner Critic is *not* you but a part you are hosting with whom you can have agency and authority.

1. **Write it down.** Externalize the voice by literally moving it from inside (your mind) to outside (on paper). Step back and ask what this voice is trying to do for you. Replace erroneous statements with new ones. (See the Inner Critic Field Day activity after this list.)

2. **Create distance.** Another effective way to manage the Inner Critic is to externalize or personify it in some way. You may recognize it as an archetypal character a part of you plays, but not the actual, real *you*.

   You can name your Inner Critic—I've had clients call theirs Fearful Fred, Mean Mary, and Timid Ted—whatever you want. Some people encourage the use of a non-threatening, even somewhat cute name such as Eugene or Agnes. You may also imagine this part of yourself as a character/persona—perhaps a pushy salesperson, a telemarketer, a bully, a mean teacher, or whatever arises naturally and fits.

   Extra Credit: Anchor this characterization by any of the following—
   - Describe it in writing
   - Draw a picture of this character
   - Find a representation of the character in media (e.g., a magazine clipping)
   - Create a mask that represents this part of you
   - Make a clay figure of your Inner Critic

   When this character shows up on the scene, you can externalize it and give it some distance from your Inner Genius so the latter may continue working its magic.

3. **Dance with it.** You can literally move the feelings stirred up by the Inner Critic through your body. There are a few ways you can do this. You can do a Shadow Dance, where you put on a song that resonates with your experience and dance with the fullness of your Inner Critic's feelings to honor them and discover what they have to teach you. You can do a Shaking Dance, where you put on a fast song and shake through each part of your body, imagining you are releasing yourself from the oppressive nature of the Inner Critic. You can also do a Free Dance, where you put on a song that makes you feel strong and empowered, and dance as if your Inner Critic has no power to shape your actions. You may also wish to do all three of these in order.

4. **Use humor.** Don't take yourself too seriously. Find a way to lighten up and let pressure out of the system. (In a healthy way!)

5. **Take action.** Often, the Inner Critic stops us in our tracks ... but only in our minds. When we get out of thinking and into *action* (i.e., we stop thinking about writing and actually do it), we can move out of the resistance or learn more about it in order to move forward.

6. **Get support.** Find champions in your life who are willing to pick you up, dust you off, and care for you when you fail or feel discouraged. They may say, "Phew, that sucked, but you were brave." These people know that if you're not taking risks and failing, you're not really showing up. They admire you *because* of your vulnerabilities, not *despite* them. Value their voices like gold.

7. **Support your Inner Genius.** See Chapter 4 for more on this!

8. **Focus on impact.** Put your energy, attention, and focus on the service, the greater good, and the impact your book will create in the world. Focus on how it will serve. Strengthen that narrative in your mind. Believe in it. Do the Rave Review activity you'll encounter in Chapter 5.

9. **Develop an Inner Coach.** Practice hearing a strong voice inside your head that champions you and encourages you even when you feel discouraged.

10. **Be kind.** Always, always be kind to yourself. The Inner Critic shows up when we are feeling vulnerable, so it is supremely important to call on your kinder, gentler (but firm and powerful) inner resources any time the Inner Critic shows up.

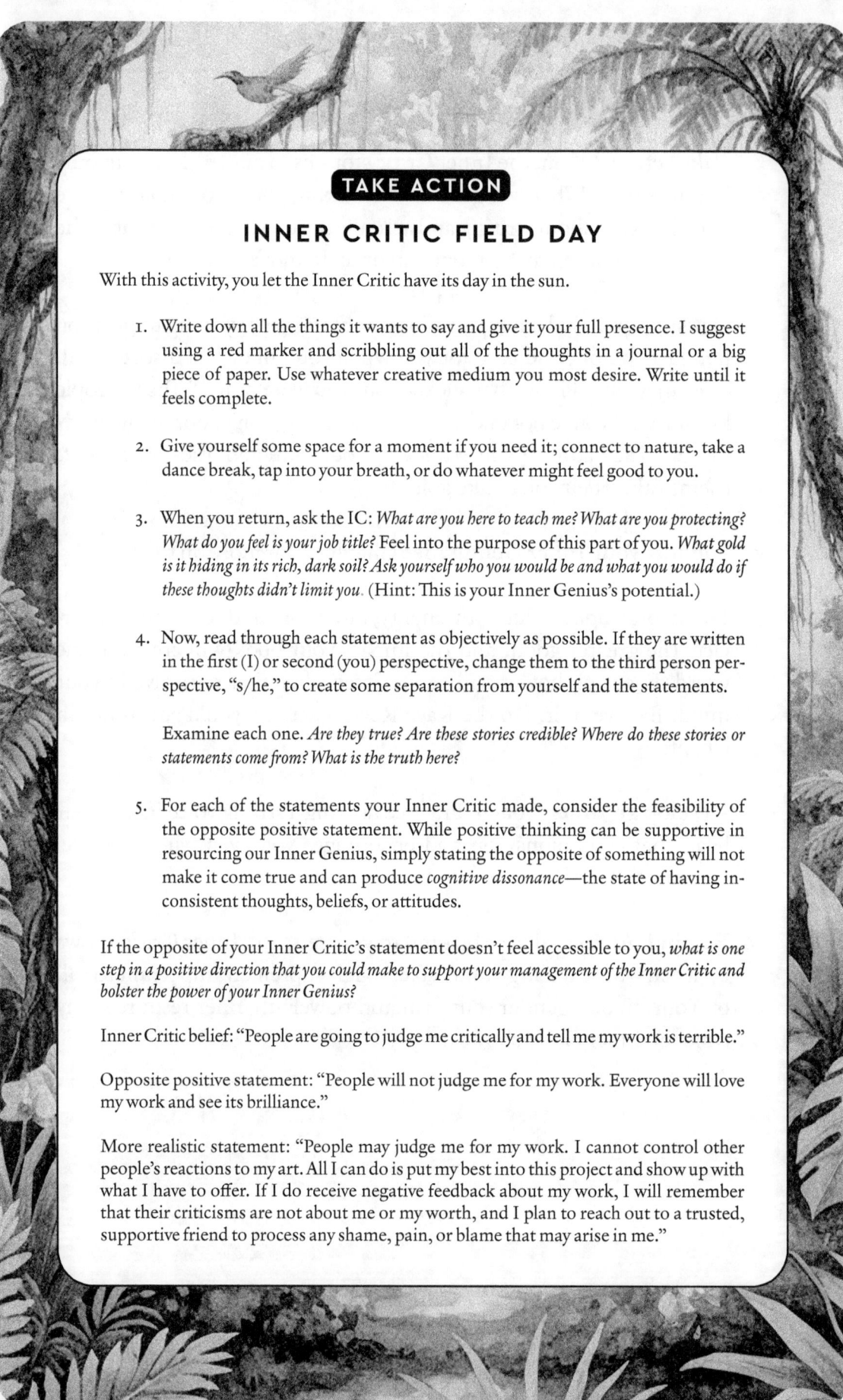

TAKE ACTION

INNER CRITIC FIELD DAY

With this activity, you let the Inner Critic have its day in the sun.

1. Write down all the things it wants to say and give it your full presence. I suggest using a red marker and scribbling out all of the thoughts in a journal or a big piece of paper. Use whatever creative medium you most desire. Write until it feels complete.

2. Give yourself some space for a moment if you need it; connect to nature, take a dance break, tap into your breath, or do whatever might feel good to you.

3. When you return, ask the IC: *What are you here to teach me? What are you protecting? What do you feel is your job title?* Feel into the purpose of this part of you. *What gold is it hiding in its rich, dark soil? Ask yourself who you would be and what you would do if these thoughts didn't limit you.* (Hint: This is your Inner Genius's potential.)

4. Now, read through each statement as objectively as possible. If they are written in the first (I) or second (you) perspective, change them to the third person perspective, "s/he," to create some separation from yourself and the statements.

    Examine each one. *Are they true? Are these stories credible? Where do these stories or statements come from? What is the truth here?*

5. For each of the statements your Inner Critic made, consider the feasibility of the opposite positive statement. While positive thinking can be supportive in resourcing our Inner Genius, simply stating the opposite of something will not make it come true and can produce *cognitive dissonance*—the state of having inconsistent thoughts, beliefs, or attitudes.

If the opposite of your Inner Critic's statement doesn't feel accessible to you, *what is one step in a positive direction that you could make to support your management of the Inner Critic and bolster the power of your Inner Genius?*

Inner Critic belief: "People are going to judge me critically and tell me my work is terrible."

Opposite positive statement: "People will not judge me for my work. Everyone will love my work and see its brilliance."

More realistic statement: "People may judge me for my work. I cannot control other people's reactions to my art. All I can do is put my best into this project and show up with what I have to offer. If I do receive negative feedback about my work, I will remember that their criticisms are not about me or my worth, and I plan to reach out to a trusted, supportive friend to process any shame, pain, or blame that may arise in me."

The Somatics of Working with the Inner Critic

Many of the practices I've shared here help you meet the Inner Critic in practical ways and through the mental channel of our being. It's all good. But there is one other hitch here. Self-protection, the domain of the Inner Critic, is also *somatic*. That means it's a bodily experience—and one that happens subcortically (below the conscious mind). Our autonomic nervous system is charged with making micro-moment assessments of our environment and experiences to determine whether we are safe, in danger, or life-threatened. If it perceives that we are somehow in danger—like, say, we are about to do something that it sees as threatening our belonging—it will come between us and that thing it perceives as dangerous. It's supremely good at what it does. Its job is literally to keep us alive. It doesn't mess around.

How does the autonomic system make these decisions? It looks at the vast database of *all* our past experiences and makes a split-second, *noncognitive* judgment. Let's say when you were in second grade, you wrote a paper about your summer vacation, and your teacher gave you critical remarks about your writing. You may have stored information subconsciously, such as "Writing is not safe. If we write something, people will judge or critique us." Fast-forward thirty years, and you are sitting down to write your first book. Except you're not. You're scrolling on social media, cleaning your house, or giving your cat a bath instead of writing.

Consciously, you want to write the book. But *you can't*. What gives? It may be that your system has decided, based on the past, that writing is not safe. We don't even have to know about the past event for it to have merit. If we are afraid of the writing, our system has a reason. It makes sense to our system. So, as we've been saying, we get to become the captains of our author-ships and give our systems new information.

That is the cool thing about neuroception (that part of you tracking every moment to assess safety or danger). It has plasticity and is always being updated. You reshape your system by *showing* it that you are safe to take the next step in your writing journey. You can't just tell your system; you have to show it with tolerable new experiences that counter the past.

So go slow, keep taking aligned action with your creative dreams, and trust that your system is being reshaped to allow you to *become* the author you intend to be. Further, somatic practices help. I suggest checking out Chapter 16, which will also be incredibly supportive. I also have a whole course, called SOMA, which is full of somatic practices you may find helpful.[4]

CHAPTER 4

ACTIVATING YOUR INNER GENIUS

We talked about the Aware Ego, or Self Energy, in the last chapter about the Inner Critic. On the same team as the Aware Ego is the Inner Genius, that wise part of us that knows how to write the book and wants to do so to support our soul's call toward expression and realization.

In *Big Magic*,[1] Elizabeth Gilbert writes about how both the Greeks and Romans believed in a daemon of creativity—an external energy that helps one in their creative works. "They called it your *genius*—your guardian deity, the conduit of your inspiration. Which is to say, the Romans didn't believe that an exceptionally gifted person *was* a genius; they believed that an exceptionally gifted person *had* a genius. It's a subtle but important distinction and [...] a wise psychological construct," she writes.

She goes on to explain that *having* a genius, rather than *being* a genius, puts some distance between an artist and their work. It keeps one's ego in check and alleviates the burden of full responsibility for what moves through them creatively. Whether the work is successful or deemed a failure, she writes, "the vulnerable human ego is protected. Protected from the corrupting influence of praise. Protected from the corrosive effects of shame."

This way of conceiving of the Inner Genius is much like how the Aware Ego bears witness to different parts or aspects of the self without mistaking them for The Self. This can have a protective effect on our vulnerable parts (which the Inner Critic exists to protect, remember). What Gilbert suggests here is for us to regard the Inner Genius in a way that acknowledges and honors the Inner Critic.

Whether we consider the Inner Genius a "part" of ourselves (much like the Inner Critic is a part) or we adopt the ancient view of the Inner Genius as a happy house elf, or we see the Inner Genius as our truest essence or Self, let's dive into what this part is all about.

WHAT THE INNER GENIUS DOES

Check all that you relate to—

- ☐ Follows ideas that seem to come from nowhere
- ☐ Takes its mission, not itself, seriously
- ☐ Is willing to take risks and make mistakes, knowing they are not diversions from the path but an integral part of the path
- ☐ Acts with humility and kindness but takes no beef
- ☐ Demands respect, not likes
- ☐ Chooses responsibility; rejects mediocrity
- ☐ Embraces the wild, the mysterious
- ☐ Doesn't feel the need to shout over the Inner Critic to be heard (s/he is the still, small voice within)
- ☐ Is infinitely imaginative and creative
- ☐ Is tapped into that which is Greater
- ☐ Runs on fuel that is not of the mind

How do you notice the Inner Genius at play in your life already?

_____
_____
_____
_____
_____

WHAT THE INNER GENIUS SAYS

- I have something meaningful to say, something that really matters to me. And I know that this work will serve me and others in some way, known or unknown to me now.
- I may make mistakes or encounter difficulties along the way, and I know parts of me are afraid to be vulnerable in the ways my book

project requires of me. I am willing to take risks and make mistakes here.
- The game of comparison does not serve me. It doesn't matter what others have lived or written and how it compares to my experience and what I have or will write. This is between me and Creation. Comparison has no place in that relationship.
- Others may have written about my topic or subject before, and that is okay. There is room here for me, too.
- I am enough. Oh, I am so much more than enough.
- I may not be a perfect writer, but there is no such thing. I know I will do my best and get support to make my book the strongest, clearest transmission of my message as possible.
- I believe in myself. I trust that my deep abiding desire to write this book is a potent validator that I have everything I need to write this book.
- Action is the best place for me to be, and I won't get stuck in thinking about my project. I will write my book. Now.

What does your Inner Genius say to you? What do you want it to turn up the volume on? Which of these do you want to write on a sticky note and put on your bathroom mirror, computer, or kitchen cupboard? Seriously.

_____

_____

_____

_____

_____

_____

_____

_____

How to Elicit the Inner Genius

- Find outside support in one or more friends, family members, or professional writing coaches/mentors who can mirror the truth of your Inner Genius to you anytime you need it.
- Do the Inner Critic exercises to calm your Inner Critic so you can hear the soft wisdom of your Inner Genius.
- Write yourself reasonable affirmations from the voice of your Inner Genius and read them often as nourishment.
- Read authors like Elizabeth Gilbert and Steven Pressfield, whose words will also elicit and support your Inner Genius. Or watch/listen to video interviews or podcasts with authors who model what it's like to let our Inner Genius lead.
- Dialogue with your Inner Genius. See Notes for details. Listen to what s/he has to say to you, especially when s/he is given space to shine through. You can also write a dialogue between your Inner Genius and your Critic to get a feel for its flavor, its truth, and its power. Do this anytime you're feeling stuck and need to process it out.
- Connect regularly to your Inner Genius in ways that are natural to you. Consider the meditation on the next page to connect with your Inner Author.
- Journal about the qualities, characteristics, and inspired actions of your Inner Author (Relative to your Inner Genius). How does s/he behave, what does s/he believe, what does s/he know, and what does s/he do on a daily and weekly basis? What is her/his relationship to this book project? How does s/he meet it?
- Take actions from your Inner Genius. This might be in direct relationship to your book or in what I call Creative Cross-training[2]—any tolerable, available step toward your creativity and self-expression that feels accessible in this moment.

A GUIDED MEDITATION
CONNECT TO YOUR INNER AUTHOR

You can listen to this meditation at: JaimeFleres.com/taa-resources/
Here is the transcript if you want to record it for yourself and listen back.

Begin by finding a comfortable place where you can sit or lie down. Have a pen and paper nearby, as you'll do some writing after this visualization.

As you get yourself comfortable, close your eyes, and begin to notice your breath. Without any need to change, or deepen, or extend, just notice how your breath is in this moment.

Maybe you notice the sensation at the tip of your nose, or your lips, or maybe it's the rise and the fall of your chest, just notice. As you're ready, begin to take three deep breaths, in through the nose and out through the mouth. And, if you wish to, on the exhale, you can take a sigh.

Allow your body to sink into the surface it is resting on. Allow your body, your mind, and your emotions, to come into the present moment. And allow everything to become calm and settled. From here, continue to notice your breath. Inhale and exhale.

Now imagine that your body is floating in a calm body of water, like a lake. As you take a breath in and release it out, just notice the soft current in this body of water, allowing it to gently rock you. On every inhale, we're going to fill up with energy, with light. And with every exhale, we're going to release any tension or stress, allowing it to just float away and dissipate in the water.

Bring your attention now to your feet. Notice if there's any tightness or stress present, and if so, just soften, just allow it to release. Let a soft heaviness come into your feet. Now, move your attention to your calves and your shins, relaxing these areas. Allow your breath to come in and loosen them up.

Now soften around your knees, breathing in and out and relaxing more deeply. Bring your attention, your breath, and your awareness, now to your quads, your upper legs. Notice if there's tension here and allow your breath to just gently guide it out into the water. Imagine any tension that's here in your legs just seeping away.

As you take your next inhalation, imagine that your breath is moving into your hips now, into your pelvis, and allowing any tension that's present here to be released. Breathe deeply into any places where you hold tension and allow it to soften into the water. Moving now into your belly, breathing deeply into your belly, your low-belly, mid-belly, into your torso. Just allow a full release here, a full relaxation of any tension, allow that to melt away.

Now move your attention to your upper back and shoulders. Use your breath here again to breathe into this space and allow any tension, or holding, or stress to

just melt away. Coming now into your arms, your upper arms, your elbows, your forearms, your wrists, and your hands. Just notice the sensations that are present here, bringing your breath to fill up every cell in your arms. With an exhale, just allow the deep release.

And moving now back up to your neck and your jaw. Take a few deep breaths here, allowing any tension, any holding to let go. Soften even your tongue and your ears. Soften the muscles around your eyes, relax your forehead, let go of any tension you're holding in the face or head, completely.

Now bring your attention to the spot on your forehead right between your eyes. Notice now a beam of light stretching out from that point on your forehead. Notice that this beam has a color or set of colors in it. Notice the quality of the light of this beam. And now notice that this beam stretches all the way up, out of the room that you're in, out above and through the ceiling, and that this beam of light stretches all the way up out of the place that your body is in and shines out into the sky.

Begin to travel along this beam of light. Bring your conscious awareness up and out onto this beam. Imagine floating up and just letting yourself walk along this beam, out of the place where you are, following the beam higher and upward. Follow this beam to take you higher and higher. Notice that the place where your body rests is getting smaller in your view.

As you travel, notice the beauty of the sky and move through the clouds. Start to see a view of your city, or town, or area below you. As you begin to travel faster and higher, start to see the whole region beneath you. Move up and up until you can see the beautiful globe of blue, and green, and white, and enjoy the view. Continue traveling upward until you're in blue-black space, silent, velvety, and dark.

And as you rest here, notice that there is another beam of light next to the one you are on, another beam of light. Notice the quality and color of this beam. Notice that this beam stretches all the way back down toward Earth. Notice that this beam stretches down toward Earth five years into the future, five years from now.

Begin to step onto this beam and let it gracefully carry you down. Notice Earth starting to come into focus again. Everything is getting clearer and larger in your view. Enjoy passing through the clouds again as you make your way down. As you begin to get closer to Earth, notice that you are going to a home, the dwelling place of your future self, five years from now.

This may be your current dwelling or a new place. But this is the home of the person who's written their book. The self that is already an author. Start to notice that this beam is taking you to meet that Inner Author, that future self. Continue riding the beam down, enjoying the views, following it all the way until it takes you to this dwelling place of your future self and drops you off.

Take a look around. What kind of place is this? What is it like here? What does it feel like? And as you notice the house come into view, make your way to the door. As you approach the door, see that your future author self is coming to greet you warmly

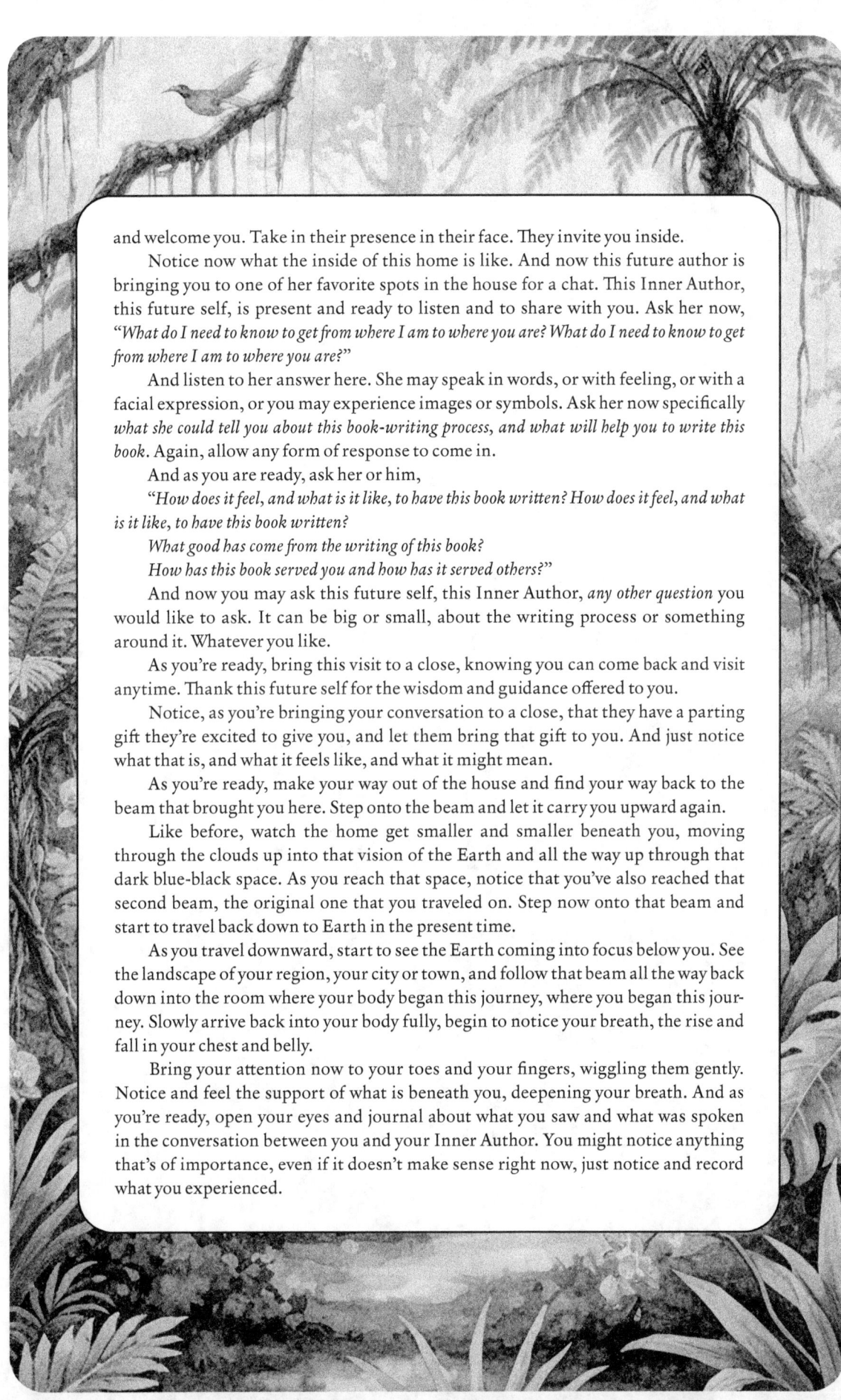

and welcome you. Take in their presence in their face. They invite you inside.

Notice now what the inside of this home is like. And now this future author is bringing you to one of her favorite spots in the house for a chat. This Inner Author, this future self, is present and ready to listen and to share with you. Ask her now, *"What do I need to know to get from where I am to where you are? What do I need to know to get from where I am to where you are?"*

And listen to her answer here. She may speak in words, or with feeling, or with a facial expression, or you may experience images or symbols. Ask her now specifically *what she could tell you about this book-writing process, and what will help you to write this book*. Again, allow any form of response to come in.

And as you are ready, ask her or him,

"How does it feel, and what is it like, to have this book written? How does it feel, and what is it like, to have this book written?

What good has come from the writing of this book?

How has this book served you and how has it served others?"

And now you may ask this future self, this Inner Author, *any other question* you would like to ask. It can be big or small, about the writing process or something around it. Whatever you like.

As you're ready, bring this visit to a close, knowing you can come back and visit anytime. Thank this future self for the wisdom and guidance offered to you.

Notice, as you're bringing your conversation to a close, that they have a parting gift they're excited to give you, and let them bring that gift to you. And just notice what that is, and what it feels like, and what it might mean.

As you're ready, make your way out of the house and find your way back to the beam that brought you here. Step onto the beam and let it carry you upward again.

Like before, watch the home get smaller and smaller beneath you, moving through the clouds up into that vision of the Earth and all the way up through that dark blue-black space. As you reach that space, notice that you've also reached that second beam, the original one that you traveled on. Step now onto that beam and start to travel back down to Earth in the present time.

As you travel downward, start to see the Earth coming into focus below you. See the landscape of your region, your city or town, and follow that beam all the way back down into the room where your body began this journey, where you began this journey. Slowly arrive back into your body fully, begin to notice your breath, the rise and fall in your chest and belly.

Bring your attention now to your toes and your fingers, wiggling them gently. Notice and feel the support of what is beneath you, deepening your breath. And as you're ready, open your eyes and journal about what you saw and what was spoken in the conversation between you and your Inner Author. You might notice anything that's of importance, even if it doesn't make sense right now, just notice and record what you experienced.

1.2
ESSENTIAL GROUNDWORK

CHAPTER 5

ANCHORING IN YOUR WHY
INTENTION, PURPOSE, AND AUTHORITY

One of the best ways to stay committed and motivated to your book project is to do what I call Anchoring in Your Why. Purpose creates drive. Knowing why you are writing, why your project matters to you, and how it will benefit others is a *huge* key to unlocking the motivation and commitment you need to start and finish your book. Anchoring in Your Why can mean the difference between a half-finished, abandoned draft collecting virtual dust on your computer and a bestselling book out in the world doing great things.

As your vision for your book begins to come into focus, take time to carefully articulate a few broad but essential elements that can serve as lighthouses through the waters of your writing process, helping you navigate where you wish to go and stay the course.

TAKE ACTION

I recommend writing out your answers and posting your intentions somewhere prominent in your writing space.

You may wish to take a quiet moment to center yourself and get connected to the creative heart of your project before you answer these questions.

Some of the prompts have a series of related questions. Please answer the ones that speak to you most strongly. If you need more space than this book permits, please take this inquiry to your journal or computer.

Intentions for Your Writing Process

What do you want to experience through the writing process? How do you want to feel through the writing process and when your book is done? What values are foundational for you?

_____
_____
_____
_____
_____

What support (through coaching, in your personal life, and beyond) do you need to make this book process a success?

_____
_____
_____
_____
_____

What permission do you need to give yourself in order to make this book-writing process a success?

_____
_____
_____
_____
_____

Exigence: Why This Book Matters *to You*

Why are you compelled to write this book? What are the specific reasons you have for writing? What is inspiring you to devote yourself to this project? Why is it worth investing your time, energy, and resources?

_____

_____

_____

_____

Why do you care about this topic, message, or story? Why does it matter to you? Will you be passionate about this topic, message, or story in a year? Five years? Why?

_____

_____

_____

_____

Why is a book the best vehicle for this expression (versus an online course or a talk, for example)?

_____

_____

_____

_____

_____

Why are you compelled to write this book now?

___

What will the world lose if your voice is not heard on this topic? (Inner Critic, step aside on this one.) What is the cost to you of not writing this book?

___

Your Book Vision

On the more practical, logistical side, what is your dream for the book? For example, is your goal to hire a big agent, land a publishing deal, and get on The New York Times bestseller list? Is your goal to self-publish and use this book to bolster your practice, serve your clients, or launch a speaking career? Or something else?

___

Purpose: Why Your Book Will Matter to Others

What is your greatest hope or intention for this book's impact on others?

_____
_____
_____
_____

What would you like your book to achieve in the world? What will it inspire people to do, think, believe, or feel? What problem will it solve? What need, burning desire, or deep curiosity will it meet?

_____
_____
_____
_____

Write a clear purpose statement for your book in one to two sentences. It's okay if your purpose changes through your process. Write what feels most resonant in this moment. To answer this question, we need verbs such as entertain, engage, inform, inspire, persuade, evoke X emotion, meet a collective need, transform, change, and so on.

_____
_____
_____
_____

Clarifying Your Inner *Author*ity

A fundamental part of laying a solid foundation for our books is to bring consciousness and awareness to who we are as the authors of our creations. This involves mindset work to stand in and own your power and authority as the author of your book. To move forward, you must see yourself as a credible author with a meaningful message, voice, and contribution.

What about you makes you the perfect person to write this book? You may think about your life experiences; your background; your formal and informal training; your beliefs, values, attitudes, and views; your personal strengths, skills, and gifts; your professional experience; your identity; and the like.

_____

_____

_____

_____

_____

What will make your voice, and thus your book, unique in the genre in which you are writing? What are you offering that may not yet exist (or how will your contribution add to or affect the collective dialogue around your genre, subject, or area of inquiry)?

_____

Finish this sentence: *I want my reader to see me as …* (give qualities, attributes, values, personality traits, and so on). *And in order to achieve this, I will need to …*

_____

TAKE ACTION

RAVE REVIEW EXERCISE

Open to a fresh page in your journal or a new digital doc. Imagine your book is written and published. About a month after publication, you get an email from someone who read your book. Your book completely transformed their life, and they are writing to tell you how and why your book was so pivotal to their learning, growth, healing, or life journey. In their voice, write this email. You might also consider who, specifically, has written you this email (we'll dive deeper into audience in Chapter 6).

While we are envisioning the future of your book (a powerful exercise!), consider also going to The New York Times bestseller list of books, printing out the page, and replacing one of the titles with your own, along with a short, accompanying description. You can display it on your wall for motivation. (By the way, you never need to make the NYT list to have a successful and satisfying authorship journey, but if that is your desire, then don't let anything hold you back from aiming to make your vision a reality.)

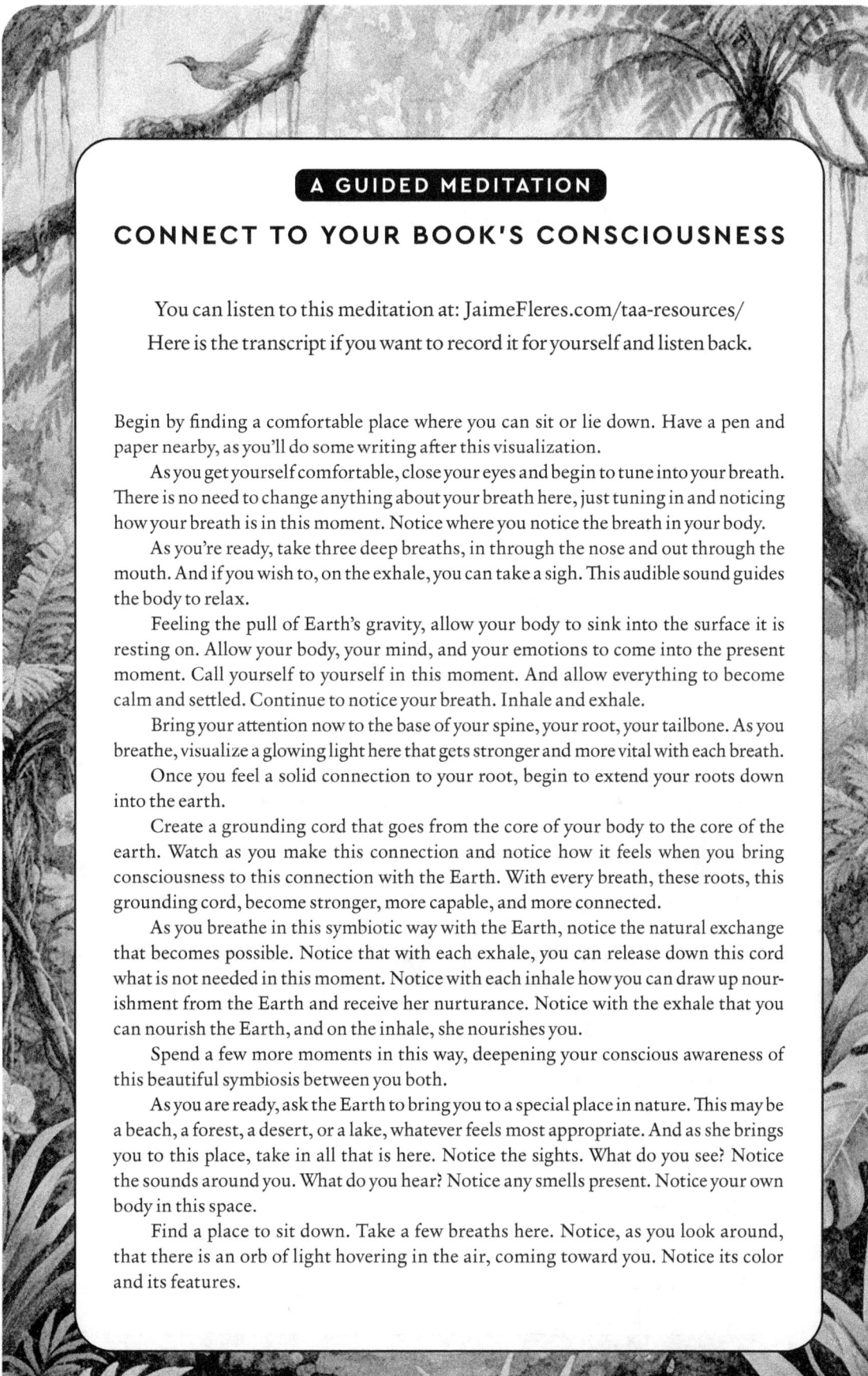

A GUIDED MEDITATION

CONNECT TO YOUR BOOK'S CONSCIOUSNESS

You can listen to this meditation at: JaimeFleres.com/taa-resources/
Here is the transcript if you want to record it for yourself and listen back.

Begin by finding a comfortable place where you can sit or lie down. Have a pen and paper nearby, as you'll do some writing after this visualization.

As you get yourself comfortable, close your eyes and begin to tune into your breath. There is no need to change anything about your breath here, just tuning in and noticing how your breath is in this moment. Notice where you notice the breath in your body.

As you're ready, take three deep breaths, in through the nose and out through the mouth. And if you wish to, on the exhale, you can take a sigh. This audible sound guides the body to relax.

Feeling the pull of Earth's gravity, allow your body to sink into the surface it is resting on. Allow your body, your mind, and your emotions to come into the present moment. Call yourself to yourself in this moment. And allow everything to become calm and settled. Continue to notice your breath. Inhale and exhale.

Bring your attention now to the base of your spine, your root, your tailbone. As you breathe, visualize a glowing light here that gets stronger and more vital with each breath.

Once you feel a solid connection to your root, begin to extend your roots down into the earth.

Create a grounding cord that goes from the core of your body to the core of the earth. Watch as you make this connection and notice how it feels when you bring consciousness to this connection with the Earth. With every breath, these roots, this grounding cord, become stronger, more capable, and more connected.

As you breathe in this symbiotic way with the Earth, notice the natural exchange that becomes possible. Notice that with each exhale, you can release down this cord what is not needed in this moment. Notice with each inhale how you can draw up nourishment from the Earth and receive her nurturance. Notice with the exhale that you can nourish the Earth, and on the inhale, she nourishes you.

Spend a few more moments in this way, deepening your conscious awareness of this beautiful symbiosis between you both.

As you are ready, ask the Earth to bring you to a special place in nature. This may be a beach, a forest, a desert, or a lake, whatever feels most appropriate. And as she brings you to this place, take in all that is here. Notice the sights. What do you see? Notice the sounds around you. What do you hear? Notice any smells present. Notice your own body in this space.

Find a place to sit down. Take a few breaths here. Notice, as you look around, that there is an orb of light hovering in the air, coming toward you. Notice its color and its features.

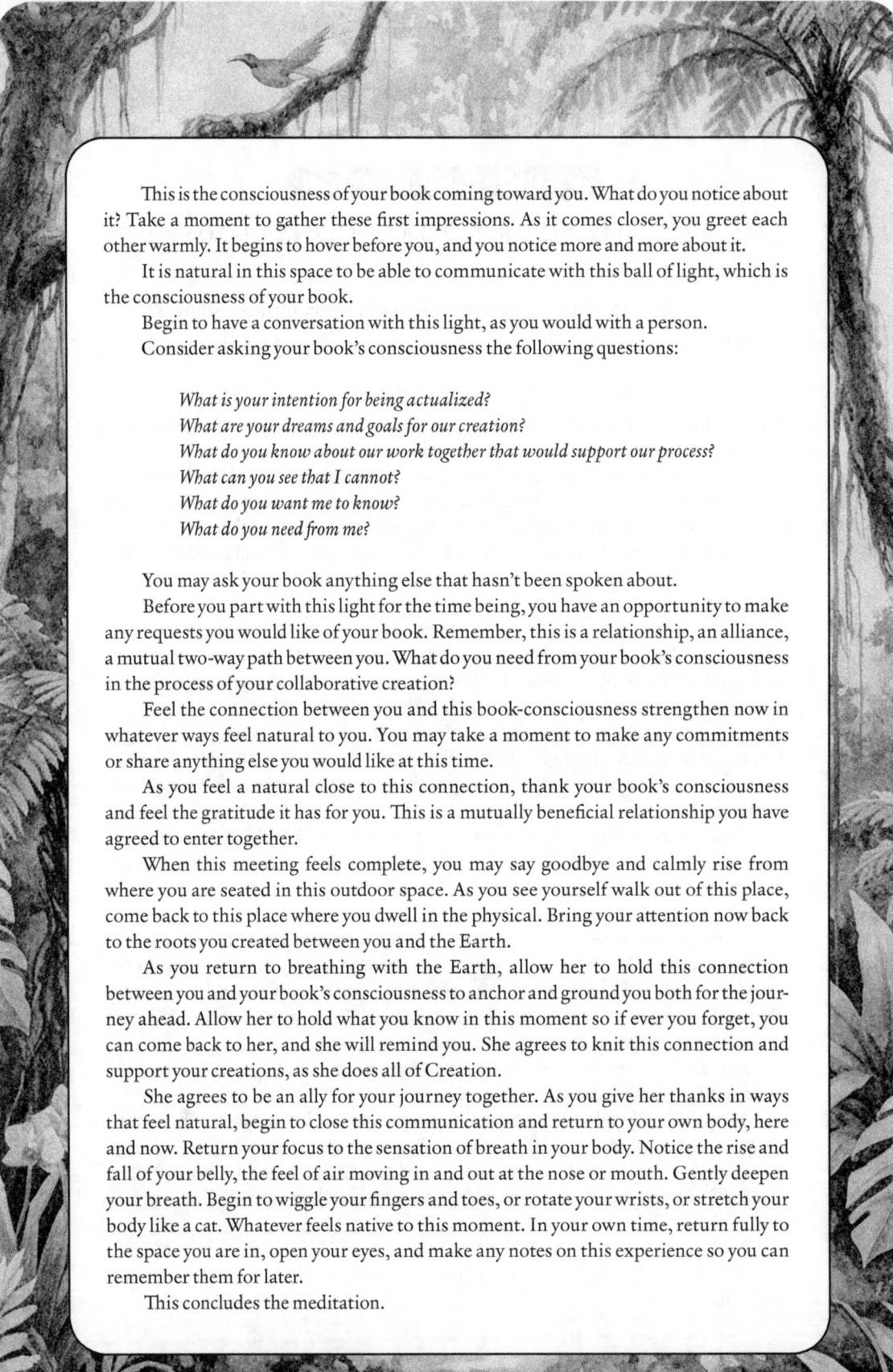

This is the consciousness of your book coming toward you. What do you notice about it? Take a moment to gather these first impressions. As it comes closer, you greet each other warmly. It begins to hover before you, and you notice more and more about it.

It is natural in this space to be able to communicate with this ball of light, which is the consciousness of your book.

Begin to have a conversation with this light, as you would with a person.

Consider asking your book's consciousness the following questions:

What is your intention for being actualized?
What are your dreams and goals for our creation?
What do you know about our work together that would support our process?
What can you see that I cannot?
What do you want me to know?
What do you need from me?

You may ask your book anything else that hasn't been spoken about.

Before you part with this light for the time being, you have an opportunity to make any requests you would like of your book. Remember, this is a relationship, an alliance, a mutual two-way path between you. What do you need from your book's consciousness in the process of your collaborative creation?

Feel the connection between you and this book-consciousness strengthen now in whatever ways feel natural to you. You may take a moment to make any commitments or share anything else you would like at this time.

As you feel a natural close to this connection, thank your book's consciousness and feel the gratitude it has for you. This is a mutually beneficial relationship you have agreed to enter together.

When this meeting feels complete, you may say goodbye and calmly rise from where you are seated in this outdoor space. As you see yourself walk out of this place, come back to this place where you dwell in the physical. Bring your attention now back to the roots you created between you and the Earth.

As you return to breathing with the Earth, allow her to hold this connection between you and your book's consciousness to anchor and ground you both for the journey ahead. Allow her to hold what you know in this moment so if ever you forget, you can come back to her, and she will remind you. She agrees to knit this connection and support your creations, as she does all of Creation.

She agrees to be an ally for your journey together. As you give her thanks in ways that feel natural, begin to close this communication and return to your own body, here and now. Return your focus to the sensation of breath in your body. Notice the rise and fall of your belly, the feel of air moving in and out at the nose or mouth. Gently deepen your breath. Begin to wiggle your fingers and toes, or rotate your wrists, or stretch your body like a cat. Whatever feels native to this moment. In your own time, return fully to the space you are in, open your eyes, and make any notes on this experience so you can remember them for later.

This concludes the meditation.

CHAPTER 6

AUDIENCE FOCUS

WE WRITE IN RELATIONSHIP + IN CONVERSATION

*"I can't write without a reader.
It's precisely like a kiss—you can't do it alone."*
— JOHN CHEEVER

When we first receive the creative inspiration to write a book, the mission often feels personal—to express our thoughts, feelings, and ideas about an issue, experience, or topic, or perhaps to tell a unique story. While this motivation is often where we begin, if we are to write a book, we must also expand our focus to include our audience/readers and develop the desire to serve them in some way with our creation. (We also expand our awareness to our cohorts engaged in the same collective conversation.)

Our book is a mode of communication between us and others. As such, it is like a conversation—and larger still, *a relationship*—we are building with others through the medium of our written words.

At the **drafting level**, audience awareness will impact what you say, how you say it, why, and when. A book only works if it impacts a reader. To write well, you need to think about who your reader is, what they need, and what would delight them.

At the **production level**, publishers and other book professionals will want to know who your book is for and how to market it to them. If you are self-publishing, audience awareness will dictate how and where you market your book.

At the **reader level**, your audience awareness and decisions around audience will determine how your book is received and how successful it is.

BIG CAVEAT: Don't let this process of audience consideration intimidate you or stop you in your process. This is one of those topics we will bring awareness to so you can allow your brain to consider this information. Then, we'll move it to the background so you can focus on your writing and what wants to come through you.

In your first draft, the primary relationship is between you and the truth. But it can be helpful in your planning process to at least consider audience as a way to shape and clarify what you'll say and how you'll say it. Also know that you can return to considering audience during the revision and editing process, *after* you've written your truth unadulterated.

If all these steps feel like too much and you only do *one* task in this chapter, skip to part four to explore where your ideal reader is in relationship to the topic or focus of your book.

You may consider coming back to this exercise during the revision, book proposal writing, or marketing stages of your book project, as this information will assist you in making decisions and taking intentional action at those stages as well. Audience matters through the duration of your book process and well into its life in the world.

We'll circle back to general audience considerations after we go through this process of moving from universal to specific audiences for your book.

Intended Audiences: Universal to Specific

Intended audiences are those you imagine you are communicating with through your book. You may have many intended audiences, and it is helpful to consider the many audiences to which your book will appeal (called *market segments* in publisher-speak).

Please note: Your book is not "for all people on planet Earth." Your book is *not* for everyone. No book is for everyone. Not even the Bible. When you try to talk to everyone, you wind up speaking to no one. You must get more specific with who you are trying to reach with your book.

PART ONE:
AUDIENCE SEGMENTING ("BUCKETING") + PRIMARY AUDIENCE

We must begin somewhere, and our level of audience awareness will range from broad to specific. The broad audience is the greater population of people to whom you'd like to offer your message. For example, in my previous book, *Birth Your Book*, my audience segment of "parents" is very broad.

It can help to be aware of your broad audience so you can communicate with an understanding of the diversity within your audience—what different values, beliefs, and backgrounds do they hold?

For my book, I needed to maintain awareness of the fact that people experience vastly different births and have a wide range of relationships to both birth and writing (and a whole lot more!).

TAKE ACTION

Brainstorm all the audiences to which your book will appeal. You can start in broad, sweeping strokes with key identifiers.

For example:

New mothers	Therapists
Mothers of older children	Birth and parenting educators
Doulas	New fathers
Midwives	Expectant mothers
Nurses and doctors	Survivors of birth trauma

_____

_____

_____

_____

_____

From here, can you identify a *single* target audience from this list? (Or perhaps two or three max, if you must.) This is your primary audience for your book. Most of us will have more than one audience, but we need to know who we are speaking to primarily, knowing that others will also read and resonate with the messages in our book.

___

___

___

___

PART TWO
DIVING INTO DEMOGRAPHICS

Segmenting and identifying your primary audiences are important steps in clarifying your audience, especially when you go to speak to prospective publishers about the general market for your book. But *don't stop there!*

Your book will greatly benefit from an even deeper dive into audience so you can meet them inside your book in a way that is effective and builds your credibility. The next step is to take your primary audiences and explore their specifics at a deeper level.

TAKE ACTION

With your one to two specific primary audience segments in mind, consider the following:

- age
- where they live
- nationality/ethnicity/region
- education
- gender
- experiences
- background
- income level
- relationship/family status
- occupation(s)

Consider how all this information may have an impact on what you say and how you'll say it in your book.

PART THREE

CLARIFYING YOUR READER AVATAR + PSYCHOGRAPHICS

It can also help to create a specific idea of your audience so you can be more effective in reaching them. It can be useful to think of the specific people or even a person with whom your book will resonate most.

I suggest you consider if it might be supportive to actually write your book to a single person, real or imagined. Consider what Elizabeth Gilbert, author of many bestsellers including *Eat, Pray, Love*, wrote on a passionate Facebook post in 2019: "Tell your story TO someone. Pick one person you love or admire or want to connect with, and write the whole thing directly to them—like you're writing a letter. This will bring forth your natural voice. Whatever you do, do NOT write to a demographic. Ugh." Publishers care about demographics and your book's saleability to that target market. But you want to move beyond that and get deeper and more personal if you want to reach your reader most effectively.

I can't overestimate how powerful this next exercise is, not only for clarifying your specific audience but also for shaping and organizing your main message in a way that will resonate and offer the benefits you are hoping to catalyze in others.

TAKE ACTION

Create an audience avatar: a single person you can imagine speaking to in your writing. You may give them a name here.

_____

Give an overview of this person's demographics (from earlier): name, job, relationship, city of residence, etc.

_____

_____

Consider overall traits. Are they: Settled? Conservative? Intuitive? Risk-averse? Spiritual? Impulsive? Adventurous? List some of your readers' key traits that may be relevant to your book project.

_____

_____

_____

What are his/her main stressors or struggles in life? His/her fears?

_____

_____

_____

Audience Focus

What does s/he love and care about? Her/his hopes?

_____
_____
_____

What do their lives look like, inner and outer?

_____
_____
_____

What media (blogs, podcasts, socials, magazines, books, music, TV) do they love? Where do they get their information?

_____
_____
_____

What books do they love, both genres and specifics? How do they consume books? Why do they read books?

_____
_____
_____

Who are their s/heroes, role models, and favorite influential people?

_____
_____
_____

How will your book land in their hands?

_____
_____

PART FOUR:

WHERE IS YOUR READER AND WHERE DO THEY NEED TO GO?

Once you've clarified your primary audience, their demographics, and their psychographics, we still need to take things one step further. This part is important. If you want to write a book that connects to and is valuable to your reader, you need to know where they are right now in relationship to the topic or issue you will focus on in your book.

What are their core beliefs, perceptions, values, and attitudes as they relate to your topic/issue/themes?

_____
_____
_____

What does this person struggle with, as it relates to your topic? What are their problems, pain points, and issues? What keeps them up at night? What do they wish were different?

_____
_____
_____

What have they tried already in order to change this thing they struggle with? How has that worked out?

_____
_____
_____

Audience Focus

What are this person's burning desires—what do they want and need? How do they want to feel as it relates to the material of your book?

What are their biggest potential points of resistance to your work?

How will your book be of value to them?

What problem will it solve for them? What is at stake for them if they don't solve this problem?

PART FIVE
SELF AS AUDIENCE

"Rather than merely analyze the audience, the rhetor [writer] becomes the audience. The two merge, become one, and the union results in action."
— CHAIM PERELMAN

We are an audience to our own book, and this is an important relationship. By necessity, we must split in two mentally in order to be in both writer-mind and audience-mind. In audience-mind, you are the gatekeeper, the liaison, between the writer (yourself, I know, this gets a little weird) and your other readers.

To take self-as-audience in a different direction, for some authors the most important and useful way for them to conceive of their audience is to actually see their reader avatar as a previous version of themselves. Perhaps the book is written to the thirteen-year-old you, or the you that was before you underwent the massive transformation you write about in your book. You can consider your audience as some present or former aspect or version of yourself. You can also bet that your life will be changed as you write this book and are influenced by it.

Considering Audience as You Write

It can be helpful to retain awareness of your audience as you write to help you connect with, appeal to, and serve your readers. There are also times when you need to throw everyone out of the room, so to speak, as you write so you can express yourself uncensored and without any limitations. What is required, and when, will depend on your unique writing process.

The best advice I can offer is to find a dynamic relationship with audience consideration. You don't want to over-focus on your audience to the point that it stifles your creative process. You also don't want to ignore your audience altogether. You want to hold audience consideration loosely in your mind as you write, particularly for the first draft. Also know that the drafting, editing, and beta reader processes are opportunities to consider your audience again and how to appeal to them.

For my book *Birth Your Story*, I'd gone as far as I could with my own audience consideration for drafts one and two, and then it was time to bring in a real test audience. I shared my book draft with a small circle of trusted people who fell into my ideal audience criteria. I asked for their feedback—what landed well, felt powerful, was useful … and what was confusing, raised more complicated emotions or concerns, and so on. This feedback was invaluable to my process. (We'll talk more about this later with beta readers.)

It would have been detrimental to my process to have invited them in as readers of my first draft. I was still in my creation mode and needed to distill my thoughts and ideas into the soup of my book before inviting a crew of cooks into the kitchen. This worked really well for me.

You, of course, will want to consider how you will engage imagined and real audiences as you work through your book-writing process.

"But What Will THEY Think?"

This is a common concern of authors, particularly those who plan to share personal information or other vulnerable or expository content in their books. In other words, most memoir writers and a good deal of nonfiction writers.

It is normal and considerate of us to care for the impact of our words on the lives of people we may speak about in our books.

Sometimes, the truth hurts.

So, how do we manage this balance?

I talk more about this in Appendix A, but for now, I will suggest this: Write the truth first. Unabashedly. Form an alliance with your expression of the truth. Without compromise. This is about you and your soul getting the truth down on paper, which is one of the bravest damn things you may ever do.

Later, during revision, you can put on a more discerning and judicious lens and decide what to keep, what to omit, and what to change. Your editor and other members of your book support team can help you navigate this.

A colleague of mine trains her memoir students to practice saying these words in the mirror in response to potential critical comments from loved ones about their book content:

"Yes, _____ (fill in the name of your sister/brother/cousin, annoying sister-in-law), I hear that's not how you experienced what happened, but it is how I experienced what happened."

So, you might consider practicing those words. In the meantime, write true and edit later.

As you write, become aware of not only the potential impact of your words on your audience (even a single member of your audience) but also your *intention*.

Writing out of spite and revenge is not an ideal place from which to offer a book to the world. When we are talking about trauma, past pain, or difficult truths, things can get nuanced, but we're in a good space when we are using the raw materials of our lives in service to the deeper truths and messages—often hard-earned and still a bit tender—that we have to share.

Use your journal for the rants (journals are so valuable), and use your book for the gold you've alchemized from the lead of your life. That said, don't be afraid to explore the grittier truths.

See Appendix A to go deeper into audience consideration.

CHAPTER 7

Your Book Concept
WHAT ARE YOU WANTING TO EXPRESS?

Here, the point is to begin to articulate your book's overall concept and how you will present what you have to say. Please keep in mind that this is an ever-changing landscape, and it will undoubtedly shift as you move through your drafting process. But you have to start somewhere. And breaking the big vision into smaller chunks and manageable pieces is paramount to your success.

Writing a whole book can be daunting, but writing *part* of a book—writing a scene, fleshing out an idea—is totally possible and much more accessible. Let's work through this with a mind for making the parts manageable and giving you clarity about what to write.

Genre and Topic/Subject of Your Book

If you haven't already, identify your book's genre or category. This may be obvious to you, or you may clarify your genre by perusing the bookstore to get a feel for books similar to yours and how they are classified.

From there, we move a step into greater specificity with our topic or subject. If you'd like further clarification on moving from genre to subject, you can look at other books' copyright pages and how the books have been cataloged with the Library of Congress (if traditionally published). Here are a few examples:

Genre	Topic(s)
memoir	early motherhood journey
memoir	travel along the Pacific Coast Trail
relationships	intimacy and sexuality in long-term partnerships

health	the female body; physiology
psychology	self-empowerment
self-help	managing money
politics	women's rights globally
spirituality	the Divine Feminine; self-care
writing	birth stories; expressive writing
family	parenting; child-rearing; child development

What is your book about? State both the genre and the more specific topic or subject of your book. You know you're still in subject territory if you are specific enough without getting into your stance on the topic (which comes next).

_____

_____

_____

_____

_____

Main Message of Your Book

"Every successful piece of nonfiction should leave the reader with one provocative thought that he or she didn't have before."
— WILLIAM ZINSSER, *On Writing Well*

The main message is the case you are making for a way of seeing, thinking about, feeling about, understanding, or acting regarding the topic. It is your central claim, main point, position on the subject, thesis, or conclusion. This is the higher-level message that covers all the key points you make throughout the book. Yes, memoirs also have a main message or key argument.

It can help to ask yourself the following questions:
- What do I want my audience to think, believe, feel, know, do, change,

or understand as a result of reading my book?
- What statement or message would achieve these aims?
- What is the solution I am offering, and for what specific problem/desire?
- What is the unifying message thread through all the major aspects of my work/book?

Examples:
- *Writing your birth story is empowering and beneficial regardless of your beliefs, birth, or background.*
- *The most effective way to fight global poverty is to empower women.*
- *As women, using the heroine's journey as a framework to understand our lives offers the potential for wholeness, empowerment, and spiritual awakening.*

What is your book's main message (in one or two succinct sentences)?

_____
_____
_____
_____
_____
_____

Key Ideas and Themes

What are the key ideas you will present to support your main idea? What are the key themes you will weave together to show your main message? Key ideas or themes can also be called claims. Your central claims will often support or be aspects of your main idea. So, we are getting more specific here. Identifying your central claims may help you gain a sense of the sequence or presentation of your ideas throughout your book.

In a more story-based book (memoir or creative nonfiction), you may consider the various themes you are threading through your book. (These may contain claims—statements or opinions about these themes—that you explicitly or implicitly make in your book.) You may want to consider your stories first in order to get to your themes. Also, themes may not fully emerge until you begin diving into your writing and discover them.

For example:
If my main idea is that "writing your story down is empowering and beneficial," my key ideas may include:
- Writing helps us remember.
- Writing helps us process and digest.
- Writing helps us (re)claim our stories as our own.
- Writing helps us heal.
- Writing helps us honor.

Addressing each of these central claims may become part of a chapter or a whole chapter.

Other ways to consider your key ideas and themes:
- What are the subtopics that your main idea is composed of?
- What are the steps you need to take your reader through to grasp your main idea? In memoir, what are the steps of learning and evolution *you* went through along the way?
- What are the aspects of your main idea that you need to guide your reader through?
- What are the skills your reader needs to gain?
- What are the criteria your reader needs to meet to fully understand and adopt/embody your main idea?
- Are there key questions or avenues of inquiry your reader needs to engage in relating to your topic?

What are the key ideas or major themes/ideas you will weave through your book (which fall under the larger premise of your main idea)?

_____
_____
_____
_____
_____
_____
_____

Evidence: Supporting Your Ideas

Getting one step deeper, begin to consider how you will support your ideas and illustrate your themes with evidence, data, and supporting information.

Here are the types of support you may use:
- Stories and scenes, real or fictitious
- Personal experience
- Case studies: detailed studies of the development of a person, group, or situation over time; specific instances used to support a general principle
- Research studies
- Definition
- Reasons/reasoning
- Facts: ideas or statements that have been proven as true; information
- Statistics: numerical data produced through surveys, research, or polls
- Examples (historical or contemporary): specific instances that illustrate general statements
- Analogies (a way of explaining something by comparing it to something else)
- Illustrations

- Interviews
- Citing experts (quotation, paraphrase, summary)
- Hypothetical situations: "what if" scenarios that describe possible effects of specific actions
- Anecdotes (short, entertaining narratives about real incidents or persons)
- Comparisons
- Shared values/beliefs (called commonplaces)
- Direct observations/sensory details
- Metaphors (using a word, phrase, or concept in an imaginative way to stand for or represent something else)

What sorts of evidence will you primarily rely on to support your ideas and claims in your book? What can you say about each type you've selected (i.e., when/where will you use them, how, and why)?

_____
_____
_____
_____
_____

CHAPTER 8

PUTTING IT ALL TOGETHER
BOOK COVER VISIONING

The content on the back of your book is your chance to tell people what your book is about and persuade them to buy or read it. This is like your elevator speech or pitch for the book.

Now that we've developed much of the foundation for your book (clarifying key details about author, audience, subject, and purpose), it's time to put it all together in a draft of your book's back cover text. This is a visioning practice to help you anchor in all these foundational elements of your book project and talk about your project succinctly. *Plus*, it's going to make it real.

I suggest taking this into Canva or another design program, if you are so inclined, and making yourself an actual draft of your book cover! You might even cover another book you have with this cover. Many of my clients who've done this process say it feels *massively* supportive.

You'll also want to return to this chapter in the Design phase of your book project when you are ready to write the final version of the back of your book.

Elements of a Book's Back Cover

Here are examples of text pulled from two actual book back covers so that you can see how each of the common elements of a book cover are woven together. I encourage you to take a few books off your own shelves and explore how they weave these elements together.

From THE BOOK OF SHE by Sara Avant Stover

Personal Growth/women's interest

FOLLOW YOUR HEROINE'S JOURNEY TO RECLAIM FEMININE POWER AND WISDOM

Women face many challenging transitions on the pilgrimage from girlhood through womanhood: menses, love and heartbreak, motherhood, menopause. Devoid of a central narrative, these rites of passage too often happen in shame and secrecy, leaving women doubting their personal power and self-worth.

Best-selling author and founder of The Way of the Happy Woman, Sara Avant Stover saw how women erroneously viewed these initiations as "curses" and **sought to present a new model** that reflected the power and wisdom unique to the feminine path.

The Book of SHE **celebrates** all that it means to be a woman, from mythological underpinnings to the cycles of our day-to-day lives. Drawing on archetypes including Mary Magdalene, the Dark Goddess, and Green Tara, Stover will guide you on a journey home to psychological wholeness, personal empowerment, and ultimately, full feminine spiritual Awakening. Brimming with **mystery** and **magic**, this **provocative** book makes ancient wisdom and healing practices accessible to every woman who is ready to revel in her full femininity - the dark and the light - through **joyfully** becoming the heroine of her own life.

"What a truthful, beautifully written guide for women seeking a feminine path to wholeness. Sara Avant Stover offers herself in these pages, and I devoured them!"
– JENNIFER LOUDEN, AUTHOR OF *The Life Organizer*

Sara Avant Stover, a yoga and meditation instructor, best-selling author, and inspirational speaker, has taught tens of thousands of women worldwide and has been featured in *Yoga Journal*, the *Huffington Post*, *Newsweek*, and *Natural Health* and on ABC, NBC, and CBS. She lives in Boulder, Colorado

Putting It All Together

From ATOMIC HABITS by James Clear

A REVOLUTIONARY SYSTEM TO GET 1 PERCENT BETTER EVERY DAY.

People think when you want to change your life, you need to think big.

But **world-renowned habits expert** James Clear has discovered another way. He knows that **real change comes from the compound effect of hundreds of small decisions** - doing two push-ups a day, waking up five minutes earlier, or reading just one more page.

He calls them atomic habits.

In this ground-breaking book, Clear **reveals** exactly how these minuscule changes can grow into such life-altering outcomes. He **uncovers** a handful of simple life hacks (the forgotten art of Habit Stacking, the unexpected power of the Two Minute Rule, or the trick to entering the Goldilocks Zone), and **delves** into cutting-edge psychology and neuroscience to explain why they matter. Along the way, he tells inspiring stories of Olympic gold medalists, leading CEOs, and distinguished scientists who have used the science of tiny habits to stay productive, motivated, and happy.

These small changes will have a transformative effect on your career, your relationships and your life.

"This engaging hands-on book is the guide you need to break bad routines and make good ones."
– ADAM GRANT, author of *Originals*

"A special book that will change how you approach your day and live your life."
– RYAN HOLIDAY, author of *The Obstacle is the Way*

(A) SUBJECT OR CATEGORIES

Take a moment to determine one or two categories or subjects your book will fall under. You can find these on the upper left corner of many books' back covers and often on the copyright page. These will determine how books are organized at bookstores and online marketplaces. They also tell people the broad subject of the book. Examples include broad topics like self-help, spirituality, personal growth, finance, and psychology. (It's likely you've articulated this already, so just note it here.)

(B) NARRATIVE DESCRIPTION

Back cover *narratives* may have any or all of the following features: leading questions or statements, project statements, central idea or argument, value statements, author's ethos, audience connection, and descriptors—which are demonstrated in the following examples.

(1) LEADING QUESTIONS OR STATEMENTS

These indicate the **problem(s)** this book will solve. Examples:

"Women face many challenging transitions on the pilgrimage from girlhood through womanhood. … Devoid of a central narrative, these rites of passage too often happen in shame and secrecy." (*The Book of She* by Sara Avant Stover)

(2) PROJECT STATEMENTS

A *project* is the *kind of work* you are doing in your book (what you are *doing*, not what you are *saying*). To say what kind of work you are doing, you need a verb. Verbs are bolded in the following examples:

"*Woman* ultimately **challenges** widely accepted Darwinian-based gender stereotypes. Angier **shows** how cultural biases have influenced research … she **offers** optimistic alternatives and transcends feminist polemics." (*Woman* by Natalie Angier)

"The book **inspires** and **supports** you to write your birth story, **takes** the intimidation and other obstacles out of writing, **offers** accessible writing prompts and support, and **includes** over 15 inspiring birth stories." (*Birth Your Story* by Jaime Fleres)

"*The Book of She* **celebrates** all that it means to be a woman … **drawing on the archetypes** …, Stover will **guide** you on a journey home." (*The Book of She* by Sara Avant Stover)

"Told with suspense and style, sparkling with warmth and humor, *Wild* **powerfully captures** the terrors and pleasures of one young woman forging ahead against all odds on a journey that maddened, strengthened, and ultimately healed her." (*Wild* by Cheryl Strayed)

"Through **case studies and lively discussion**, Perel **demonstrates** how exciting, playful and even poetic sex is possible in long-term relationships." (*Mating in Captivity* by Esther Perel)

Examples of *project* verbs are: exploring, investigating, challenging, presenting, critiquing, explaining, comparing, connecting, proposing, clarifying, and illustrating.

Writing statements like this can be a little awkward or confusing at first, so don't worry if it doesn't feel quite natural.

③ CENTRAL IDEA OR ARGUMENT

Whereas your project is what you are *doing*, your central idea or argument is what you are *saying*. In other words, what is your central claim, main point, stance, assertion, or conclusion? What case are you making for a way of seeing, understanding, thinking, or feeling about your subject? This is an umbrella statement that covers all the key points you make throughout the book.

"Kristof and WuDunn show that the most effective way to fight global poverty is to unleash the potential of women." (*Half the Sky* by Nicholas Kristof and Sheryl WuDunn)

For memoir, this may be the main theme or key message of your book. For example, and some of these might sound cliché, but they are common memoir claims: "Love conquers all," "I found myself, my power, my identity, or my purpose," "True love lets me be myself," "Tell the truth," "True strength comes from within," "We must discover what serves our soul's purpose," "Mending our collective and personal wounds, discovering our sovereignty, and owning the freedom to make our own choices are the essential tasks of the modern woman."

"When one person dares to speak her truth, it challenges us all to live our own." (*Red Hot and Holy* by Sera Beak)

④ VALUE STATEMENTS

"*Playing Big* delivers real and easy-to-implement strategies that will **enable you to have the impact, the influence, and ultimately the life you want.**" (*Playing Big* by Tara Mohr)

"You'll also find your inner identity and your external 'tribe' of like-minded people, experience the spark of inspiration, and take action to make a lasting impact on the world." (*Finding Your Way in a Wild New World* by Martha Beck)

⑤ THE AUTHOR'S ETHOS (BACKGROUND AND CREDIBILITY)

"Even as a little girl, **Harvard-trained theologian** Meggan Watterson knew something was missing from traditional religion." (*Reveal* by Meggan Watterson)

"**Bestselling author and founder** of *The Way of the Happy Woman*, Sara ..." (*The Book of She* by Sara Avant Stover)

"Martha Beck **has helped hundreds of clients** find their own North Star, fulfill their potential, and live more joyfully." (*Finding Your Own North Star* by Martha Beck)

⑥ AUDIENCE CONNECTION

"You probably have sensed that you have a higher calling and a quiet power that could change the world." (*Finding Your Way in a Wild New World* by Martha Beck)

"No matter where you rest on the spectrum of spirituality ... this story is about the desire to shed what is holding you back." (*Reveal* by Meggan Watterson)

⑦ DESCRIPTORS

Many narratives offer adjectives to describe the book. Examples include, but are definitely not limited to: bold, provocative, sparkling, wise, witty, revelatory, serious, playful, encouraging, suspenseful, straightforward, uplifting, honest, transformative, and unapologetic. You might integrate a few of these types of descriptors into your own back cover content.

Ⓒ ENDORSEMENTS

If you're in the drafting stage, you obviously won't go collect real endorsements for this exercise, as that will be a step you'll take once the manuscript is complete. But here, I invite you to think of two to three experts or influencers in your field whom you might want to ask for a blurb or endorsement of your book. Don't be afraid to think *big* right now. Even if you think someone might be out of reach, you'd be surprised. (For advice on how to get endorsements, see Appendix E.)

If you want to get really visionary right now, write out what these experts might say in praise of your book.

(D) ABOUT THE AUTHOR

This is your chance to write a two- to five-sentence paragraph about your background and credibility.

You may want to include your:

- name
- professional title(s)
- certifications, degrees, or licenses; awards or accolades
- statement of your credibility
  (what qualifies you as an expert on this topic)
- relevant experience
- past publications (books and articles)
- personal details you wish (e.g., where you live)

YOUR TURN:
WRITE THE BACK OF YOUR BOOK

Here is the visual example of what to put where on the back of your book. Use the prompts and writing spaces to follow to develop each element of your book's back cover. Then, I encourage you to go into a program such as Canva, to format everything as it would look on your actual back cover.

Ⓐ YOUR SUBJECT/GENRE $_____

Optional tagline, title or blurb

_____

Ⓑ One to three paragraphs of *narrative*, where you offer some combination of the seven narrative actions described earlier in element B.

_____

_____

_____

_____

Ⓒ Offer one or two *blurbs* here.

_____

_____

Ⓓ Write a single *About the Author* paragraph here. You may have an image of yourself here too.

_____

_____

Credits and Publisher Icon go here   BAR CODE GOES HERE

CHAPTER 9

STRUCTURAL FRAMEWORKS OVERVIEW

> *"The first principle of composition is to foresee or determine the shape of what is to come, and pursue that shape."*
> — STRUNK & WHITE, *The Elements of Style*

Determining the structure and organization of your book is one of the most challenging yet crucially important elements of book writing for most authors—it is also what often stops writers in their tracks and prevents them from moving forward in writing. Determining the structure of your work may not be easy, but it is essential and doable. The chapters of this section are meant to support you as much as possible in developing a structural plan that will work for your book.

While I am not a big proponent of a formulaic approach to book writing and structure (I find that most books have a unique essence that rebels against oversimplified formulas), there are some "moves" and organizational frameworks that serve as useful launch points for our work.

We can't steal other authors' ideas and stories—*what* they say—but we can study and steal structure—*how* they do it.

Here is an overview of different broad structural frameworks you may find useful. This is also intended to be like a menu, but don't let the options confuse you! The point of a menu is to find what sounds delicious to you. These are various options.

Please note that, as I say elsewhere, writing is a process of discovery, which means you learn about your topic and your book as you go. Therefore, your structure will evolve and develop as you actually write. The point of exploring structure before you write is to create enough of a plan that you can move forward with focus and some semblance of a container. I want to help you avoid free-falling through book space and getting lost in other dimensions, but not create a forced structure that feels more like a straitjacket than a warm hug. Let's reach for the latter when it comes to your book structure.

Structure creates freedom. Your job in the planning phase is to explore your topic, stories, ideas, and evidence enough that you can sketch a rough plan that will allow you to move forward *and* have the freedom to modify, develop, and refine your structure as you go.

Biggest Issues with Structure That Writers Encounter

As a developmental editor, I see a handful of major structural issues in books all the time. They are:

1. **Flow:** Chapters don't have a logical flow, the sequencing of information doesn't make intuitive sense to the reader, they aren't able to follow from one idea to the next, the writer doesn't stay focused on one idea at a time but is all over the place or in many places at once.

2. **Repetition:** Ideas are repeated over and over again throughout the book, without taking the reader's journey meaningfully forward; thus, making the book "fluffy."

3. **Tangents:** The writer goes on major tangents and offers information that is not in line with the focus of a particular chapter, section, or their overall message or topic. Out-of-scope coverage of topics and themes is also included here.

4. **Gaps:** There are gaping holes in the content or major leaps made without adequate bridges or transitions. Perhaps the reader is expected to guess how to fill those gaps.

While developmental editing can point out these issues after a manuscript is written, you can do a lot on the front end in structural and organizational work to avoid these major issues. This will save you a lot of time and mental energy later on.

Finding a Basic Structure

BEGINNING, MIDDLE, AND END

This is the simplest of all book structures. If nothing else, you may want to map out what will come first, second, and last in your book. Some examples:

- problem(s), solution(s), benefit(s)/results
- before the rupture, the rupture, after the rupture
- old way, transformation opportunity, new way
- a way of looking at something, the components of applying this approach, the impact of this approach
- departure, initiation, return (see Hero and Heroine's Journey details to come for more on this option)

This is obviously not as refined as a working Table of Contents, which we want to move toward at the appropriate stage in our book process. But this can be a helpful first step in considering structure.

Seeking Structure in Other Works

As I mentioned, you never want to steal content or ideas from others, but you can study the structure other writers use and adapt it to your book's needs. Most of the time, we read books for content, and if the structure is executed well, we don't notice it. However, as a writer, I encourage you to re-read your favorite books or those that are well-regarded, and study structure. Look at what a writer *does*, not what they *say*. Notice *how* they do what they do. If you find a structure you love and can adapt to your work, use that as your starting framework. You might consider looking at the structure of books that don't share the same topic or scope as your book, so it is easier to separate out content from structure.

What's to Come

In the next three chapters, we will be exploring a number of rich options for you to consider as you develop a framework for your book. First, we will look at nonfiction structures most appropriate to when you have ideas and concepts driving your book. We'll also talk about a hybrid option called a teaching memoir. That will take us into some ideas about structuring memoir, which is story-based. From there, we'll dive deeper into exploring story-based structures, which will help both authors of nonfiction and memoir. There are many options here, try not to let it confuse you! I recommend reading all of these, giving yourself some space, and allowing these options to inform, not force, you into developing a structural plan for your book.

CHAPTER 10

FRAMEWORKS FOR NONFICTION

In this chapter, we'll explore a menu of options for developing the structure of your transformational nonfiction book; that is, a book driven by ideas, concepts, or a body of work. Technically, memoir is a subset of nonfiction, but we are going to treat it as its own animal in Chapters 11 and 12, given that memoirs are story-driven. In this chapter, we will also talk about the blend between idea-driven and story-driven books.

Transformational Book: How-to/Process or Thought Leadership

Most transformational nonfiction books fall into this category. A process-based book solves a problem or satisfies a need or desire in readers by guiding people through a process. A thought leadership book guides people through a new way of thinking. Often, a book does both, which is why these types are combined here. For most books of this kind, you'll want to determine whether your content lends itself to a *sequence* approach or a *component* approach. In a sequence approach, you'll present steps in a process that are usually carried out in the same order you present them in the book. This is common in how-to books or books based on a specific sequence of steps you want your reader to take. An example of a book that takes a sequence approach is my client Cissi Williams's book *Your Heart Knows How to Heal You*.[1] The book takes readers through a specific sequence of steps or explorations that are meant to be completed in a particular order.

A component approach presents aspects of your topic you want your reader to consider. The order of these aspects doesn't necessarily have to be in sequence. However, you might present them in an order most advantageous to your reader, especially if the components build on each other. Many transformational nonfiction books use this approach. An example of a component-based book is *The Seven Principles for Making Marriage Work* by John Gottman and Nan Silver.[2]

At its simplest, this book looks like:
- Introduction
- Step/aspect 1
- Step/aspect 2
- Step/aspect 3
- Step/aspect 4
- Step/aspect 5 …
- Conclusion

Situation, Solutions, Benefits

The structure may also be based on the problem/situation, solution, and benefits. Here are some questions to help you map a situation/solutions/benefits structure. These can be parts one, two, and three of your book, or you may present an overall situation/solution in your introduction, and for each chapter or section, you look at one aspect of the situation and present the corresponding new way and its benefits. Then, the conclusion brings it all together.

SITUATION / OLD OR CURRENT WAY

- What is the situation?
- What is the challenge/struggle/problem/suffering/injustice/blanket insanity that is relevant to your reader?
- How much are they aware of this problem? (This will indicate how much explaining you may need to do in your book in order to establish the situation.)
- How will you need to talk about this situation to your audience in order for them to connect to what you are saying?
- What aspects of the situation are relevant to explore?
- What might be their reaction to how you express the situation, and how will you address this?
- What is your connection (direct experience/passion/relationship) to this situation? What are your relevant stories?
- What evidence do you have to support the picture you paint about the situation?

SOLUTIONS / NEW WAY

- What is the new way (this could be a new mindset, a new understanding, or new actions) that you are presenting?
- What is the insight, the moment of transformation, or the shift you are advocating?
- What will it take for your audience to understand and embrace your New Way?
- What stories and other evidence will you present to illustrate and support this New Way?
- Application: What steps or shifts does your audience need to make in order to adopt and apply your New Way?

BENEFITS

- What are the benefits to the New Way?
- What would/will life be like for your readers if they apply/adopt your New Way?
- How do these benefits link up with your reader's needs, longings, and desires?

The Mountain Climb Structure

This is one of my favorite structural support tools for those writing transformational how-to or thought leadership books. It calls on the metaphor of your book journey as a mountain climb. Consider the extent to which this frame may support the work you want to do in your book, and simply take what is useful to you. You can adapt this as you find most helpful.

PART ONE: THE CALL TO ADVENTURE + OVERVIEW OF TERRAIN

- Get to know the group: Check in about what's happening at home right now that has called each to this adventure. *Assessment: Where are you in your life right now?*
- Guide explains this "common" situation (problem/desire) and how

it connects to the climb ahead: *What are we all doing here?*
- Guide frames this situation in a particular way by presenting their overall idea/philosophy, making a case for *why this mountain, why you as a guide, and why climb it in the way you suggest?*
- Guide's experience with the mountain: Your own story of having climbed this mountain before or your relationship to the mountain now.
- Orientation to the overall terrain you'll encounter (book's introduction).
- Connect back to the group: Address fears and concerns, hopes and expectations.

PART TWO: ESTABLISHING BASECAMP

- *What needs to be established before we can set off on the adventure?*
- A shared view: Explores core principles in greater detail
- Right gear: Overview of the tools you'll need for this climb
- Technical terms: The names of things (definitions)

PART THREE: HOW TO CLIMB THE MOUNTAIN

First, consider if you are taking a *chronology or components* (or a hybrid) approach. If you're taking a chronology approach, what are the steps/sequence/segments of the climb? *What happens first? Then? And so on? (Do you have to descend before you can rise?)* If you're taking a components approach, what are the aspects/elements/features/principles you'll encounter on the journey?

- **Invite** us into the segment of the journey with a **story** or something else that hooks our attention and orients us to the next leg of the journey
- **What** the aspect or step is
- **Why** it must be navigated
- **How** to navigate through each one
- The **specific tools** you'll need and the **actions** you'll take to succeed

in traversing each step or aspect
- How to **get the most** out of each leg of this journey
- **Evidence** that what you suggest works or is a good idea (examples, case studies, stats, stories)
- The **common risks, obstacles, or pitfalls** with each leg of the journey
- How will we measure **success**?
- At each step, how do we **reflect** on our progress?

PART FOUR: WHY GO AT ALL + DESCRIBING THE VIEW FROM THE TOP

(This part is movable; it may come at the beginning, at the end, or interwoven through part three)

- Benefits of climbing
- Results: How this climb changes you
- What life is like at this elevation, with inspiring examples
- How this satisfies the trekkers' (your readers') goals, dreams, needs, and desires
- What does the vista (future) look like from here?
- What is the next mountain to climb?

Main argument (what): What is this mountain in the first place? Why climb this mountain in this way?

Project (how): What this journey/process is about or entails.

Purpose (why): What is the overall outcome or effect of having climbed to the top?

Interview Book or Anthology

This is the book where you showcase the ideas or stories of others. Even with these books, you are the chief curator and at the helm. For an interview book, you'll want to digest and shape your raw interviews, covering only what is most interesting, essential, and relevant to your book's main point. You may present them in an interview or narrative style. You might group/order interviews by common themes/topics related to your message and frame interviews with your own introduction and conclusion (summarizing key learnings and giving readers an idea of where to go from here).

Barbara Huson (formerly Stanny) does an incredible job with a mostly interview-based book in *Secrets of Six-Figure Women*.[3] I also love what Hilary Hart did in *The Unknown She*.[4] Another anthology you might consider as an example is *Labor Day*,[5] edited by Eleanor Henderson and Anna Solomon.

For an anthology, you'll want an introduction that presents your main idea or area of exploration. I encourage you to look at the introductions of anthologies to study the "moves" they make. (I cover the contents of an introduction in great depth later in this book.) You will also want to consider how a reader will move through the stories; you are still responsible for creating a narrative arc or a sensible order from the stories you include. This may include introducing each contributor in some way prior to including their work, and framing or shaping your reader's experience of the piece after you've presented it.

The Teaching Memoir

If you are struggling to decide whether you should present your ideas via a story-based memoir or an idea-based nonfiction book, there is an option to do both. As I see it, all of this is a matter of proportion along a spectrum between story and idea. In a nonfiction book, you lead with your ideas and use stories (yours or others) to illustrate and support your ideas or your proposed process. The ideas lead, and the stories support.

In memoir, you are using your story as the central vehicle by which you share your messages. The stories do the work, and the messages or concepts are more implicit than directly conveyed (they are revealed, not directly told).

In a hybrid, you have more of a balance between the story and the message. The hybrid has more story than the nonfiction book and less story than the memoir. The hybrid has more of a direct setting forth of the ideas or processes you advocate around the themes, issues, or topics of your book.

I do see some writers get tripped up in the process of developing such a hybrid. Usually, the trouble happens when it's not clear whether the story or idea will be driving the book forward. It is often difficult, I've found, for the ideal sequence of concept presentation to fit in perfectly parallel with one's chronological story threads.

For example, I worked with a therapist who wanted to both present a body of conceptual work around her theme, and her chronological story of living the experience she was writing about. We worked a lot on how to find a structure that really served both aims: her telling her story and her sharing her ideas. The trouble was in not deciding clearly which one would lead. Like in a dance, they were stepping on each other's toes. In my experience, you do need to decide which one will lead and which will follow. If the concepts are leading, the stories may come out of chronology and be chosen for how well they illustrate an idea. If the story is leading, your conceptual framing needs to be connected to what each piece of the story reveals.

You can apply the framework options in this chapter to develop a hybrid structure. For example, you may lead each chapter with a story from your personal journey and reference that story and your experience throughout the chapter as you articulate the central teaching tool, principle, or step in a process that you are sharing with your reader. You can blend your personal experiences with your ideas to shape a deeply personal and compelling transformational book.

Since we are in a gray zone territory with the hybrid, I do want to caution you against a tone that may be experienced by your readers as preachy (unless that is what you are going for). Remember to allow your stories to reveal their lessons without feeling like you have to explain every part to your readers. (I talk more about this in Section Two.) Also, as with any frame you use, keep your reader and their needs, desires, and experiences present and in focus as you write a hybrid book. The content is about you and your ideas, but it is all in service to *them*.

CHAPTER 11

Frameworks for Memoir

> *"There on the bed, in her pigtails and pain, my daughter was me—the little girl I once was, the woman I am now, still struggling to answer the questions: How can I be expansive and free and still be loved? Am I going to be a lady or am I going to be fully human? Do I trust the unfolding and continue to grow, or do I shut all of this down so I fit?"*
>
> — GLENNON DOYLE MELTON, *Love Warrior*[1]

Your memoir is not a chronological account of your life (that is an autobiography). Memoir is about you, and it is not. Technically, it focuses on your life experiences and how you choose to weave them together. But memoir transcends the personal by allowing readers to see themselves, and the universal, through your specific story. It is about a universal truth (or truths) as illustrated by a well-considered and presented collection of your life experiences. It's not what happened; it's what you did with it. It's about the truth, wisdom, healing, insight, and perspective you gained from it all.

Memoir, like other nonfiction, has an argument: It advocates for a way of seeing things and speaks to a universal truth. This is what takes your personal story and makes it meaningful to your readers. This truth or argument is the bridge between you. *What have you learned, or what wisdom do you now carry, as a result of what you have been through? How does that connect to your readers? Might it help them access this universal truth? Might it compel or inspire their own growth, healing, or transformation? May it solve a problem or meet a burning desire of theirs? Might it offer them a road map or make them feel less alone?* Readers read memoir for their own transformation, and your story is the catalyst.

Two Approaches: Story and Message

What makes memoir effective is having a specific story you want to tell or a single message you want to share, and then sharing the experiences/scenes/stories that are relevant to that message/story.

For the story approach, think of your memoir as sharing a single chapter of your life. Ask yourself: *When did that chapter begin? When did it end? What did I learn along the way, and how will it benefit my readers?* Having a container around what you're going to share will help you stay on track. The best way to get to the truth about something is to share the big things in the small details of your experience.

For the message approach, get crystal clear on the message you want to share. *What are the questions your book sets out to explore? What are the messages it will convey?* Is it about regaining self-love, building a successful business, or adapting to a new culture? Once you are clear on your message, break it into subtopics you want to discuss. Then, for each of those subtopics, think about anecdotes/stories/scenes from your life that are relevant to that specific subtopic.

In either approach, you'll only want to share the parts of your experience that drive the story forward and serve your purpose. You'll need to be highly selective in what you choose from the giant storehouse of your life story and leave the rest behind. You'll also want to show your transformation, growth, and healing—let your reader witness this change and experience life's wonders through your journey. Otherwise, you are just taking us on a trip through your day planner.

Here are examples of structure that you may want to consider for your memoir.

Ways to Structure Memoir

Strict chronological. The easiest structure is beginning your story at the earliest point in time and progressing to the latest point in time. However, this structure can lack dramatic tension or, at worst, end up as a boring repetition of "this happened, then that happened." If you want to use a strict chronological structure, take extra care that each chapter contributes to the main message of your story and contains ample tension for your readers to want to keep reading.

Open with the turning point. Open the story with a dramatic event, then drop back in time and relay the events that brought the narrator to the dramatic climax. Many novels and movies use this technique quite successfully. Similarly, you can determine what your cornerstone story or scene is, upon which the rest of the book can be built, because it provides the sturdiest foundation for the rest of your story (this may or may not be the "climax.")

Two timelines. Another variation is to carry two timelines forward simultaneously, alternating chapters, until the two timelines meet and merge in the end.

Reverse chronological. You can reverse the order of events chronologically, starting with "how things turned out" and working your way back in time to "how it all started." NOTE: This structure can be difficult to pull off. If telling the story backward enhances character development, dramatic tension, or important and essential windows into the narrator's journey, then a reverse timeline may be worth considering.

Thematic. Ordering scenes along one or more thematic threads is another way to structure a memoir. Themes may include any elements the scenes have in common, such as relationship conflicts, illness, geography, or repetitive historical events. The scenes do not have to occur in chronological order and, in fact, can jump all over the place in time as long as the transitions between jumps are strong and do not confuse your readers.

Please see the next chapter on story-based structures for an even deeper look into how to structure your memoir.

Choosing Your Memoir's Structure

Ultimately, you need to figure out what works best for the story you are telling. And you might need to experiment with a few ways to arrange your story before finding the right one. Ideally, you'll know your approach before you begin writing, but you might also need to do a lot of writing (or pre-writing) before you fully understand your underlying themes and the focus of your story.

To get to structure, you might first want to determine a chronological timeline of events/stories/scenes that may be appropriate for your memoir. So, at least you are clear about what happened in what order. Then, you can begin to make decisions about sequencing and scene selection based on the structure options just described. I recommend diving into the next chapter about story-based structures before you settle on a structure for your memoir.

Additional Tips

STUDY MEMOIRS YOU LOVE

Remember, you can't borrow or steal another's content/ideas/stories, but you can steal structure. And it is wise to study the greats. Analyze the structure of one or a few of your favorite memoirs:
- Draw a timeline and locate the events of each chapter on the timeline. Does the author move straight through her story chronologically? Or does the narrative move back and forth through time?
- Identify the theme or themes for each chapter. Are the themes organized in clusters, or are the themes threaded throughout the story?
- If the memoir includes more than one voice, note how the author organizes the voices and the transitions between them.
- Look at transitions between chapters and between events on your timeline. What techniques does the author use to effectively transition from one theme or time to another?

Notice what other memoirists do and how they do it so well. Cheryl Strayed divided her book *Wild*[2] into five parts. Elizabeth Gilbert structured *Eat, Pray, Love*[3] into three sections based on her location (in Italy, India, and Bali), but she also divided the book into 108 parts like the beads of a *japa mala*, with each section having thirty-six parts (she writes about her structural choices in her introduction). Sophie Strand's memoir, *The Body is a Doorway*,[4] is divided into twenty-one chapters that follow her chronological story, but are named by the themes she presents in each chapter.

THE BINGE SHOW EFFECT

When you write memoir, include enough tension at the end of each scene or chapter to keep the reader engrossed and wanting to know more. More formally, this is called narrative drive. Narrative drive is the jet engine that propels your reader through your book and keeps them curious, engaged, and wanting to read more. It's delicate and fragile: it can be broken with one clunky scene or paragraph. It's also Eiffel Tower tough: it can hold up the entire architecture of your story or argument. When narrative drive is lacking, a book starts to lose momentum and risks a crash and burn.

CONSIDER TRANSITIONS

When you are considering the order of your scenes and stories, pay attention to the effectiveness of the transitions you make between them. Read the last paragraph of A and the first paragraph of B and see if they work together. I cover transitions in greater detail later when we discuss the drafting process.

REMEMBER, WRITING IS A PROCESS OF DISCOVERY

You will learn a lot about your themes and the meaning of your stories by writing them down. The first draft is a process by which you discover and make a mess of things ... revision is for making sense of everything and cleaning/shaping it into something ordered and cohesive. Don't be afraid to make a mess and discover along the way.

The point of structure consideration at the outset is not to set some plan in stone but to plan enough that you can move forward with focus and flexibility to further develop and refine your plan as you go.

CHAPTER 12

Story-Based Frameworks

You'd be surprised how many books, films, TV shows, and other story-based communications are based on the classic five-part structure and the hero's/heroine's journey. Here, I am presenting three related frameworks: the general five-part narrative arc, the hero's journey, and the heroine's journey. The five-part narrative structure traces back through literary and theatrical works for centuries, the hero's journey is considered the monomyth told cross-culturally, and the heroine's journey was developed by feminist scholars as an adaptation to the monomyth that fits the feminine more aptly.

These latter two frameworks, the hero's and heroine's journeys, are perfect for transformational nonfiction; and they have a lot of overlap. They are currently in a more binary gendered expression, in part because the hero's journey is what was first set forth as *the* journey of transformation, and feminist scholars critiqued the framework as being male-centric, posing that for female-bodied beings, the journey looks different.

That all said, the truth is that any being can navigate either of these frameworks in their own life quests. The point is to find yourself in these frameworks, if they are resonant for you, and notice if this framework is supportive for the story or message you have to share. I personally like to think of these as reflections of one another: one is an interior journey of transformation, and the other is an exterior journey of transformation, though they each contain and mirror one another.

The Five-Part Narrative Arc

The five-part narrative arc is a long-lived, enduring story structure. It is sometimes called Freytag's Pyramid, after a nineteenth-century German novelist and playwright, yet it was developed long before him. Some attribute it to Aristotle[1] and his work *Poetics*, some claim that Shakespeare was the developer of this structure, while others attribute it to Horace,[2] a Roman poet and playwright who wrote about drama in his *Ars Poetic* in 19 BCE, though it had its limits for book-form applications.

For any story you are telling in your book, you may want to consider this basic story structure.

1. **Exposition:** The exposition introduces important background details, including setting (time and place), events that occurred prior to the main story or topic, and the characters' backstories. It may also include the hook or the (emotional) appeal to draw us in and keep us engaged and reading further.

2. **Rising action:** A series of related moments that build toward the point of greatest interest (climax). The entire plot depends on these details.

3. **Climax:** The turning point; the moment that changes the protagonist's fate (if things have been going badly, she can now draw on her strengths like never before and is often required to).

4. **Falling action:** Comprised of the events after the climax; it wraps up the plot and leads toward resolution. It may contain a moment of final suspense.

5. **Resolution:** *Denouement* in French, this includes events from the end of the falling action to the end of the story. Conflicts and complexities are resolved, creating a new normal or reality for the protagonist.

The Heroine's Journey

This work has been developed by several scholars, feminists, and writers, including, but certainly not limited to, Maureen Murdock,[3] Sara Avant Stover,[4] LiYana Silver,[5] and Heather Jo Flores.[6] This arc is situated inside a contemporary context of some cultures alive on our planet today, including most Western cultures.

The Illusion: Protagonist in a state of illusion. She's rejected the feminine and/or her own soul essence in her search for identity and strives for success in a patriarchal, capitalistic, culturally conditioned system that has taught her to source her own power, goodness, worth, and identity from outside herself, which has harmed her.

Prepares for Journey: She decides or is forced to leave normal life; a rupture/crisis/inciting incident casts her onto the journey; the unbearable nature of, or ejection from, current reality may unfold. This journey may be inner, with or without an outer counterpart(s).

The Descent: She navigates some great loss (which may or may not include depression/anxiety/mental illness, dysfunction, physical illness, breakdown, betrayal, relationship loss, death, a move, and so on). This stage can also be described as the Catalyst, where she is driven by curiosity and a desire for her own wholeness. Here, she often must:
- navigate the darkness/death
- strip away illusions and false sources of power
- confront pain and trauma
- go deep within
- face the shadow: abandoned, discarded, rejected, suppressed, or unmet parts of herself
- reckon with broken systems that have failed her
- reclaim what has been cast below or rejected; reclaim what is whole, true and essential about her nature

This phase may involve intense resistance, doubts, trials, and confronting one's own past and non-serving beliefs and values. She may experience a set of challenges and tests here, building to a climactic shift in the next stage.

The Initiation: This is often what we may call the darkest hour and that moment of first light where old life becomes unrecognizable; this may involve a deeper invitation into death, a deep rite of passage, and a more complete transformation one has been preparing for (knowingly or unknowingly). This stage may kick off the process of ending the fight, or represent a shift in consciousness. This stage can include unlocking some new gift or wisdom. The initiation comes with the cost of the former life or consciousness, and may involve other losses. Thus, this stage likely includes grief (mourning loss of the old self and other losses) and acknowledging that the journey is not without a cost.

The Ascent: In this stage, a rebirth unfolds and greater access to wholeness is gained. This can be called the inner marriage. Some aspect of essential power is returned to our protagonist; she ventures into uncharted territory and finds renewed passion/connection to nature, creativity, life force, her body, and her own Self. She may re-identify with essential parts of herself, heal old wounds, transcend old dualities, tame and turn resistance into resilience, incorporate and honor the potency of her shadow, alchemize lead into gold, forgive self and others, find freedom from perfection, shift her relationship to the pain of the past, and so on. This adventure is often deeply relational.

The Homecoming: Here, she returns to life in a new way as a more authentic version of herself. She discovers true success and makes choices on her own terms. She is more self-defined, self-validated, sovereign, discerning, embodied, and rooted to her center. She may have a greater understanding and alignment with her soul's purpose/niche, her own essential inclinations and strengths, and so on. Here she writes her own story about who she is and what her experiences mean to her. At this stage, she may offer what she has learned to her wider community and empower others to embark on their own heroine's journey.

The Hero's Journey

This is the structure of the monomyth, based on Joseph Campbell's work in *The Hero with a Thousand Faces*,[7] originally published in 1949. The monomyth is the universal narrative arc of transformation that runs through many mythic traditions and tales worldwide and cross-culturally. Here I am using the word *hero*, but feel free to substitute *heroine*, *protagonist*, your name, or whatever else fits for you.

The **Departure**:
- **The Ordinary World:** In this stage, the hero is introduced and shown in their Ordinary World, "old" world, or native environment. The hero may be unaware of greater forces creating dynamic tension under the surface of their lives, yet they may feel dissatisfied or unfulfilled, be aware of an unmet yearning, or need to grow emotionally or psychologically. This world contrasts with the new or Special World later visited in the story. The reader gets a glimpse of what the journey ahead is about.
- **The Call to Adventure:** The hero receives information or has an experience that shakes up the situation and serves as a call to adventure. This change can be internal or external (e.g., feeling unhappy inside or losing a job or marriage). Nevertheless, the hero is prompted to leave the Ordinary World for the Special World, and a new stage begins.
- **Refusal of the Call:** The hero refuses to answer the call and turns from the adventure, perhaps due to feelings of insecurity, obligation, or fear of the unknown; yet the lure of the adventure becomes more powerful than the resistance, and the hero proceeds forth on the adventure.
- **Meeting with the Mentor**: Here, the hero meets a guide, protector, or other helper who offers support and guidance. The Mentor often knows more about the journey ahead and offers wisdom, tools, encouragement, and support along the way. The hero may also begin to develop or connect to an inner source of wisdom and support.
- **Crossing Threshold to Special World:** Here, the hero commits to leaving the Ordinary World and crossing into adventure in the Special World, an unknown and dangerous place for which the hero doesn't know the rules. The Mentor has led the hero to a threshold, but the hero has to cross it on his own. This threshold is protected by a Guardian or Gatekeeper, and the hero must prove worthy to pass.

The **Initiation**:
- **Tests, Allies, and Enemies:** The hero explores the Special World, experiencing tests and trials in this unfamiliar setting. They gain knowledge and skills in preparation for an ordeal to come. The hero doesn't succeed at every test and knows what failure feels like (because this produces growth). Here, they encounter new characters and discern friends from foes. While new friends may help the hero through tests and trials, the journey is still daunting, and complications may continue to build.
- **Approach the Innermost Cave:** Here, the hero prepares for some ultimate challenge in the Special World—perhaps by facing greater challenges and more difficult obstacles and guardians. Here, hope hangs in the balance; they may want to turn back, they may experience a big defeat (love lost, for example), or it may even seem like the antagonist is gaining an edge. They must find inner reserves of strength they may have never had called forth before. (Thus, internal transformation begins.)
- **The Ordeal:** Here, the hero faces the greatest challenge yet in the form of an antagonist (character, or situation). This is where the hero must confront death or their deepest fears; they may hit rock bottom. Yet, they are equipped with the knowledge and skills gained in previous stages of the journey. Here, a new choice must be made.
- **The Reward:** Hero receives or takes the "reward or treasure" won by facing this ultimate challenge, marking triumph over the antagonist. However, they may not recognize or be able to enjoy the reward just yet because they are still in the Special World and have to make it back out. (Real dangers may still lie ahead.)

The **Return**:
1. **The Road Back:** Now, the hero must return to Ordinary World with the reward or treasure. It can often be as dangerous to *return* as it was to *start*. This stage may include a chase scene that signals urgency and danger, or the antagonist may rally for a second round.
2. **The Resurrection:** The Hero is once again tested on the threshold of Ordinary World return. The hero experiences a final moment of death and resurrection on a higher, more complete level than before.

Resurrection may be literal or symbolic, as the hero wakes to a new world and transformed life.
3. **Return with the Elixir:** Having transcended fear and death, the hero returns home with a reward or treasure they can use to improve the Ordinary World. This *elixir*, as it is called, is meant to help someone *other* than the hero; what the hero gained on his journey benefits those beyond himself. This stage of storytelling may involve a luring twist to take us into the next book/story. The hero may be ready for new adventures or happy to settle back into life, seeing it anew.

ARCHETYPAL CHARACTERS IN A HERO'S JOURNEY

- **Hero/ine:** The protagonist or main character (even narrator) of the story.
- **Antagonist:** The antagonist can be a "bad" guy, organization, or system; an opposing/opposite or contrasting force; something inside the protagonist, such as a doubt, fear, flaw, or regret.
- **Herald:** The messenger who comes to signal the call to adventure.
- **Threshold guardians:** Those who ensure the hero is ready and prepared to cross the thresholds into and out of Ordinary World. They may put up a roadblock, yellow light, or speed bump in the road to ensure readiness (can also be a secret helper).
- **Mentors:** Guides, protectors, and teachers who come to help the hero/ine look within to find the wisdom and resources they'll need. A dark mentor may be a teacher who comes to reflect to the hero/ine their worst fear.
- **Allies:** Friends and kin who help the hero/ine along the journey.
- **Enemies/shadows:** Those who try to derail or thwart the hero/ine's progress.
- **Trickster:** Those who complicate matters for the hero/ine, yet unexpectedly lead the hero/ine toward new and necessary growth.

CRITIQUE OF THE HERO'S JOURNEY

There has been some critique of the hero's journey for how it has traditionally positioned women, privileged some while marginalizing others, and offered a limited view of the ways of transformation beyond the white, cis male world. Feminists (e.g., Catherine Bailey Kyle[8]) have developed criteria for a female-friendlier version of the hero's journey. Story must:

- Contain at least two females, who connect over something more than a male character
- Represent round, whole, and dynamic women (not just the damsel in distress, the mistress, or the witch)
- Contain at least one female "helper" or ally
- Include at least one instance of nonviolent problem-solving
- Account for multiple subjectivities
- Show effective, heroic women who are neither married (partnered) nor dead by the end
- Reject the "chosen one" archetype of hero in favor of voluntary heroism
- Not pointlessly sexualize characters

How to Use These Frameworks for Your Book

If one of these or some combination of them is resonating with the story you have to tell, consider the following. Take out a large piece of paper (butcher paper or kids craft paper in a roll can be great for this) and some colored pens. Divide the paper into the phases of the journey. For each journey, note the major events of this phase in your story, the internal experience that unfolded during this time, the meaning or thematic threads, the central tensions or "tasks" of this phase, and the other characters involved. You might consider reviewing Chapter 25, Layers of a Story, to capture the main levels of each story.

From here, you might do some character development work. This includes getting into your own hopes, fears, perspective, and experience at each stage. Getting back into the consciousness you had during that stage of your journey will help you write a compelling story that takes your reader along as you lived it (as opposed to just telling it retrospectively from the consciousness you hold now). This part also includes noticing what role each of your characters is playing in your story and doing some character development work on them as well. You might actually refer to Chapter 6 under "Reader Avatar and Psychographics" and use these questions to develop your characters.

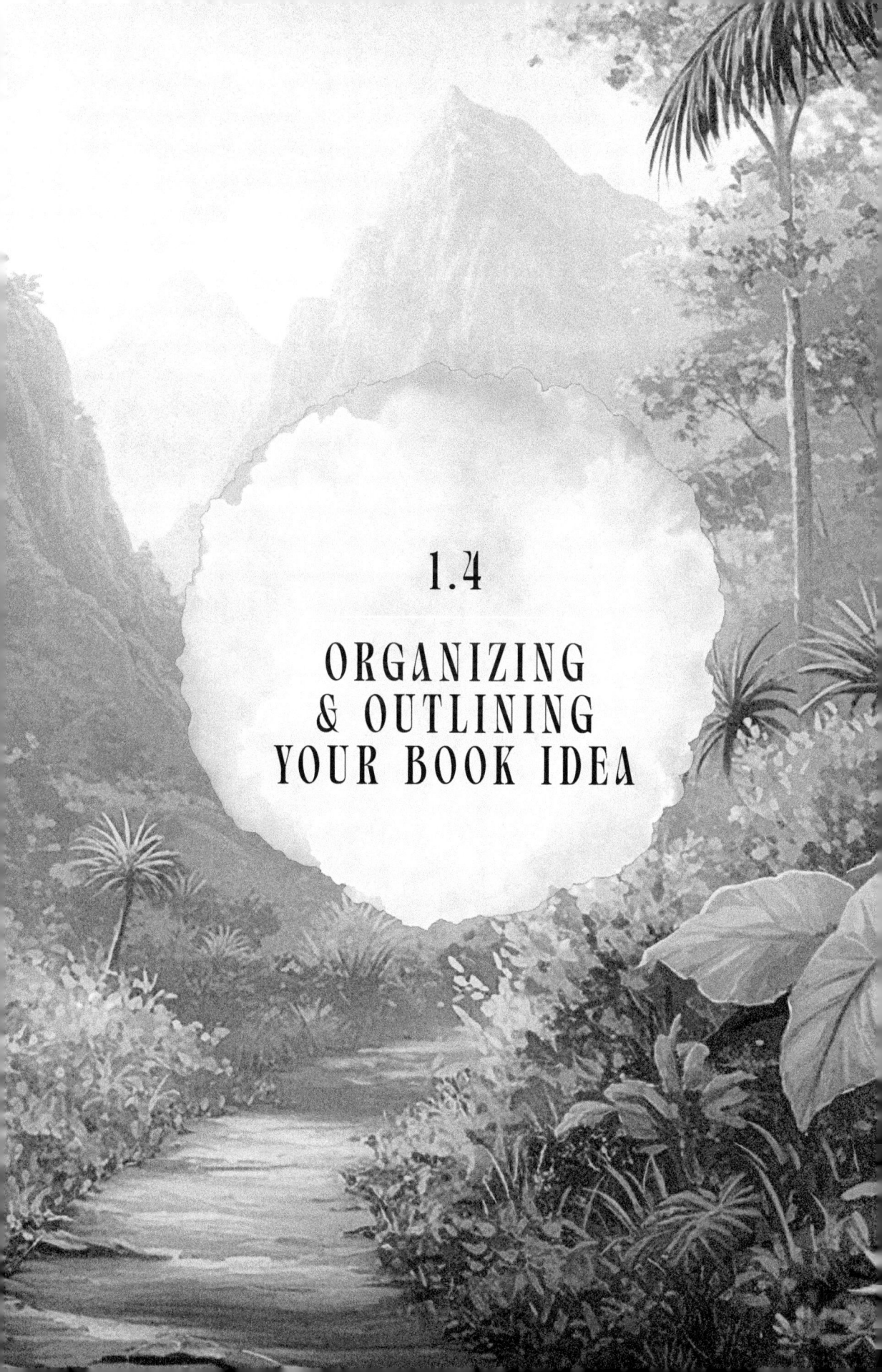

1.4

ORGANIZING & OUTLINING YOUR BOOK IDEA

CHAPTER 13

Organizing Your Ideas

Mind Mapping

A mind map uses both the left and right hemispheres of our brains to create a visual and organizational representation of our book ideas. A mind map has a radiant structure—it begins with a central theme or idea in the middle of the page, then you add smaller ideas around it, and for each of these ideas, you add subtopics or details. This radiant structure mimics the natural way our brains work. When we add shapes, colors, and images, we harness the power of our right brain to further enhance the left brain's functions of processing information, making connections, and generating ideas.

A simple mind map template. In the graphic below, the central large circle is where your main idea goes. From there, the mid-sized circles are your major points, your steps in a process, the parts of your book, or your stories (if memoir). The smallest circles are your subtopics or key points for each of these topics; it can also be your evidence, your story elements, or whatever else feels natural here.

Mind maps have been used for hundreds of years by brilliant creatives, including da Vinci, Darwin, Picasso, Einstein, and Edison. Studies show that mind maps improve our memories, idea generation and organization, ability to stay focused, ability to see the big picture, connections between our ideas, and connections to the central idea we are expressing in our book project. I have also seen mind maps make confusing concepts and ideas much clearer and more manageable and illuminate insight about a topic that hadn't previously been accessible. When you can get your key ideas on paper, see the relationships between them, and organize them in an intuitive way that you and your readers can follow, your writing process is often more effective and feels much better.

You can use mind maps for your whole book and for specific sections or chapters of your book. From your mind map, you can begin to shape "content clusters" or groupings of related content that feel like they go together. Here are a few approaches to mind mapping practices—find one that works best for you.

POSTERBOARD

Get a posterboard or large piece of paper and put your topics/subject/central theme at the center, with your main message underneath, if you have it articulated.

Surrounding it, in whatever way feels most natural and intuitive, begin to add in the details and get more specific. You may cluster a set of themes, order/arrange steps or elements, or list key points or subtopics. You can also write elements you want to weave into these larger themes. You can write questions to yourself and make a note of what your audience's concerns might be with a particular point or idea. Whatever arises and serves you best.

I encourage you to use color—perhaps choosing one for main messages; one for subtopics, steps, or components of your work; and another for stories, evidence, and details.

The posterboard matters because big ideas need space. And it also gives you space to get out of linear thinking, if that is what will best serve you. You can also use this technique with each chapter, story, or section of your book.

POST-IT NOTES AND INDEX CARDS

Post-it notes or index cards can be another way to generate and organize your ideas for your book. The benefit of these tools is that they are movable: you can put your ideas down and then move them around to begin sequencing your ideas (how you might present them in your book) or cluster them in a radiant, hierarchical way in mind map fashion.

Beyond using different colors for first-, second-, and third-level ideas, you can also use specific colors for types of information. For example, blue can signify quotes you want to use in your book. Green might be for types of evidence, such as stories, interviews, case examples, and studies. (Or you can designate a different color for each.) You may also use color to track major themes.

For index cards, you may want to create a strategy for what you'll put on each card. For example, you may decide to write (in a specific color?) the main idea or topic at the top. On the front side of the card, you might list (or mind map) your main points and the evidence (stories, facts) for such points. On the back, you might include relevant quotes. You decide, based on your subject and preferences, how you'd like to make use of the cards.

You can use a posterboard, the floor, a table, or a dedicated wall in your workspace to move things around as you begin to generate, refine, structure, and organize your ideas. While your cards or Post-its are not laid out somewhere for your viewing or engagement, you can keep them in a folder or binder, or take pictures of them laid out so you can later review the organization you created.

DIGITAL MIND MAPPING

If using the computer is your jam, numerous software programs and apps are available that offer mind mapping support. Examples include mindmup.com, wisemapping.com, and coggle.it. Apple also has programs, especially for the iPad, (such as MindNode) which I recommend you research, as these are changing all the time. You might explore your App Store or do a quick search to see what software is recommended for digital mind mapping.

TIMELINES

A bit different than mind mapping, timeline work is also supportive in the organizational process, especially if you are working with stories (as in memoir) or a step-by-step process you wish to lay out in your book. A timeline can support your process in sequencing your ideas or the events that took place in an area or around a theme in your life that you'll be exploring in your memoir. This can also serve as a precursor to using a mind map, as it helps you discover sequence or chronology, and from here, you can decide how to organize it.

See Chapter 11 for more information about how to work with chronology.

OTHER ORGANIZATIONAL APPROACHES

I encourage you to creatively explore and develop your organizational strategies. I have had clients make lists, labyrinths, and complex spreadsheets to generate and organize their book ideas. You may choose to use a dedicated journal. You may use PowerPoint slides. You may use an online tool such as Evernote or Google Sheets.

Tracking Your Ideas and Stories

In addition to generating and organizing your ideas right now, it is wise to create a system for how you will track what you want to write about as you journey through your writing process. Many of the same strategies for idea development and organization can also be used for tracking.

You can use:
- a digital program like Scrivener, Microsoft Word, Microsoft Excel, or Evernote
- paper note cards or index cards
- a dedicated journal (perhaps small enough to carry with you)
- a file system with hanging folders
- the voice recorder on your phone (you can even have these transcribed)
- the notepad app on your phone or device

- Post-it notes (maybe you have some by the bed, in the car, and in your purse)

Your specific strategy of idea tracking is less important than the *act of creating a strategy* that you can commit to and that will work for you.

What kind of system do you want to use to keep track of your ideas as they come in? If you feel drawn to a few options, how will you test them, and when will you make a clear decision on what to commit to?

_____

_____

_____

_____

But What About Research?

Some authors will not do much research for their books, while others will create research-heavy books. You don't need to be doing any heavy academic work to bring research into your writing process. If you plan to quote anyone, integrate another's ideas into your book, reference fellow experts in your field, or the like, you'll need to consider your research process. Please see Appendix C for more about book research.

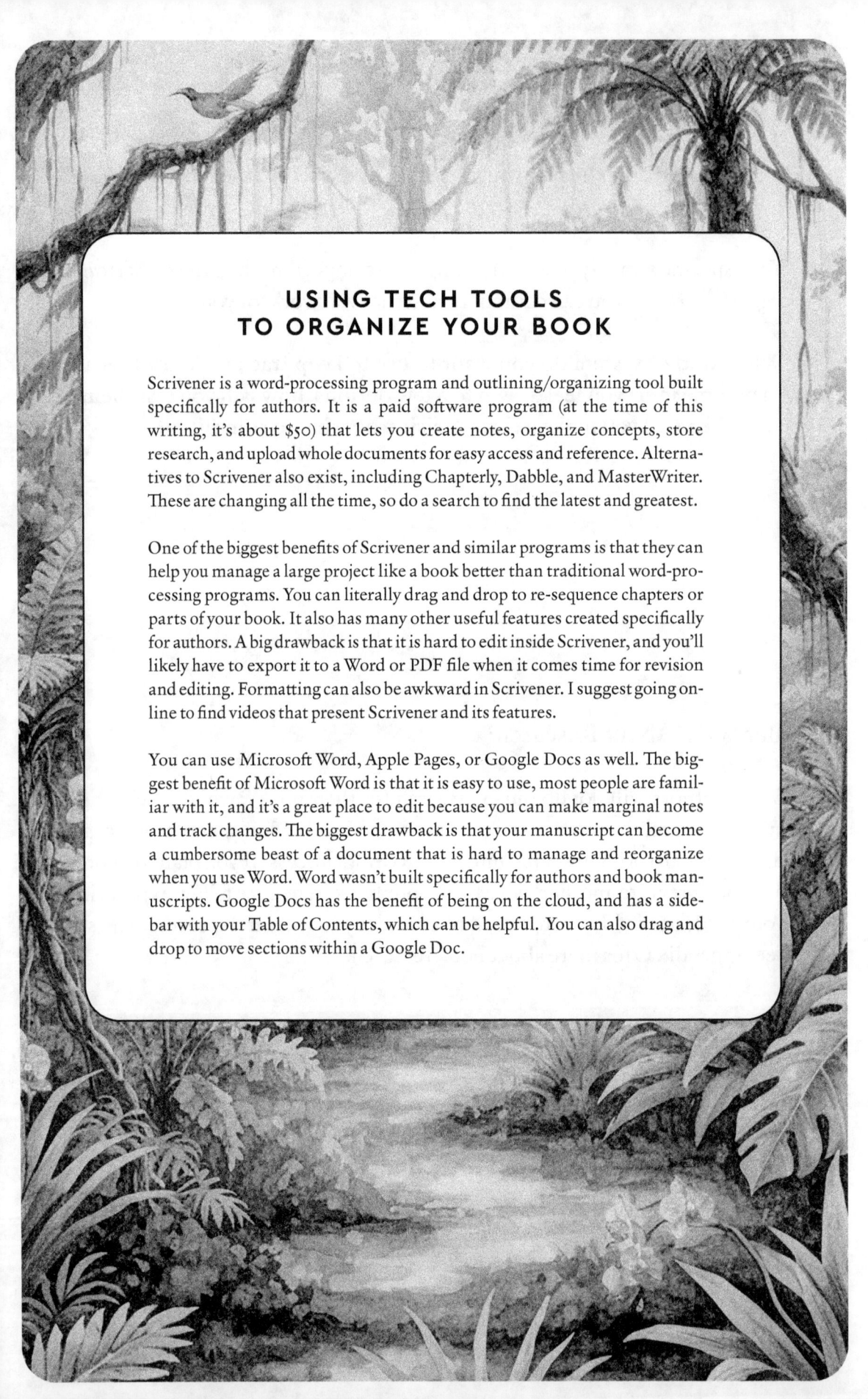

USING TECH TOOLS TO ORGANIZE YOUR BOOK

Scrivener is a word-processing program and outlining/organizing tool built specifically for authors. It is a paid software program (at the time of this writing, it's about $50) that lets you create notes, organize concepts, store research, and upload whole documents for easy access and reference. Alternatives to Scrivener also exist, including Chapterly, Dabble, and MasterWriter. These are changing all the time, so do a search to find the latest and greatest.

One of the biggest benefits of Scrivener and similar programs is that they can help you manage a large project like a book better than traditional word-processing programs. You can literally drag and drop to re-sequence chapters or parts of your book. It also has many other useful features created specifically for authors. A big drawback is that it is hard to edit inside Scrivener, and you'll likely have to export it to a Word or PDF file when it comes time for revision and editing. Formatting can also be awkward in Scrivener. I suggest going online to find videos that present Scrivener and its features.

You can use Microsoft Word, Apple Pages, or Google Docs as well. The biggest benefit of Microsoft Word is that it is easy to use, most people are familiar with it, and it's a great place to edit because you can make marginal notes and track changes. The biggest drawback is that your manuscript can become a cumbersome beast of a document that is hard to manage and reorganize when you use Word. Word wasn't built specifically for authors and book manuscripts. Google Docs has the benefit of being on the cloud, and has a sidebar with your Table of Contents, which can be helpful. You can also drag and drop to move sections within a Google Doc.

Chapter 14

Outline or Working Table of Contents

Once you have considered potential structural frameworks, generated your ideas, and begun to organize them into an arrangement you feel confident in using to proceed, you can develop an outline or working Table of Contents for your book.

Skipping this step is often a perilous mistake, and it is common to many first-time writers. A solid outline or working Table of Contents helps you focus your train of thought, stay true to your intentions, avoid gaps and redundancies in your idea expression, know how to transition between ideas or stories, avoid major tangents, develop consistency in your chapters, and wisely guide your readers through the experience you want them to have in reading your book.

Essentially, this process is taking that radiant or other structure you've used to clarify and organize your ideas and turning it into a linear plan for your book. This important step helps you develop a plan for writing a book that takes people from start to finish.

Remember, this is a living document and will be modified as you go. But it should be articulate and developed enough that you can reliably use it to guide your process forward. I recommend writing short chapter summaries (or a bulleted list) that explain what each chapter will cover and how it will contribute to the book and your readers' journey through the book. This is required in book proposals and is a helpful exercise in the planning stages of writing a book.

Do your best to create a working Table of Contents that provides some level of structure and detail, but allows you some room for revision and refinement. Changes and refinements will inevitably occur. But this working Table of Contents or outline will serve as a supportive scaffolding through your drafting process.

Here is a template to help you develop a chapter summary:

In Chapter #, I introduce the concept of P. To help engage reader's attention and interest, I will open the chapter with the story of D. I will write about how [give a high-level overview of the story]. Then, I will help readers understand how this story illustrates the idea of P (main concept of the chapter) and say more about this idea. From there, I will go into supporting my main idea by talking about J, K, and L. For each of these supporting elements, I discuss A, B, and C, using [kind of evidence you are using, see Chapter 7]. This chapter will help my reader understand W. This will be important before we talk about X, which comes next.

The letters here are just stand-ins. Feel free to make this chapter summary your own. If you choose to use bullets under each chapter, consider including points about your main idea, the way you will support it, the stories or other evidence you will use, and any practices you want to include.

Here is an example:

Chapter 6: Herbs and Astrology
- History of Medical Astrology
- How herbs connect to the planets
- Exploring your astrology chart
- A section for herbs associated with each planet (give planet attributes, give three plant examples)
  - Sun
  - Moon
  - Mercury
  - Venus
  - Mars
  - Saturn
  - Jupiter
  - Neptune
  - Uranus
  - Pluto
- How to work with Herbs and Astrology
- Practice: Apprentice with a plant

DEVELOPING AN OUTLINE MID-DRAFT

What if you are in the middle of writing a book for which you have no working Table of Contents beyond your chapter titles? If you are in the middle of writing your book and you want to get a clearer sense of what you have written and what you want to write next, you may want to take a pause and do the work of creating a detailed working Table of Contents with chapter summaries. You may also want to check out the resource in Chapter 30 on charting, which will help you reverse outline what you've written so far.

1.5 ACTION PLAN

CHAPTER 15

Fitting a Book Into Your Life

This chapter is all about creating a plan of action to help you fit book writing into your actual life. Developing a concrete plan can hold you accountable to yourself and your project. The intention here is to create a plan that actually feels *good* for you to carry out, and one that realistically fits into your real life in this moment. Follow this process to develop your personalized action plan.

Match Your Real Life with Your Writing Goals

There are two ways in: starting with your real life or starting with your writing goals. It isn't either/or, and you will likely need to explore it from both angles to find the happy place where your writing goals align with your real life.

GET REALISTIC ABOUT YOUR TIME AND CLAIM TIME SOVEREIGNTY

Pull out your calendar and take a realistic look at your schedule for the next three to six months (or whatever time frame feels appropriate to you for this project). What is coming up? What do the rhythms of your life currently look like? For example, are you traveling a lot for business? Are you seeing clients on Mondays, Wednesdays, and Fridays? Do you have a personal commitment every Sunday? You may want to do a time audit, where you spend a week tracking how you actually are spending your time. Don't forget to track things like basic tasks of living and internet scrolling time.

Look for the places where you can create space for your writing project.

If life is feeling more than full right now, this is your opportunity to reclaim your time and create alignment between your priorities and your commitments. And to acknowledge that you have a choice. We have more autonomy in our lives than we are often led to believe. We just have to claim it. To take greater personal responsibility for how you choose to fill your life, you may trade "I am too busy for _____" statements with "I have chosen not to prioritize _____" statements.

For example, if you've decided that this book is a priority, but you have a schedule filled with social commitments you're not even all that jazzed about, consider what you can decline or elegantly bow out of. Or if you'd love to write at night after work, but you tell yourself you don't have the energy, yet you can find the energy to binge-watch a show, perhaps take a look at that. Consider this as an opportunity to remove nonessentials and activities that drain your energy rather than feed it.

Consider also that your book is here to feed you, not drain your energy. Read that sentence again; it's important. At the end of this fine and precious life, you will not lament that time you took a month off Facebook or woke up early every morning to work on your book. You may lament never getting your story or ideas expressed and shared.

Remember, one of the major tools of resistance is to keep you scattered and attempting to do too many things at once. This book project is an opportunity to get clear on your priority and organize your life around it.

FIVE WAYS TO MAKE TIME

1. Reduce or eliminate **social media** information consumption. You can go into settings and have certain apps shut down at certain times or after a certain duration of use. I promise you won't die or be forgotten. You can also bring more intentionality to your usage; for example, I will only go on at 3 p.m. to check my business page and reply to any direct messages for a period of twenty minutes max.

2. Limit **email checking** to only one or two times a day. Consider an automatic "vacation responder" that lets your email contacts know

you are working on your book and will be slower to respond than usual. Feel great about that. It gives them permission to do the same. We all win.

3. **Delegate.** Get support for the **household responsibilities** that are not essential for you (specifically you) to do. Order **groceries or food delivery** if that is accessible to you. Meal batch or meal plan to save time in the kitchen. When I was busy with my Kickstarter campaign for my book and had a three-year-old at home, I ordered from a meal service, and it was a great decision. What do you do now that you can get someone else to do?

4. **Automate** anything that can be automated in your business, your personal life, or wherever it makes sense.

5. **Wake up an hour earlier.**

What are three ways you can make more time in your life for writing?

_____

_____

_____

_____

Start with Your Clear Goal and Reverse-Engineer Your Writing Project

Okay, let's say you have a clear target date by which you'd like to have your manuscript's first draft complete. You may even have a manuscript deadline from your publisher. You can work backward to determine what you need to accomplish monthly, weekly, and daily to reach this goal.

Let's take an example. You decide you'd like to have your first draft done six months from now. Let's say you want to aim for a 250-page book, which is approximately 62,500 words. This would be a little under 10,500 words per month or about 2,600 words per week. That's about forty-two pages per month and ten to eleven pages per week. Perhaps you do a little tracking experiment for a few writing sessions and find that you write about three pages per hour. That means you will need to dedicate approximately three to four hours per week to your writing.

FINDING THE SWEET SPOT

Based on what is true in your real life right now (i.e., how much time and energy you can and will choose to realistically devote to your project) *and* the quantitative insight you gathered about how often and how much you'd need to write to reach a certain book deadline, you can begin to come up with a writing schedule that is realistic for your life and your desires for your book.

How many hours per week or blocks of time do you feel you can realistically and sanely dedicate to your book project in the next three, six, or nine months? We're looking for that sweet edge of your comfort zone that stretches you but also feels good and doable. When is your desired date for the completion of your manuscript?

_____

_____

_____

_____

SIMPLE BOOK MATH FOR YOU

The average nonfiction book is between 200 and 300 pages. A standard guideline is that there are 250 words per page. (Of course, this may be different if your book is physically larger or smaller than the industry standard or if you use a bigger or smaller font on your pages, but let's just go with this.)

Standard Guidelines:
200-page book = 50,000 words
250-page book = 62,500 words
300-page book = 75,000 words

To get an idea of how long your book may be, pull books off your own shelf that match your desired length and check the page count (remember, this page count may also include pages like titles, dedications, Forewords, and Tables of Contents).

Also note that many authors eliminate content in the revision process (it depends on your book, but some sources say it's an average of 5000 to 7000 words), which is a consideration in your book's time-factoring.

Two Humbling Wild Cards:
Your Book's Organic Pace + the Creative Life Cycle

HONORING YOUR BOOK'S ORGANIC PACE

I find time and again that our creative projects have a life and pace of their own. They are like children—we have our ideas for their pacing, and they have theirs. Theirs usually wins. We can assert our desires and our will, but only to an extent, and we must be humbled by this fact. It's a relationship; it's a two-way street between us and our creation. We show up for what we can control, and we leave room for our creative project to teach us about its organic pace of development.

Sometimes, an idea, concept, or new connection needs to work in us awhile, and it just may take time before we understand it well enough to write about it. Sometimes, we discover a new way of seeing something we've been working with, and we need to let that new perspective fully arrive before we can share it. All of this is normal and natural. What we do want to watch for is that we don't stall our pace because of an unexamined/unaddressed Inner Critic flare-up or creative block, but those will inevitably arrive as well.

HONORING THE CREATIVE CYCLE

Here's another reality check for you. Not all book project time will be in production (summer) mode. Remember Chapter 2 about the seasons of creativity? Here is a quick synopsis:

- Spring—the research and idea-generation stage
- Summer—production/manifestation (the only season in which you are actually sitting down and progressing on your page count)
- Fall—the reflection/reflexive process, which may involve some revision as well
- Winter—the fruitful darkness from where all creativity comes, but it may make us feel like nothing is happening

In recognizing that summer only makes up 25 percent of the creative life cycle, we are wise to factor all the seasons into our process. With careful planning and organic readiness, winter and spring can largely be journeyed through before our drafting process. In other words, the ideas have sprung from the fertile darkness, we've spent our time researching and planning our books already, and we come to the drafting stage in full summer mode. In such cases, I suggest using the eighty/twenty rule. In your summer season of draft writing, plan that 80 percent of your time will be in production mode, and the other 20 percent will be in another season.

What does this look like? Some days, you will sit down to write, and you will not feel the clear capacity to begin cranking out new words. Maybe you need to review the last three chapters to get clearer about where the next chapter needs to lead. Maybe you need to return to your outline to assess where you have been and where you are going. Maybe you review and adapt your working Table of Contents (all fall-like activities). Perhaps you realize you are missing some piece of information to develop an idea, and you need to turn back to your research (spring).

All said, let summer be mostly summer. Sometimes, you have an errant cold or rainy spring or fall-feeling day in summer, meaning you might need to turn your attention to planning or reflection activities—but let summer be summer, meaning let your focus be on forward progress, writing your manuscript when it is time for this work. Don't get bogged down in wanting to edit everything you've written as you go or be forever in pursuit of more information to support your claims.

Land Your Writing Plan

So far, we've been at the 10,000-foot view. Let's bring it down to 5,000 feet, then all the way to the ground. Based on the information we gathered about that sweet spot between your life reality and your book intentions, let's explore in greater detail how often you can and will dedicate your time, energy, and attention to your book project.

What are the feasible days of the week that will be best for you to write? Do you have consistent availability (e.g., every Tuesday and Friday), or does it feel better to dedicate a certain number of hours or sessions per week, which varies by week, to your project?

___

___

What times of the day are you most creative? Are you more of a morning person or an evening person? If you're not sure, track your energy for a week to identify your most productive and clear times in the day, and aim to write during these hours if possible.

___

___

For how long can you engage in your book project at any given time? Two hours? Three? Four? Most creatives find that three to five hours in one sitting is optimal, and anything beyond that, they start to see a diminishing return on their creative efforts. However, there are some outliers who do their best with intense "binge" sessions and can go deep into their process over a period of an entire or even multiple days. Consider also the minimum time you'll need. Anything under an hour or even two is often too short a time to get into the flow of your writing project.

___

___

CREATIVE RHYTHMS SCOUTING MISSION

Okay, let's say you have *no idea* when your ideal creative times are or how long you should write for. Or any other specifics for creating a personalized, feel-good plan for your book project. No sweat. We just need to go on a little exploratory mission. Use the "Tracking Your Creative Rhythms" resource at the end of this chapter.

PUT IT IN THE CALENDAR. SERIOUSLY, PUT IT IN THE CALENDAR.

I always joke that if something isn't in my calendar, it doesn't exist. While I am clear on my calendar co-dependency, in some ways, this is true for all creatives: if we don't schedule our creative time, it likely won't happen, or at least not in any real, progressive, intentional way.

So, the next step is to get out your calendar and schedule your writing time. Schedule it like you would your kid's doctor visit, lunch with your best friend, a prospect meeting, your client sessions, or whatever other calendar items are valued and nonnegotiable.

WHAT CAN YOU SAY YES TO RIGHT NOW?

If you find yourself resistant to showing up for the time you've scheduled, and you're thinking of going for brunch or hitting up Netflix instead, try this. Do one small, simple action that serves your book project. It could literally be this: Write a single sentence. Do the smallest manageable "yes," and then celebrate. Literally say out loud, "I'm amazing. I did it." This isn't to overinflate simple tasks but to begin in a place of beginning. If the bigger commitment feels inaccessible, look for what is accessible and do that. Do this consistently to develop the *habit* of working on your book. Even in the tiniest of bites. And then you can slowly work up to bigger book commitments. The key is to let yourself feel good and celebrate, to be gentle with yourself, and to develop the habit of weaving your book into your life.

Determine Your Optimal Writing Environment

What do you ideally need in your environment to write? Will you write in public (e.g., a coffee shop or library)? On retreat? Alone at home? At the office? What is your optimal writing environment? If you are not sure, how will you find out?

_____

_____

_____

_____

_____

You can use the "Tracking Your Creative Rhythms" resource to help you track where you write best as you explore options. Some of us need the bustle of other creatives in our space as we write. I suggest noise-canceling headphones if you choose to write in loud places. Some of us absolutely need solitude and silence. Some of us need to write in the same place each time we work on our project. And some of us are adaptable and can use other constants to ritualize our writing process.

Support Your Success

PLANNING FOR CHALLENGES

It is important to visualize your ideal situation and to create a plan for when the ideal isn't possible.

What do you anticipate will be your biggest practical obstacles in keeping to the plans and intentions you've just outlined?

What will you do when you get stuck emotionally or energetically somewhere along your creative cycle? What will you do when resistance rears its head, which it is certain to do?

Name at least three ways you anticipate challenges arising and, for each, list one to three ways to navigate these challenges.

_____
_____
_____
_____

WHEN YOU GET STUCK

When you get stuck, you might want to revisit the important groundwork we covered in Chapters 1 through 5. Putting your book "down" and going for a walk can do wonders. Find a way to let some pressure out of the system. Put on a good song and dance. Talk with your Inner Critic.

One concrete thing you can do when you feel stuck is to write down five to ten ideas you have for your book. For example, "I want to interview so-and-so," or "Include an actionable step my readers can do at the end of every chapter," or "I want to add this specific healing practice or meditation in the appendix of my book," or "Use the pub crawl story as the lead to chapter 6." Then choose one and see if you can write a paragraph about it, or create an outline, or something that feels doable.

Read or listen to an audiobook by a creativity champion like Steven Pressfield (*The War of Art*) or Elizabeth Gilbert (*Big Magic*).

Don't take yourself so seriously. Have a little fun to lighten the mood if you can.

Remember that in the creative cycle, not every day is summer. Ask yourself what season you are in, and act accordingly.

Go back to your *why*. The why of this book for you. The why of this book for your reader. Write yourself a letter, maybe from the perspective of a future reader whose life will positively change because of your book. Have her ask you to keep going, and have her say why. Get out of the ego-limitation mind and into the creative-service mind.

What support do you need to have in place to enact this inspired plan of action?

_____
_____
_____
_____

What permission do you need to give yourself?

_____
_____
_____
_____

What support do you need to request from others?

_____
_____
_____
_____

Track Your Progress

How will you track your progress? Will you add a note in your calendar once a month or once a week to check your word count and compare that to your stated goals? Will you base your check-ins around chapter or scene progress? Will you go by an inner sense of progress?

How will you consider adaptations to your plan as you learn and journey through this book-writing process?

My Progress-Tracking Plan

Consequences: Rewards and Punishments

I have a colleague who suggests that people write a $500 check to the organization they despise the most (political or a cause) and give the check to a good friend with the directive to send the check to said organization if the writer has not met such-and-such a goal on their book by such-and-such a time. I mean, that is definitely one way to motivate. If that's your jam, run with it.

I'm generally in favor of positive reinforcement. And I love a good party. If you feel like reward is your jam, you might alternatively consider designating milestones along your book-writing journey where you will consciously pause and celebrate your progress. This might be a little happy dance when you reach twenty-five thousand words, for example, or it might be something bigger, like a dinner party with your favorite people after your first manuscript is complete. You might celebrate smaller wins, such as a seven-minute writing session. (As stated earlier, this can provide positive reinforcement to get you going on your project.) What little carrots can you dangle that might motivate and celebrate you as you go through this journey?

My rewards plan:

_____

_____

_____

_____

_____

Make a Clear Statement of Intent

After working through your answers to these questions, create a single-paragraph declaration of your plan, and put it where you can see it to remind yourself of this plan so you can return to it anytime you stray. Ensure it is in the highest service of your intentions for this book, and let it feel *good*!

Fitting a Book Into Your Life

Write a single-paragraph declaration of intention for how you'll fit writing into your life.

_____

_____

_____

_____

_____

_____

When it comes to developing a writing lifestyle, take a little time to get inspired by other authors and how they approach writing life. See the resources listed in the Notes for this chapter.

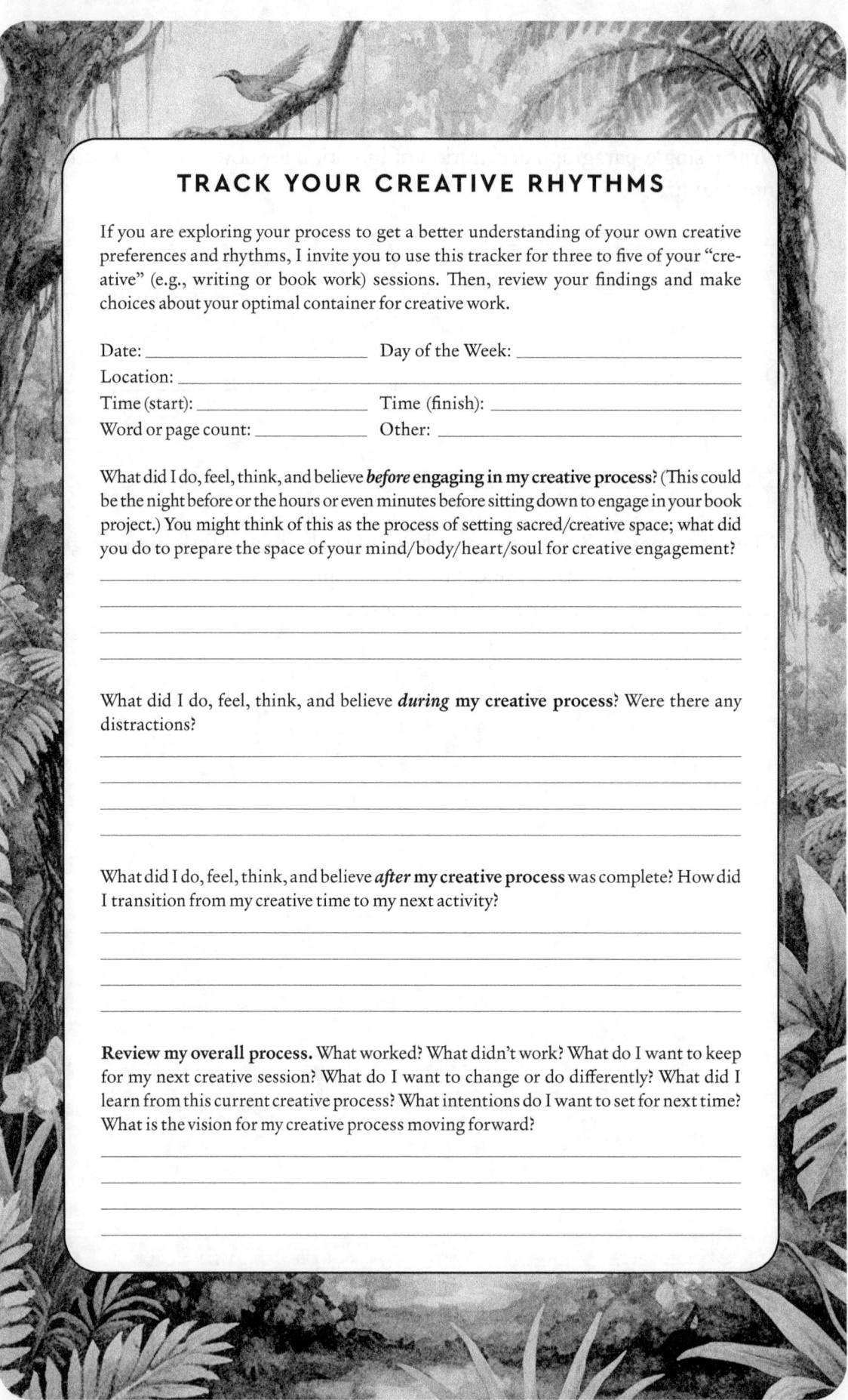

TRACK YOUR CREATIVE RHYTHMS

If you are exploring your process to get a better understanding of your own creative preferences and rhythms, I invite you to use this tracker for three to five of your "creative" (e.g., writing or book work) sessions. Then, review your findings and make choices about your optimal container for creative work.

Date: _____   Day of the Week: _____
Location: _____
Time (start): _____   Time (finish): _____
Word or page count: _____   Other: _____

What did I do, feel, think, and believe *before* **engaging in my creative process**? (This could be the night before or the hours or even minutes before sitting down to engage in your book project.) You might think of this as the process of setting sacred/creative space; what did you do to prepare the space of your mind/body/heart/soul for creative engagement?
_____
_____
_____
_____

What did I do, feel, think, and believe *during* **my creative process**? Were there any distractions?
_____
_____
_____
_____

What did I do, feel, think, and believe *after* **my creative process** was complete? How did I transition from my creative time to my next activity?
_____
_____
_____
_____

Review my overall process. What worked? What didn't work? What do I want to keep for my next creative session? What do I want to change or do differently? What did I learn from this current creative process? What intentions do I want to set for next time? What is the vision for my creative process moving forward?
_____
_____
_____
_____

CHAPTER 16

RHYTHMS AND RITUALS OF WRITING

Because I believe a good birth metaphor lands a point about creativity more often than not, I liken writing rituals and rhythms to the comfort measures and coping mechanisms we use during (birth) labor. I also believe that creative space is sacred space and that when we recognize this, we can harness the power of rhythms and rituals that support our creative process.

Establishing creative rituals can offer us a number of benefits. One, the brain responds positively to routine, which can remove the need to constantly make new decisions about our process or behavior, help us focus, and alleviate nervous jitters. Rituals can act as conscious and intentional openings and closings of our creative space. Creative rituals can also get us into our bodies and the present moment so we are more available and clearer for our creativity to come through us. Ritual creates a consistent container in which your creativity can be invited in to work its magic. I also call creative rhythms and rituals the Creative Cave because it is the process of entering the cave, a sheltered, contained place, where you can work directly with your creativity unimpeded and uninterrupted.

At its simplest, a creative ritual can have a beginning (something you do before you write), a middle (something you do while you write), and an end (something you do intentionally to complete your writing work before initiating a new activity). These can be elaborate or simple, as you desire. The point is to find your unique rhythms and rituals that support your creative process.

Fun fact: Beethoven is rumored to have sprinkled water around his flat before he composed music.

Opening Your Creative Space: A Buffet of Options

Nervous system regulation practices—Many of the activities I suggest count as nervous system regulation activities. We want our nervous systems to be in a place of calm and safety so we can open to our creative genius. You may want to go deeper into these practices and explore further options, such as my online somatic healing program, SOMA.

A movement activity—Movement can include yoga, running, walking, or dancing. Writing is actually an embodied practice that requires our full attention, focus, and presence. A ritual that gets us into our bodies can be a supportive way to open space for our creative work. Getting into our bodies can also assist us in getting out of mental spaces that do not serve us, such as worries or preoccupation about the past or the future, feelings of resistance, and distraction.

Time in nature—Getting connected to nature—creativity herself—can also be a supportive way to slow down and enter creative space. This may be sitting on your porch listening to birdsong, taking three deep breaths with your feet in the dirt, looking out the window at the snow sparkling outside, or taking a walk.

Time spent in pleasure and enjoyment—If you have any resistance or nervousness before entering a creative space, do something you enjoy and find pleasure in to train your brain to connect these activities to the creative process that follows. Activities that help you feel confident and effective can also be supportive.

Make/buy tea—If you're at a coffee shop, part of your opening ritual (in addition to the act of getting yourself there, which is part of the ritual) may be to order your favorite drink. If you're at home, it might be the ritual of brewing your favorite green or herbal tea.

Meditate—Practice forms of meditation while connecting to your breath, inviting in a compassionate witness, shifting to a calm state, envisioning the outcome of your creative time, connecting to your creativity, meeting your creative genius or other allies, and slowing down. All of these and other aspects of meditation can be used to open your creative space in a powerful and supportive way.

Mantra—You may repeat a meaningful mantra to yourself that helps you ground your intentions for writing. You may also read your *why* for writing this book, your rave review, or something that connects you to your greater purpose and service in writing this book. You might also write yourself permission slips: What permission do you give yourself today as it relates to your writing process?

Clear your workspace—Some people have to clean the house before they enter into a creative space. Declutter, put away distractions, turn off the phone and any alerts on any devices, hang a note on the door, and put on your noise-canceling headphones.

Warm-up writing—You may write as a way to clear the workspace of your mind. Maybe you need to blow off some steam or express what is on your mind or heart. Maybe your Inner Critic needs to get out her piece so she can sit quietly as you begin the work of your book project.

Another creative activity—You might engage in another short creative activity you enjoy, such as doodling, drawing, painting, or gardening. This could serve as a creative warm-up for your writing process. I suggest giving this a clear time frame so you know when you are done and ready to move into writing.

(For more inspiration, check out the book *Daily Rituals: How Artists Work* by Mason Currey.)

Whatever you choose, make sure this is not an act of resistance to your writing process but serves as a powerful portal into your creative space. It doesn't have to be elaborate at all—it can be as simple as pouring a glass of water and turning your cell phone to silent. It can be as simple as taking one conscious, slow breath as you open up your computer.

As far as rhythms, they are movements toward routine and regularity in your creative process, such as writing at the same time or in the same place each day. These can also be powerful cues to your Inner Creative that it is time to come out and play.

What will you do to get started? Do you know what already works for you? Do you feel called to explore one or two options from these examples (or something not on the list)?

_____

_____

_____

_____

_____

_____

During: Establishing Your Creative Cave
DISTRACTION KILLS CREATIVITY

> *"You can play with your phone, or you can change the world. You don't get to do both."*
> — ROBIN SHARMA

Turn off the internet and your phone while you write. (Better to put it out of the room altogether.) Hang up a Do Not Disturb sign. Write in a place free of distractions. Take care of your needs for food and drink.

As Steven Pressfield writes, "[The professional] eliminates chaos from [her] world in order to banish it from [her] mind. [S]he wants the carpet vacuumed and the threshold swept, so the Muse may enter and not soil her gown." Chaos is counter to creativity.

Keep your space clear of distractions that your resistance may argue are necessary or useful. This can even include reference books. If you know you are going to use a specific book for reference today in developing your next chapter, it can remain for the time it is needed.

But if you think you might be tempted to stop your own writing and see what so-and-so said about X or how they put this idea into words, *stop*.

Write your own book. Actually write. Research is not writing, social media is not writing, and doing your business is not writing. Writing your book is writing. Write your book. In your own words. Stay in your own lane. Watch your own bobber, as fisher-folk say on the lakes of Minnesota. Trust yourself and the words you will use to convey your ideas. We want to read your book, not some version of someone else's. We want you.

Sitting to write is like entering the boxing ring. It's just you—hands outstretched and poised for action, gaze steady on the heavyweight champ called Creation—dancing around in a box. You may have a coach on the sidelines, loved ones cheering in the front row, or the spirits of those who've come before you stoically holding space in the darkness. You may even hear a heckler out there in row five. You may be tempted to hear your inner voice as it thinks about the last time you were in the ring. Pay all of them no matter. This is between you and creation. Let it be pure. Focus your attention only on the One in the ring with you and the dance you are doing. If you shift your focus to Row Five Dude, you will find yourself on the ground seeing cartoon stars in no time.

Be a channel for creation. There's a small catch. Creation often whispers. So you've gotta get real quiet and focused to hear it. You can't be a channel, you can't clearly listen to creation, if you're doing or focusing on a bunch of other stuff at the same time. It's like having five radios on at once. Plus, a five-year-old playdate dance party in the background. With a strobe light. Mind-scrambling.

Get super focused in your Creative Cave and watch the magic happen.

During the writing process itself, you might also consider any rituals, rhythms, or intentions here.
With what tools will you write?
Will you write anything by hand? All by computer? Will you dictate? Will you use a program like Scrivener to help you create your drafts?
What will you do when you hit a snag? Will you shake it out by literally shaking through your body, or will you buzz your lips, or will you stand up and stretch?
When will you take breaks?
How will you ensure your space is distraction-free?

My Creative Cave Plan

_____
_____
_____
_____
_____
_____
_____
_____
_____
_____
_____
_____

After: Closing Rituals

How and when will you know you're done? By the clock, by your progress, by your felt sense of completion?
What will you do to close your creative space? Will you simply close up the computer?
Will you read what you wrote?
Will you look at what your intentions are for the next day?
Will you take a deep breath?
Will you get up and celebrate?
Will you track your word count progress?
Will you leave one space and go to another?
Will you do any of the activities offered as ways to open your creative space?

I really recommend writing yourself a note after each section that shares with future you: your current thinking about the book section you're in, what you are tracking that needs to still happen in that section, and what you want to do next time you sit down to work on this section. Future you will thank you.

My Closing Ritual Plan

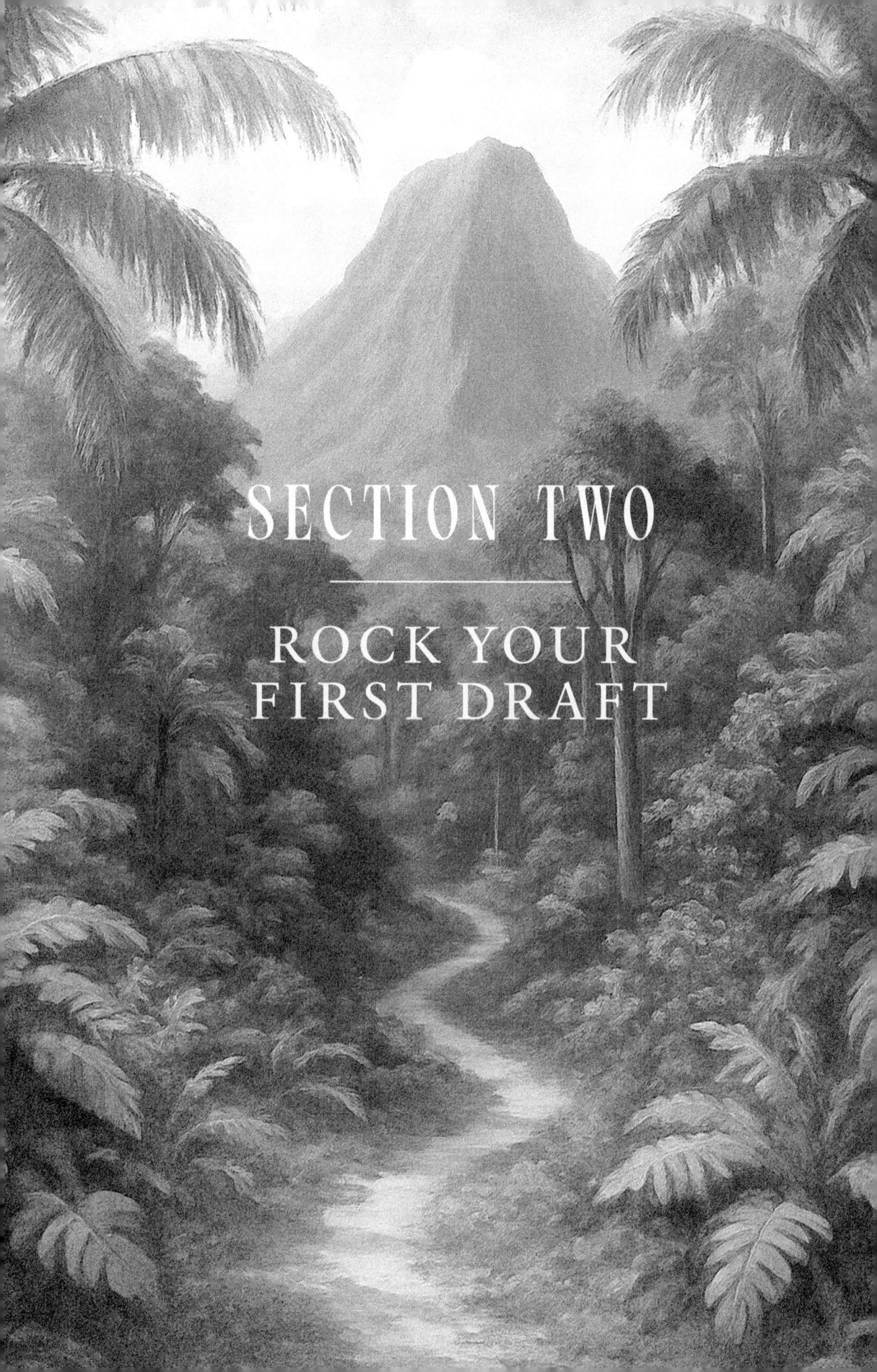

CHAPTER 17

First Draft Best Practices

> *"One rule for first full working drafts: get them done ASAP. Don't worry about quality. Act, don't reflect. Momentum is everything. Get to THE END as if the devil himself were breathing down your neck and poking you in the butt with his pitchfork."*
> — STEVEN PRESSFIELD

Have an Outline or Working Table of Contents

Do your best to create a rough outline or working Table of Contents, which we explored in Chapter 14. Major bonus points if you have chapter summaries or at least a bulleted list of what you want to include in each chapter. While you may not have this outline in front of you as you write, you can reference it as a map at various points along your route. This will also help you greatly with the next step of making micro-progress.

Make Micro-Progress

> *"Writing is like driving at night in the fog. You can only see as far as your headlights, but you can make the whole trip that way."*
> — E.L. DOCTOROW

Zoom in when you write. Resist the urge to zoom back out until you're done writing.

It's difficult for the mind to hold in its awareness the concept of writing an entire book. It gets overwhelming. Just as a builder has a plan to build a home but then focuses on smaller, manageable steps of the process—one day and one part of the project at a time—so, too, must we approach our writing. A builder doesn't go to the job site on Tuesday thinking, *Today I shall build a house.* No. They go pour the concrete for the foundation. Or add the drywall to the upstairs bedrooms. Or tile the roof. Or install the sink in the kitchen.

When you sit down, don't think to yourself. *Today, I shall write my book.*

Consider instead a plan for how you will choose the next wisest project or task, and focus solely on that.

Today, I will write that scene from my son's birth.

Today, I will explain the first of five key ways that people struggle with their relationships in early parenthood.

Today, I will explain how the brain gets a steady hit of dopamine with regular Facebook-checking, and I will describe the three-step process to detox from this habit.

Break your book into a series of sections, chapters, stories, and scenes. Take one step at a time. Focus on making steady micro-progress toward your larger goal, giving your attention and focus to the steps, not to the whole. The key is to make the next step just the right size that your brain goes *Ah, this is a tolerable and doable next step!* That is the sweet spot.

As you enter your writing space, you may reference your outline or working Table of Contents to help you select your focus for the day, but then release the bigger plan. Zoom in and focus right where you are. As you write, if distracting thoughts come in—*where will I put this other idea or point? Where should this idea go? How will I include that story about the monkey? Ooh, I should go research Steve Jobs's childhood hobbies*—jot down the question or idea on a Post-it and put it aside to consider after your focused time. Place these notes out of sight or out of your space and keep going.

After you close your writing time, you can span out again to reflect on how what you wrote will fit into the whole, and you can address those other questions or ideas that came up. But when you're writing, stay focused and zoomed in. Remember, you only need to see what's just in front of you in order to keep going. And if you are trying to be everywhere, you are effectively nowhere.

Write Authentically

Write in a way that comes naturally, using words and phrases that come readily to mind. Don't mentally force yourself to sound a certain way or to present in a particular voice. That is a guaranteed setup for discomfort, for you and for your reader, who will feel it. Your job is to do the work of expressing what you want to say in the ways that feel most natural to say it. You don't have to sound like Liz Gilbert. Or Cheryl Strayed. Or anyone else. You have to sound like *you*.

The best way to get to your voice is to let it develop. Yes, you can think about stylistic techniques like writing in active voice, in present tense, and in a tone appropriate to your audience. All that. But truly, when you're writing, give yourself permission to be you. To speak truly and authentically the way you do.

When one of my dear friends read my book in the beta reader phase of my book project, her first comment to me was, "Jaime, when I read your book, it's like I can hear your voice as if you were sitting here talking to me." It was her favorite part of reading my book because she felt connected to *me*. It was my favorite piece of feedback because I knew then that I had nailed my voice. I'd managed to write in a way that was authentic, natural, and true: *me*. I wasn't afraid to let my personality and voice come out in my work. I didn't try to sound like anyone else; I sounded exactly like me.

Sound exactly like you. Those four words are the best advice I have about developing your writing voice. Boom.

But I'll say one more thing. Finding your voice is a lot like sculpting. You are not creating something from nothing; rather, you are taking away all that is not you, that is not your piece of art, that is not your creation, and getting it out of the way for your creation to fully shine through. When it comes to your voice, get everything out of your head if it is not your voice—other authors' voices, your parent's/partner's/teacher's voices, and your editor's voice. Just listen for your voice. Sound exactly like you.

Leave the Introduction for Last

Don't start writing your book by tackling the introduction. This is the last part of your book that you should write. That's because your introduction includes an overview of what you say in your book. And if you start there, and you haven't written much yet, you're only just guessing about what will follow. Write the rest of your book first and come back to the intro.

That said, some people do feel deeply compelled to start at the beginning. If that is you, I recommend writing just a rough sketch of your introduction, not the full version. It can sometimes be helpful to articulate your main message, or do some of the other big moves of an introduction (which you can learn all about in Chapter 20). But don't get stuck here, and don't try to "finish" an introduction before you move on to the chapter material.

Trust me when I say that writing your full introduction is best done after most or all of your chapter material is complete. And when that time comes, definitely head to Chapter 20 to discover how to rock out your introduction like a pro.

Look for the Place Where It Feels Good

Here, I borrow a line from my work in Qoya (an embodied dance practice I teach): "Look for the place where it feels good to move." In this case, when you sit down to write, "Look for the place where it feels good to start writing." Or at least good enough. Go to a place that piques your interest, a place where desire lives for you. You may be the kind of author who can only write chapter by chapter, point by point, in the order you will present your ideas in your book. But this isn't the norm. Most authors move about in their drafting process. This is largely because ideas don't give two hoots about linear processes and keeping you comfortable in predictability. Creation is messier than that. So why not have fun and enjoy yourself? You can do this by looking for the place where it feels good to write.

While you want to bring some spontaneity and now-moment aliveness to your choice of focus as you write, you don't want to be free-floating in space, just picking up whatever happens to float across your field of awareness at any given time. This is why you have your working outline. Because you can choose a place *from your plan* to dig in deeper on any given day. You may work through Chapter 3 for four consecutive writing sessions, but when you are ready to begin another micro-project (ahem, see earlier), you may long to write Chapter 7. You just can't wait to see what you discover there. You just know something juicy lies in those lines you have yet to write. (Or maybe you're full of doubt but still curious anyway—all good.)

Bring play, pleasure, and curiosity into the drafting process. They are excellent antidotes to pressure, pain, and fear.

Hush Your Inner Editor and Orient to First Draft Reality

"Every writer starts in the same place on Day One: Super excited, and ready for greatness. On Day Two, every writer looks at what she wrote on Day One and hates herself. What separates working writers from non-working writers is that working writers return to their task on Day Three. What gets you there is not pride but mercy. Show yourself forgiveness for not being good enough. Then keep going."

— ELIZABETH GILBERT

One of the first hurdles to any major creative process is the moment before you begin. This is the moment when your Resistance reminds you that you can turn back. *It's not too late. You can turn back around, and no one ever has to know that you even had a desire or intention to write a book*, it whispers menacingly. You can even convince yourself that you never had such a desire.

Often, resistance to sitting down and *writing the freaking book* is the biggest way the Inner Critic shows up here. You make a date in your calendar to write, and then you find yourself cleaning out the garage, scrolling social media, talking on the phone, baking cookies, doing something for work, or *anything else* besides of writing your book.

First drafts are messy, unrefined, and likely to feel subpar in our minds. It's normal. You'll feel better if you can just accept this as part of the process. All good authors start with a Sketchy First Draft. I also call it Emptying the Bag—the first draft is you taking the contents of your brilliant mind and heart and pouring them onto the page to see what you've got. You have to do that first before you can decide where everything goes. Please see Appendix B for more on Sketchy First Draft support.

Don't get bogged down trying to get everything perfect. Don't wear your writer hat and your editor hat at the same time; your head will feel too heavy, and so will your writing process. Use marginal comments or a color code for your own Notes to Self about places you may want to return. Create strong boundaries with your inner editor, but ensure him/her that they will have their space to shine after you've written the first draft.

Fact: Nothing is less efficient than perfectionism.

Another way Resistance shows up in the drafting process is that you get stuck in the research phase, feeling like you have to read everything under the sun before you can sit down to write your book. Or you have to go teach your material for another day or another decade before you can write. Or you have to "live the conclusion of your memoir" before you can start the draft. *Classic not-enoughness.*

Honestly, the best antidote to all this crap is to GET YOUR ASS IN THE CHAIR. AND WRITE. Sorry, I didn't mean to yell, but seriously, do whatever mental gymnastics are required to get writing.

Cue the Rihanna song "Work" now. Or whatever gets you going.

Chapter 18

Principles of Composition

Make the Paragraph Your Unit of Composition

The paragraph is to the book what the cells are to the body. Like cells in the body, your paragraphs are the basic building blocks of your book.

The paragraph is intended to present and support a single idea, which means you don't present multiple ideas in a single paragraph. One idea per paragraph. It sounds simple, and it works.

I read this book once, where I loved the author's ideas but had a hard time getting through the book, and I couldn't figure out why. I went back with my writer's eyes and noticed that she consistently presented multiple ideas in each paragraph. She also didn't stick with a single point until it was fully developed before moving on. The writing felt like a four-year-old hopped up on candy searching for Easter eggs, bounding here, there, and everywhere. It was dizzying and a definite turnoff for readers.

Stay with one point, develop it fully, and then logically transition to your next point. Also, any work you don't do for your reader—in terms of being crystal clear, making connections, and orienting them to your ideas/stories—is work you are making them do. No fair.

Now, it may take you more than one paragraph to make your point. And you may divide your idea into parts and treat each one in a single paragraph. That's cool. Just stick with a point or idea and develop it fully before moving on.

For each paragraph, begin with a sentence that suggests the topic of said paragraph or that helps with the transition from the last paragraph. You may begin with a concise and comprehensive statement that serves to hold together what follows. In some ways, you can think of that first sentence as a summary of the paragraph.

Paragraphs can vary in length from a couple of sentences to several.

While this rule has changed in marketing as we move toward a greater conversational style of communication, a written paragraph ideally contains more than one sentence.

In dialogue, a new paragraph begins with each new speaker.

Charting, covered in Chapter 30 in the next section, is seriously golden when it comes to checking your paragraph coherence and tracking the expression of your thoughts and ideas. It helps you discover what you are *doing* in your writing and helps you see any errors of communication you couldn't see before.

For example, you may notice that you make the same point four times in a chapter in different ways without moving your ideas forward or presenting anything new. Or you may see that you took eight paragraphs to offer one example that was fairly tangential to your point.

> **BECAUSE I LOVE BODY/ANATOMY METAPHORS:**
>
> **Your book** = the body
>
> **Sections of your book** = regions of the body, e.g., torso
>
> **Chapters** = body parts, a limb or an organ
>
> **Subsections in a chapter** = muscles, bones, skin, tissues
>
> **Paragraphs** = cells
>
> **Sentences** = parts of a cell (nucleus, mitochondria, golgi apparatus, which isn't mentioned in book coaching nearly enough)
>
> **Words** = DNA

Be Clear, Concrete, Specific, and Definite

Vague, abstract, and general will get you nowhere in the writing world. Confusion kills. Aim to be clear, concrete, and specific in your language, in your expression of ideas, and in the ways that you support each of your ideas.

The thing about your book and its messages is this: It will only be as clear as you are about your topic. It will only go as deep as you have journeyed to understand the depth of your topic. We need you to be crystal clear and able to dwell in the details and the particulars in order to communicate with us effectively. (*We*, as in your audience.)

When it comes to detail, don't aim to be exhaustive but rather selective. We want to give significant details with accuracy. Engage the senses; give us a sense of immediacy. Be accurate and arouse the imaginations of your readers. No big deal. You can do this. And it's okay if you don't get it on the first try; that may be an unrealistic expectation. Instead, head in this direction and keep going.

Create Unity

Unity is the staple of good writing. Consistency. Cohesion. Gold.

This principle helps keep you in line and *immensely* helps your reader follow along with your writing and enjoy and extract the most from your book.

Components to decide and keep consistent:

- **Point of view:** Consider first person "I/we," second person "you," or third person "he/she/they." Do your best to keep these consistent. If you mix and match, at least keep the point of view consistent in each paragraph or treatment of a particular subject or set of materials.

- **Tense:** Generally, choose either present tense or past tense. The exception is if you are using tense as a tool for managing and expressing time. But still, choose a principal tense and know why (what effect this tense has). See Chapter 21 for more on tense.

- **Tone and voice:** If you're casual and conversational, keep that tone throughout. If you are cheeky or provocative, thread that through your work. If you're more formal and academic/professional, keep it consistent without throwing in a super casual conversation for good measure.

- **Key terms:** If you are calling something *soul*, don't suddenly switch to calling it *spirit*, *daemon*, *guardian angel*, or *muse* … unless you explain to your reader that these will be used interchangeably. If you give a name to a step in your process, keep it consistent.

- **Chapter length:** All chapters should be roughly the same in length, unless you're using chapter length as a creative narrative device intentionally. They don't have to be the same word count exactly, but they should all fall in the same length range.

- **Basic chapter "moves":** (See the next chapter, Chapter 19, for more on this.) Follow the same moves (such as tell a story, frame your story with your main idea for the chapter), or include the same ingredients (personal story, main idea, client examples, application) in every chapter.

CHAPTER 19

Chapter Structure

As a developmental editor, one of the primary things I do for every book is check two things: one, does the structure of the whole book make sense and feel optimal to the reader experience; and two, do the chapters have a repetition and rhythm that will also optimally suit the readers' experience of the book.

Just as your book has a beginning, middle, and end, so, too, will your chapters. Think of them almost as mini-books, self-contained in terms of an overarching theme and idea (in a way that is similar to your book as a whole) but also connected to one another like links on a chain.

A simple chapter structure for nonfiction books is effective, interesting, and easy for your readers to follow. Of course, writing them can be a bit more complex, but there is a structure you can use to build your chapters and, therefore, your book.

A chapter is like your favorite soup recipe; it should have roughly the same ingredients every time you make it because that is what makes it delicious. Your chapter soup might include a leading story, one main idea, support for that idea through quotes and case studies, and a section on how your reader can apply the idea via practices, for example. Those are your main ingredients. You might slightly tweak the recipe every time you make it—adding a little dash of this here or a little more of that—or maybe you change up the order of when you add the ingredients—but it should basically stay the same. Now, I am talking about structure here, not content, of course.

Parallelism in chapter structure is a crucial strategy we can use as writers to serve our readers and ourselves. We are supported because we don't have to reinvent the wheel every time we go to write a new chapter; we already know its basic structure. Our readers are supported by our chapter parallelism because they can intuitively know what to expect in every chapter. They ideally won't notice your structure, but it will be one of the main contributing factors to their sense of the cohesion, clarity, and unity of your book.

Getting Started with Chapters

If you've been working through the materials of this book, you know your book's overall message, the key points you want to make, and the kinds of evidence you will use to support these points (e.g., stories, facts, expert testimony), and hopefully, you have a rough working outline.

So, the next natural step is to dive into your chapters or sections of the book. For each chapter, you may consider doing a mind map or creating an outline if this helps create structure and sequence for you before you write. A little planning can go a long way in saving you time and avoiding wasted energy, frustration, and confusion.

One of the *key* things to do at the drafting stage is to discover the natural rhythm and structure of your chapters. Once you discover a pattern for how each chapter is organized, you can use this structure for *all* your chapters, as we've covered. I use the word *discover* intentionally here. Don't feel like you need to *force* a structure right at the outset. Instead, let it emerge as you write your first chapters. But do be mindful of seeking and replicating that basic structure throughout your book.

The PSA Structure

While you may discover your chapter structure organically as you write, which is what I recommend, there are some tried and true basic structures to writing a transformational nonfiction book. The simplest structure for a nonfiction book is the point, support, and application (PSA) formula.

The Point: What is your key overall point or message in this chapter? What are the parts of this message or point you need to walk your reader through in this chapter? (These may become your chapter subheadings.) The Point can be a few simple sentences or several pages, depending on your topic and what you want to convey.

The Support: Give us the evidence and support for your points. Make your case. Are you going to build it through storytelling, by offering us reasons, or by giving us examples? Are you going to tell us why it matters, what is at stake, and what the benefits are?

The Application: Give us specific tools, resources, action steps, or reflection opportunities so we can integrate your ideas into our own lives.

SANDWICHING THE PSA

Because the chapter is a distinct unit, it also needs a beginning and an end. Simply, in your chapter introduction, the first words, sentences, and perhaps paragraphs should introduce us to The Point in an engaging way. The introduction may also contain a transition from the last chapter to this new one.

In your chapter conclusion, you may summarize your key points and transition us to the next chapter, compelling us to want what you offer next.

Key points:

- **Clarity** matters here more than building suspense, though you may offer a bit of a teaser-transition to encourage your reader on to the next chapter.

- The PSA doesn't necessarily have to be in one-two-three **order**. Sometimes, you'll lead with a powerful story (S) and then frame the story with your main point (P). Sometimes, your application (A) will be woven into the support sections as they are relevant. You'll have to find the combination and sequencing that work best for you and your ideas.

- **Follow the same general format/composition for every chapter** to create rhythm and cohesion between chapters. When you find a specific chapter composition that works for you, stick to it. *Rinse, repeat.* This is where structure creates freedom (and clarity and effectiveness) both for you and your reader. As the author, you begin to get into the rhythm of each chapter and don't have to create a new structure each time. And for your reader, this uniformity creates predictability and makes it easier for them to follow, understand, and engage with your ideas.

- Bring balance to the **length of each chapter** as well. They don't each need to be 5,555 words exactly, but they should be about the same length. (The exception would be if you are changing the length stylistically with intention, but this should still have its own rhythm and purpose and be executed with uniformity.)

Memoir Chapters

As usual, some of this wisdom applies to memoir, but memoir also has its unique considerations. As with other nonfiction, you'll want to think of your chapters as having a unifying theme or project.

In your chapters, you may develop a single story, or you may weave stories together. In the former, your story is the unified theme or unit that makes it a chapter. When weaving stories together, they may be held by a theme or a "season" of your life. You'll want to consider how your chapter division makes unified wholes of each chapter (and then the next step is their sequencing).

As with nonfiction, you may develop a rhythm to your chapters. They may each be similar in terms of length, level of detail, and how stories are shared. For example, one of my memoir clients was weaving together the theme of identity/belonging through two key threads: 1) her faith experience and 2) her work as a midwife. In each chapter, she shared a story that revealed some aspect of each of these—i.e., she told a faith story, and she told a birth story. She revealed to us what they had in common and how they came together. In each chapter, she offered the same kind of evidence—quotes from the sacred text of her faith, scenes, and narrative. There was a rhythm and predictability that tied each chapter together, even though each one was completely unique in its content.

In Sophie Strand's memoir *The Body Is a Doorway*,[1] she uses a few key ingredients in each chapter. She tells some of her personal story and weaves it in with stories from the natural world. For the latter, she weaves in facts about different species, their behaviors and characteristics, and parallels that with something she is illuminating about her own human experience. Each chapter makes these "moves," which create unity and cohesion throughout the book.

Chapter Structure

If you have favorite memoirs, go back and read for chapter structure. Notice not what the reader is *saying* but what they are *doing* in each chapter. See what key ingredients they weave into each chapter. Then find your own perfect recipe.

CHAPTER 20

Book Introductions

Confession: I totally geek out on book introductions. The part of my mind that loves structure and universality loves the predictable nature of an introduction. Most books move out from this home base in wildly divergent directions, but we often all begin at the same place, covering the same things. Ah, the sweetness of structure (says my Venus in Virgo).

Here, I will demystify the introduction of a book for you. In many ways, this can be a step-by-step process, or at least you can use this resource as a guide to ensure your introduction has what it takes and does its job well.

Before we dive in, though, I have a suggestion. As I mentioned in a previous chapter, I recommend that you write your introduction *after* you've written and arranged the rest of your book. You may sketch out a higher-level, rough outline of your introduction earlier on, but hold off on diving into your full introduction until the rest of the book is written. Trust me, you'll have a much easier time writing it at the end than trying to get it written before you have anything else articulated. This is a place where many new writers get stuck—and with good reason. A lot goes into the introduction!

What is the Job of an Introduction?

In some ways, your introduction is like an elevator pitch for the rest of your book. It's more in-depth than the back of your book but is still part of a courtship phase where you are inviting your readers deeper into your book and giving them a reason to read the rest.

In the introduction, you are making a solid case for what your book is about (the what) and why it matters. It is also super important from the get-go, here in the introduction, to connect deeply with your audience and establish your ethos/credibility as someone who understands them and is qualified to lead them on the journey that follows.

The introduction is the summary or overview of the whole book.

"Moves" Made by Effective Introductions

- Introduce your *what*—that is, your topic, in a meaningful and attention-grabbing way (the hook).

- Make your case (for *why* what you do works or your way of seeing things is optimal).

- Establish why it matters: *So what? Who cares?* Here, you may outline the problem, what is at stake around your issue, why you specifically care, and why your audience should too. Why should people read your book? Your book is an investment of your reader's time, energy, and attention (all precious resources). Make the case for why your book is a valuable investment. You might talk about the benefits your book may bring to your reader.

- Give context and background about your issue or topic. What do we need to know at the outset to understand what will follow?

- Tell your personal story. Explain why you are writing this book, how you came to be an expert in this area, and how you are connected to the topic. (If the personal story you want to share is more in-depth, you might consider a fuller account in an early chapter, and stay more high level here.)

- Establish your credibility (see Chapter 22 for more).

- Indicate the gap—what is missing in this conversation—and your unique value statement and contribution to your field or topic.

- Present your main claim. What is your main, overarching idea or message in the book? (Revisit Chapter 7.)

- Share your intentions, reasons, and purpose for writing. What do you hope your book will do for your reader? What will it help them to do, believe, feel, and understand? (Revisit Chapter 5.)

- Describe how this book is organized. Give us an idea of the structure of your book and what ideas and features your reader should expect.

- Suggest how to use this book. Do you recommend reading it in a specific order or from start to finish? Is this the kind of book you can open to any page and just start reading? Do you want to instruct your reader to take breaks for integration, the exploration of processes, application in their real lives, or something else? Do you want to encourage your reader to go to the parts they are most drawn to first? Will some parts not be relevant to everyone?

- Share caveats and disclaimers, address objections and concerns, and offer necessary qualifiers.

- Define key terms. (This may come here or in an early foundational chapter.)

- Create a desire in your reader to continue reading. Develop momentum. Establish the "world" of your book.

Don't feel like you have to make every one of these moves in your introduction, but do try to cover much of this. If you want to see an application of these moves, open any well-written nonfiction book and read with the lens of watching for the "moves" authors make. You'll be surprised to see the similarities in many effective introductions.

Introductions for Memoirists

Obviously, some of these suggestions will apply to you, and some will not. You may go through the list and ask yourself, *What here can apply to my book? What of this can I make work for me?*

Here are a few ideas to consider in the introduction of a memoir, specifically.

1. The Hook: Engage your readers—definitely draw your reader into your story and the world of your book as quickly, powerfully, and effectively as possible. Bring us into a scene filled with action or tension, for example. Lead us on through the story, paragraph by paragraph, creating interest and momentum. Show us a potent scene that gives us a glimpse into the intriguing story or stories that will follow.

    Self-intrigue test: Notice if you are engaged and invigorated by the start of your book. If you are not super interested in this beginning, you can't expect that your readers will be.

2. Develop your ethos—reveal to your reader that you are at the helm, commanding this ship and leading us in a clear direction. Don't let your reader get lost or confused or have to do the job of filling in gaps or background details. Build trust.

3. Establish your book's purpose and personality (through tone and language use)—what are the compelling questions you are setting out to explore in this memoir? How might you reveal these through your writing?

4. Develop your connection to your reader—illuminate for your reader who you are and what the journey of your book will be like. Memoir often requires an intimate relationship with our reader. We reveal ourselves—with vulnerability, transparency, humility, courage, and openness—to build that connection.

5. Lay the foundation for what is to follow—what do your readers need to see, experience, or understand about you or the world you are creating in your book? Recall in the five-part narrative arc (in Chapter 12) that the first part is the exposition, which includes important background details and settings, events that occur prior to the main story, and character backstories.

6. Evoke your reader's emotions—go with the heart here more than the mind. We don't need your CV; we want your heart right out on page one.

CHAPTER 21

STYLISTIC AND LINGUISTIC CHOICES

Now that we've explored drafting best practices and insight on chapter structure, let's shift into the craft of writing and some techniques you'll want to consider as you write. In this chapter, I invite you to explore some of the more general stylistic techniques you may want to employ in your book. Chapters 22 and 23 will walk you through some important strategies all good nonfiction book authors employ, including strategies of effective communication and how to make more practical moves, such as quoting and making transitions. In the remaining chapters of this section, we'll dive into storytelling strategies.

Here are a few stylistic and linguistic choices you may consider as you dive into the drafting phase of your book. These will influence your degree of impact and how you are received by your reader. You don't need to have a full, robust, articulated answer to each of these (especially in the name of Resistance), but it's wise to at least consider them.

Language choice: Will you write in a casual, conversational, or more formal style? Do you use swear words? Slang? How much technical language from your areas of expertise will you use, and how much defining will be required to show goodwill toward your audience? To what extent do you use qualifiers (words like some, most, virtually, all, just, and hardly)?

Tone: What is the most appropriate tone to establish goodwill and credibility with your audience, given their position on your topic? Will you be serious? Funny? Laid back? Authoritative? What effect will that have?

___

Perspective: Will you write in first person (using "I" or "we")? Second person (where you address the reader "you" directly)? Third person (using "he" or "she")? *The effect of third person is to create more objectivity, authority, and distance, while first and second are more personal, establish more intimacy between reader and author, and can be more casual and informal. Second person is the domain of advertising, something to be aware of as you consider its effects in your context.*

___

Tense: Will you write in present tense or past tense? *Present has more immediacy and gives the audience a sense of participation in the scenes and events you present. Past tense gives more of an onlooker effect on events that have already occurred (hence, greater distance).*

___

Voice: Will you use active or passive voice? *Active puts emphasis on the agent of the action (I did the laundry), lessens distance, and means you must take more responsibility for your statements. Passive puts emphasis on the action/object (the laundry was done), increases distance, and can "hide" a writer from their statements (which can diminish ethos). Generally, active voice is more powerful, but it depends on context and your desired effect.*

Now, some of these will unfold naturally as you write, and you may use more than one strategy or stylistic technique as you write. This chapter is merely meant to bring more conscious awareness to some, though not all, of the major stylistic and linguistic techniques you might want to consider as you write.

CHAPTER 22

PERSUASIVE WRITING STRATEGIES

I'm pulling out my master's degree in Rhetoric and Writing Studies and going classic Greek education here for a minute (hat's off to you, Aristotle). In this chapter, we'll look at the three "rhetorical appeals" or three major strategies of persuasion—ethos, pathos, and logos—that we want to use in our writing. These strategies also connect to what we call the Rhetorical Triangle, a framework for understanding and developing effective communication, consisting of the author (ethos), subject (logos), and audience (pathos). All good writing utilizes these three strategies.

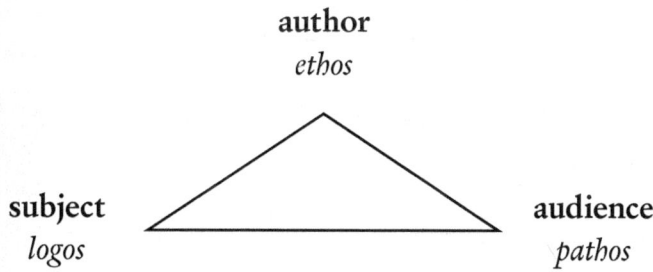

Ethos: Presenting Yourself as Likable, Competent, and Trustworthy

Ethos is connected to the *writer* (speaker/author) in our communication triangle. Ethos is our likability, trustworthiness, competence, and expertise in the eyes of our readers.

There are two major ways to establish our ethos. One, we establish it outside our book's content—by our existing reputation as a professional in our field, as well as through our presentation of a book that is well-edited, aesthetically pleasing, and well-regarded by other experts. Two, we establish it inside our book by the way we present ourselves to our reader—how we write and what we write. Both are important, but let's turn our attention to the inside of the book since we are in the drafting phase.

In our book, we want to show that we are considerate, intelligent, caring, trustworthy, reasonable, honest, knowledgeable, informed, moral, and have goodwill toward our readers. Here are a few ways we can develop our ethos.

DEMONSTRATE INTELLIGENCE AND EXPERTISE BY DOING YOUR HOMEWORK

Writing a book on a subject requires a *deep*, thoughtful, and thorough investigation of your subject matter. You have to know it more intimately than most people do. And you have to do your homework. You may have already done extensive "homework" by being a leader in or deeply engaging with your field or subject for some time. You may also "do your homework" through research, deep contemplation, and synthesis of ideas. (See Appendix C for more about book research.)

How, where, and what information will you share about your **background and qualifications?**

_____

_____

_____

_____

_____

Do you have a solid stance on your issues that comes from having **done your homework** (either through study or lived experience)? Will you offer **evidence** from your field, your personal life, or other experts? (And to what degree? You want to provide information your audience may not already have but not repeat information they already know.)

We also want to acknowledge our biases and be honest and transparent about where we are coming from, how we are approaching our subject, and why. Ideally, we have the reader's best interest in mind.

How will you acknowledge your **own bias** and be honest in your expression?

ADDRESSING NAYSAYERS

Part of creating a strong ethos is to demonstrate that you have a full understanding of your subject area and the various ideas and perspectives held by others. Now, most of our nonfiction books advocate our way of looking at an issue, but this perspective is subjective and one among many. To assume that everyone would agree with us and not acknowledge the potential criticisms, concerns, hesitancies, and dissenting opinions can make us look less credible and connected to the conversation about our subject. So, what can we do?

We can anticipate and address the opposing points or our reader's potential objections directly and overtly in our writing. Though it may seem counterintuitive, this often strengthens our writing and our ethos.

Templates for addressing counterarguments:

Now, I know what you might be thinking right now ...
Many smart readers at this point might be wondering ...
You may be reluctant to believe ... so allow me to explain and offer another example ...
You may not like what I am about to say, but ...

You can present the opposing ideas and take them in your own direction by:

1. Refuting the naysayer perspective completely with your own reasons and evidence.
   I disagree completely, and here's why ...
2. Make concessions while still standing your ground.
   While it is true that ... it doesn't necessarily follow that ...
   On the one hand, I agree with X that ... however, on the other hand, I still insist that ...
3. Empathize with another perspective, but show why yours is ultimately the most valid.
   I totally understand how X would feel this way because ..., but let me illustrate why this is ...

How will you **anticipate and answer** the potential thoughts, feelings, values, concerns, and ideas of your reader as you present your ideas?

_____
_____
_____
_____

DEMONSTRATE GOODWILL THROUGH DEEP EMPATHY AND AWARENESS OF OTHERS

To show goodwill toward our audience, we need to demonstrate that we've taken the time to deeply understand our reader's needs, feelings, and beliefs and that we deeply empathize with them. We have to show that we understand and genuinely care about them. Often, we must make ourselves open and vulnerable to make these authentic and meaningful connections. We also have to be generous to our readers in all the ways we can—because of the communication context, we are in the position of giver, and our reader is the receiver. Giving generously, thoughtfully, and authentically to our reader is a huge ethos-builder.

Will you tell personal **stories**? With what degree of transparency, depth, and vulnerability? And what is the intended effect of this storytelling? (Note: personal storytelling can have a powerful and lasting effect on readers, often because of its emotional appeal, relatability, and memorability.)

_____

_____

_____

_____

How will you compassionately **connect** to what your reader is feeling and needing? How will you offer them solutions to problems they know they have? How so?

_____

_____

_____

_____

What is the **power differential** between you and your audience, and what effect does it have on how you present yourself and your work in this book?

_____

_____

_____

OTHER WAYS TO ESTABLISH YOUR AUTHORITY

In addition to these ways of establishing your ethos, you will convey your authority through the presentation of your book at a practical, tangible level. **These all come *later*,** so don't worry about them too much now, but simply note that these will also have an impact on your ethos.

Editing: Part of establishing ethos is making your writing clear, organized, and error-free. Books with several typos or errors are seen as less credible and damage the author's ethos because it seems like they didn't take the time to edit their work sufficiently.

Blurbs or endorsements: You can boost your book's credibility by having endorsements from known and reputable experts in your field or fellow authors writing in your genre (or similar).

Design: The physical and spatial design of your book can also support or harm your ethos: Is the book layout user-friendly, attractive, and suited to the kind of book it is? Is the cover attractive?

Again, these all come way later but are part of how you convey your ethos in your book.

Pathos: Appealing to Your Audience's Emotions

Pathos corresponds to the *audience* aspect of our communication triangle.
   The communication strategy pathos is the writer's artful appeal to their reader's emotions. As you write your book, you may consider how you are evoking your audience's emotions and to what end. Emotional appeals can be incredibly persuasive (and should be used responsibly!). Consider what emotions you want to arouse in your audience, and *why*. The primary emotions are happy, sad, angry, disgust, fear, and surprise.
   Here is a partial list of additional emotions; I recommend checking out Nonviolent Communication lists of feelings (and even needs) for a more robust list:

When needs are met

adventurous	hopeful
engaged/ interested	thrilled
loving	warm
excited/ thrilled	encouraged
fascinated/ curious	empowered
awe	open
peaceful/ calm/ relaxed	empathetic/ sympathetic
playful	grateful / reverence
confident	passionate
content/ satisfied	inspired
happy/ delighted/ joyful	refreshed

When needs are not met

Scared	Lonely
Afraid/ Alarmed /Nervous	Troubled/ disturbed
Nervous/ Anxious/ Tense	Discouraged
Confused	Disconnected
Angry	Longing/ yearning
Agitated / flustered / annoyed	Helpless
Embarrassed	Hopeless
Overwhelmed	Jealous / envious
Ambivalent / torn	Shock
Protective	Pity
Sad/grief/heartbroken/ devastated	Aversion
Disappointed	

To arouse emotions, you need to know:
- Your reader's current state of mind (what they are already feeling) and *why*.
- How you can reach them in this place.
- What you can offer that will elicit the emotion you desire to evoke—one example is *enargeia*, through which you depict a scene or events so vividly that the reader feels like it is happening. Your word choice, tone, and presentation of evidence are influential as well.
- It may also be important to know the audience's attitude toward you.

One of the best ways to use pathos in your writing is to tell stories: stories are so potent and tend to stay with us longer than facts. One of my mentors says, "Facts tell, stories sell" because stories are so persuasive and connecting. We are wired for story. As you weave stories into your own writing, consider the ways they connect to and evoke emotions in your reader. This is often what makes them most powerful, and we want to use them wisely, consciously, and responsibly. See Chapters 24 to 26 for more.

Logos: Making Logical Sense in Your Writing

Logos connects to the *subject* aspect of our communication triangle.

In our writing, we want to ensure we're making logical or reasonable sense to our audience as they move through our ideas, and the reasons and evidence we use to support those ideas. A whole body of work, both classical and contemporary, looks at how we can make logical arguments. It involves a lot of great Greek words but is beyond the scope of this guide. So, I'll try to give you what is most useful.

Essentially, we want to make strong, viable, and valid logical arguments in our writing and support them adequately with appropriate and real evidence. We want to avoid logical fallacies or methods of faulty or shady reasoning (which you can Google if you want to learn more).

Here are high-level basics about making logical sense of your idea development.

All arguments are based on a premise that is a) observable with the senses, b) generally agreed upon by most people, c) in existence in law or custom, and d) what is admitted or accepted by writer and reader in a given context. There are also arguments based on what is *probable*, especially in the realm of human conduct (which is often less than predictable!). Another way to think about premises is that they are assumptions, often implicit, that we make about our topic before we begin to build our case for seeing it in a particular way.

For our purposes, we want to make sure the assumptions you make about your subject will be accepted by your reader. If you need to do some work to get them into agreement first, doing so will support the strength of your message and its reception.

From solid working premises, we can move out in a few directions.

We can move from one or more particulars (e.g., examples, case studies) to a universal conclusion.

We can move from a universal truth toward a conclusion that is more specific and particular to one application.

Another major move we can make in building a logical argument is to use examples. Examples can take many forms—they can be historical examples, fictional examples, personal examples, expert examples, analogies (hypothetical), and similar/contrary examples (compare/contrast). This covers many types of evidence, but do refer to Chapter 7 for a full list of types of evidence you can use to support your ideas. Providing facts/stats/data and defining your terms are two other major ways to adequately make solid arguments in your writing.

CHAPTER 23

Summarizing, Quoting, and Transitions

BRINGING IN OTHERS' VOICES: THE ART OF SUMMARIZING AND QUOTING

Summarizing and Paraphrasing

To make a solid case for your way of seeing things, you often need to position your ideas relative to others involved in the discussion about your topic. For this reason, it is important to be able to summarize what other people say in a way that keeps your ideas central and moves them forward.

You want your summary of another's ideas to remain true to their original intentions while also being expressed in a way that is relevant to your points. To remain true to the original author's ideas, you have to go back and "listen" with an open mind to what they are saying. To express what will benefit your book, you need to read with an eye for how you will present this idea or information for your purposes and to filter out what's unnecessary so you can concisely articulate what is relevant.

Now, you may present summaries of others' ideas in your book as evidence or support of your argument or to illustrate a point. You may also use a summary as a launching point for disagreeing and presenting a new way of looking at something (which we explored in the ethos section).

Verbs to indicate agreement with another's points:
- Acknowledge, admire, agree, endorse, praise, celebrate, reaffirm, corroborate, support, verify

Verbs to indicate disagreement with another's points:
- Renounce, repudiate, deny, qualify, question, refute, reject, contradict, complicate, complain, deplore, question

Generally speaking, summarizing another's ideas with attribution is considered "fair use" (speak with a copyright attorney to be sure). This is a way to cover a lot of ground without having to directly quote them, which often requires rights permissions (see Appendix D for more on fair use). Lean on using summarizing— or paraphrasing, which is getting one level more specific—over direct quoting if you are concerned about fair use guidelines or are seeking to cover a lot of ground in accounting for another person's ideas. And always accurately offer attribution (citations) for another's points and ideas. (You generally do not have to provide a full citation for epigraph quotations, like those at the beginning of a chapter, according to The Chicago Manual of Style.)

Quotes

Sometimes, the most powerful way to support your points is to quote an expert verbatim in your book. Here is how to do that.

When I taught college composition, I taught my students to create "quotation sandwiches," and while a bit *cheesy*, this is a great tool for professional writers as well. This is a quotation sandwich:

- **Part one (top slice of bread):** Introduce, set up, or frame who is speaking and what it's about (any important context details).

    Examples:
    In her book, _____, X maintains that …
    According to X, in her book about Y …
    X illustrates this idea perfectly when he writes …
    As the prominent climate change researcher Y states in his report titled B …

- **Part two (the meat/veggies):** Include the actual quotation in quotes and the appropriate citation or superscript to indicate a full citation lives in the Endnotes.

- **Part three (bottom slice of bread):** Explain the quote or frame it for your readers to understand its relevance to your point or to carry your case further.

Examples:
In other words ...
X's point is that ...
In making this point, X is saying ...
X shows us that ...
What I love about X's statement here is ...
What this statement reveals is ...

Example from *Half the Sky*, a book by Nicholas Kristof and Sheryl WuDunn[1]

> "A senior World Bank official told a maternal health conference in London in 2007, with typical enthusiasm: 'Investing in better health for women and their children is just smart economics.' Now, that's certainly true of educating girls, but the sad reality is that investments in maternal health are unlikely to be as cost-effective as other kinds of health work."

Generally, if you are quoting less than four lines (in your book) of someone else's words, you include them in the text without any special treatment regarding formatting. If longer than four lines, you often begin a new line and indent the whole passage (your editors and designers will likely do this for you, but just FYI). Also, if you are indicating what someone was *thinking*, not what they said, you often show that by using *italics*.

Transitions

To help your reader follow you where you lead them, you need to make strong transitions from one idea to another, one move to another. This happens at different levels—between sections, chapters, paragraphs, and sentences. Often, readers get lost because a transition has not been offered in these places. Writing can feel disjointed or lack a smooth flow without transitions.

Transitions are simply gestures (words or phrases) that point back to what you just said or point forward to what is coming next. In this way, you articulate the relationship between each of your statements and take the guesswork out of it for your reader.

I like to think of this as creating the chain that connects each part to the whole or as the subtle hand that holds the continuity within your writing.

When transitions are made well, they are barely noticed by a reader, but when they are lacking, the reader can feel the disconnection, confusion, choppiness, or lack of cohesion.

Here are transition terms you may want to use:

To introduce an example
After all
As an illustration
Specifically
Consider
For instance
For example

To elaborate/clarify
Actually
In short
That is
In other words
To put it bluntly/succinctly/another way
What I mean is
Point being
I'm not saying
Ultimately

To add to
Also
And
Besides
Furthermore
Additionally
So too
Moreover
Indeed
In fact

To compare/contrast
Along the same lines
Likewise
Similarly
In the same way
However
But
By contrast
Nevertheless/Nonetheless
On the contrary
Conversely
Even though

To show cause/effect
Since
Hence
Thus
Therefore
Then
So
Accordingly
As a result
Consequently

To conclude
In summary
Therefore
Consequently
To sum up
To summarize
In short
In conclusion
Hence

To concede/qualify/hedge
Admittedly
Naturally
Of course
To be sure
Although
Granted
Yet

Other transition templates:
Having just explained x, I now want to complicate the point/add/examine ...
Now that we have a solid understanding of x ...
Building upon that ...
Even more importantly ...
X naturally leads us to consider ...
First/second/lastly
What comes next is ...

You can also use pointing words, which point or refer back to the concept in the previous part. But use these words carefully and make sure they have only one possible reference object. These words include *this, these, that, those, their, such, his, her, he, she,* and *it*. Most of us are pretty comfortable using pointing words.

A third way you can make connections and overall cohesion in your writing is to develop and repeat key terms and phrases throughout. These, when extracted, give your reader a solid sense of your topic and perhaps your stance. Using them stylistically can build a sense of momentum as well.

Lastly, you can build bridges by repeating yourself, but in a way that is interesting and varied enough that it helps you build a solid foundation and advances your ideas without sounding insulting or redundant. Think of the way a rock climber ascends a rock wall: they get a secure hold on the position they've established before reaching for the next ledge.

CHAPTER 24

SCENES AND SUMMARIES IN STORIES

> *"Whenever you can, tell stories instead of explaining stuff. Humans love stories, and we hate having stuff explained to us. Use Jesus as an example: He spoke almost exclusively in parables, and allowed everybody to draw their own lessons from his great storytelling. And he did very well."*
>
> — ELIZABETH GILBERT

Often, I'll suggest places in an author-client's book—whether fiction, nonfiction, or memoir—where I believe it may be more powerful for them to *show* rather than *tell*. When I say this, I am often greeted with a blank stare. What does this mean, exactly?

As much as possible in storytelling, we want to give people experiences, not information. This means you want to paint them a scene and draw them into the action so they feel they are present in the moments you are creating (*show* them), as opposed to *telling* your reader what happened in the past, which I'll call "narrative summary."

Really, both scene-building and narrative summary have their roles in our writing and storytelling. Here, we'll explore the characteristics of each and when it is best to use them.

Before we get there, I want to further my case about the importance of using storytelling and scene-building in your book, whether a thought book, teaching memoir, or other type of transformational nonfiction book. One of the things we do at Whale Song is help our clients write book proposals to submit to agents and publishers. And sometimes we get to see the feedback publishers give to our authors.

Here are two responses to two different book proposals, both of which showcase the importance of storytelling in your book (and, in this case, your ability to secure a book deal if you want to go the traditional publishing route—more on that in Section Four).

> *"You put together a solid proposal for your book —well-prepared, creative, and with a strong point of view. The passionate energy in your writing was infectious, and we really resonated with some of the key terminology you use for your work.*
>
> *While we were drawn to your creativity and overall concept, we believe your writing could benefit from a slowed-down approach that allows the reader to sit in the moment with specific, carefully selected scenes from your story. Remember that the more the reader can put themselves in the scene, the more they will be able to resonate with your story, and it's important to choose stories and key details that will serve the reader on their journey. We hope this feedback is helpful as you work toward making this proposal and future book the best it can be. Wishing you only success in your publishing journey!"*

Here, the publisher praises many of the strengths of this proposal and book, but decides to pass on it because it is lacking that "slowed-down approach ... of crafting carefully selected scenes." And the publisher goes on to explain why that matters. Here is a second example, this one from an agent about a different book.

> *"You both have excellent credentials, and this is a very interesting topic for a book. I did not, in the end, feel a connection to the material in the book in the way I need to offer representation. I wanted to have a better and deeper sense of how each person you describe experienced things and came to learn from their experiences."*

Here, the agent passes up on a book proposal from a well-qualified author-duo, leaders in their field really, with an extremely interesting topic, because of its lack of compelling storytelling that gave her a better and deeper sense of the characters' experience in the book. That crucial ingredient of storytelling was missing, and it cost them a book deal. (They kept tweaking their book proposal and had a publisher pick up their book. Happy ending!)

So, what is the difference between scene-building (showing) and narrative summary (telling)? Let's look at an example next.

Showing Versus Telling: An Example

This is a passage from Michael Crichton's memoir *Travels*[1]. He is *showing* us what is taking place.

> "Look here, don't worry about it," he said, laughing and slapping me on the shoulder. "I was just joking."
>
> "You weren't."
>
> "I promise you, I was."
>
> "What do you want to bet I make it?" I said.
>
> "Look here, Michael," he said. "It was just a joke. You're taking this entirely too seriously."
>
> I persisted. "I'll bet you a dinner, when I get back to Nairobi," I said, and named a French restaurant that he had mentioned as expensive and good.
>
> Mark agreed to the bet. "Right," he said. "Now, how will we verify that you actually get to the top?"
>
> "Do you think I'd lie?"
>
> He raised his hands. "I'm just asking how I'll know. A bet's a bet. How'll you prove it?"
>
> "Well, there'll be pictures," I said. "I'll have pictures."
>
> "They won't be developed yet."
>
> "I'll develop them in Nairobi for you."
>
> It turned out that you couldn't get color processing done in Nairobi; the film was all sent to England, and it took weeks.
>
> "I'll get a statement from the guide or whatever."
>
> "Could be forged."
>
> "Well, Loren will tell you whether I made it or not."
>
> "That's true," he said nodding, "she'll tell me whether you got up there."

> So we agreed, back in Nairobi, if Loren and I had climbed Kilimanjaro, he would buy me dinner.
>
> Then a thought occurred to me. "What if Loren doesn't make it?"
>
> Mark shook his head. "The boys are six to two that she'll make it to the top. We're not worried about her. We're worried about you."
>
> "Great," I said.

In that passage, we learn a lot about Michael, Mark, and even Loren, as the author shows us their character and actions through dialogue, inner thoughts, and actions. Crichton is *showing* us a lot about Michael's upcoming trip to climb Kilimanjaro.

Now, consider how this might be presented in a narrative summary:

> Mark and I had a close brother-like relationship and bantered in a friendly way. But I felt competitive and like I had something to prove. I wanted him to believe I could climb Kilimanjaro successfully; I wanted him to believe in my abilities. But I couldn't tell him that. So I made him bet me that I could do it. We labored around the logistics: how would he know I'd actually climbed the mountain? I suggested that maybe I could take pictures or get a note from the guards, or maybe Loren could vouch for me. Mark thought Loren had a better chance of making the climb than I did, so I was determined to make it. I made a bet with Mark that if I did it, he'd take me to the fanciest French restaurant in Nairobi.

These are both solid but have a different impact. One brings us into the immediacy of the scene as if we are watching it unfold; the other tells us a lot about the characters from the narrator's after-the-fact reflections. Which one feels more alive and engaging to you?

Scene-Building

Let's look at scene-building in greater depth. A scene is your (re-)creation of a moment or moments in time by showing your reader the real-time events as they are happening (in present tense) rather than describing them after the fact, as with narrative summary. This gives your readers the feeling that they are watching the events as they transpire, drawing them into the world you are creating, making them feel a part of it, and, ideally, allowing them to get "lost" in your world. Scenes give your writing a sense of immediacy and transparency. Scenes engage the reader's emotions more than their minds, generally speaking. While scenes are so powerful, they can be harder to create than just telling your reader something, and it can take practice to develop confidence in their use.

Scenes are created through action, dialogue, and interior monologue (see Chapter 26 for more). They engage the senses and emotions. You offer specific locations and actions that readers can picture so they can imaginatively enter your scene. You show them things about your characters through dialogue, their actions, and their inner thoughts. You can show details of a character's motives and behavior rather than just telling us. You can reveal why a character feels or acts the way they do.

When creating a scene, a writer will have to discover the just-right level of detail to offer. A good guideline is to use enough detail to jumpstart your reader's imagination so they can picture your scene themselves. Be wary not to create scenes that are totally exhaustive and non-plot-moving. Scenes can be immediate and engaging, but can also be relentless and exhausting if overused.

Good storytelling employs both narrative summary and scene-building in wise proportion. It is wise not to tell your readers something you've already revealed through dialogue and action. You must trust your readers to have gathered this information from your scenes.

Narrative Summary

Narrative summary is when you *tell* people about a scene rather than *show* them. You tell your reader about your characters, their location, what they are doing, and what has happened. It's a secondhand report and can create a sense of distance between your reader and the action you are presenting. Narrative summary engages the reader's mind, not their emotions. While it lacks that potent immediacy of scene-building, it is a necessary contrast to scene-building and has its place in our storytelling and transformational nonfiction books.

WHEN TO USE NARRATIVE SUMMARY:

When you want to slow down the pace: Using the right proportion of narrative summary to scene can vary the rhythm and texture of your writing. It can slow things down to give your readers a chance to catch their breath if the action has been fast-paced or intense.

To account for a long period of time: Using narrative summary can give continuity to your story on a larger scale—it can capture weeks or months of slow, steady growth or change that a scene can't capture, for example.

When you are accounting for repetitive action: Using narrative summary can be appropriate when you are accounting for a repetitive action, something that a character does again and again. You can use narrative to summarize the first few of a series of similar actions (e.g., track races for an athlete character).

For brevity: You can use narrative summary when some events don't justify having a whole scene dedicated to them.

QUESTIONS TO CONSIDER WITH SCENES AND SUMMARIES

How often do you use narrative summary when you are writing stories in your book? Are there long passages where nothing happens in real time? Do main events take place in summary or in scene?

What is the proportion of summary to scene? Are there some summaries you could convert to scenes, and vice versa? Good places to write scenes are those with major plot twists or surprises and those involving main characters.

Are you describing your character's emotions, or can you show us how they felt through action, dialogue, and monologue?

CHAPTER 25

LAYERS OF A STORY

When you are writing memoir or developing a story for your nonfiction book and are working to build and add fullness to your storytelling, consider taking some time to work with the three layers of your story. You may take this out of your book for a moment for some journaling, exploring, and planning as you use the writing process as a way to explore and discover your truth and what you wish to convey in your storytelling.

Here, we explore the three layers of a story: the surface skin, the midlayer of story muscle, and the deepest layer, the story bones.

Top Layer: Our Story Skin

The skin of our bodies is what is seen and what we reveal to the world; it covers and protects our deeper structures. The skin of our stories is also the outermost layer—what we most often show of our experiences socially and what serves to protect the deeper aspects of our truth. This story skin is where "what happened" takes place—it is the keeper of the facts, the timing, the setting, the chronology, and the what, where, when, and with whom.

Our story skin, comprised of these facts, is what any observer might see of our story. Like skin, it blankets the story in a surface layer of continuity—it could even be seen as holding the story together, offering a container for all the deeper structures. Our story skin is often what we feel most comfortable showing the world.

The story skin speaks in nouns and verbs; it loves quantity over quality; it favors the concrete and the physical.

The story skin registers the external landscape of our experience—what we can see, touch, hear, feel, and taste.

In the context of storytelling, the story skin correlates with the setting, context, and action of our story. At the skin level, we are the actors, enacting roles and displaying traits by performing behaviors in the presence of others.

We all begin our stories at the skin. We need this place as our starting landscape, as the first thing we encounter as we explore the body of our story. The facts provide the physical landmarks we can use to guide ourselves deeper into the terrain of our experiences and come back out again. We need to know what happened and how it happened.

The story skin is also the acceptable social script from which we are expected to read. When someone asks, "What was [a particular personal experience] like?" we are often expected to answer from our story skin—reflecting the surface-level facts, not the heart or soul of our profound experience. *Just the facts, ma'am.*

Without reflection (and courage), many of us remain at our story skin. Given the deeply vulnerable nature of our most potent stories, we deem it safest to stay on the surface. We can use our story skin to hide behind, to keep people out, and to keep ourselves disconnected from the deeper layers of our experience. This may be appropriate self-protection—like our physical skin keeps the harmful bacteria out—but sometimes, sharing only our story skin with another protects us from the non-supportive response we risk when we reveal what lies beneath.

While the story skin can protect us socially, we must remember that it requires a degree of permeability to let in the goodness—like how our skin absorbs vitamin D from the sun. Opening past our story skin can offer nourishment, such as fulfilling our deep need to feel heard and seen by others as we reveal the tender, vulnerable aspects of our experience.

Vulnerability research pioneer Brené Brown said, "I spent a lot of years trying to outrun or outsmart vulnerability ... my inability to lean into the discomfort of vulnerability limited the fullness of those important experiences that are wrought with uncertainty: love, belonging, trust, joy, and creativity, to name a few." The possibility of fulfilling these fundamental desires—to be loved, to belong, to experience joy—lies beneath the skin of our stories.

In our data-driven world, it is easy to mistake the *chronology* of events for our actual story. This is not our story. It is the scene in which our *experience* unfolded.

One of the amazing things about a book is that it lets us sneak, skip, and scribble past the social conventions of staying at the skin of our stories. It allows us space and a proper context to go into the deeper layers—of our stories, of our beings. I often feel that if someone really wanted to know my truest truth about a thing, they'd do best to ask me to write about it. I can be much more fully me and explore the whole of my experience with much greater ease when I am writing, versus any other medium of communication. So, let's dive deeper, shall we?

Middle Layer: Our Story Muscles

Going a layer deeper, we move from the external landscape of our experience—the facts—to the internal landscape of our experience—our thoughts, feelings, needs, relations, and the quality of our experience. Our story muscles reveal how we feel and what we think about what happens to us. This layer of our story is like the muscles and connective tissues of the body in that they serve as the prime movers of the body. They generate and coordinate action and the effects of such action, they protect what lies even deeper, and they store and release energy.

The female body is made of approximately 40 percent muscle (for men, the percentage is higher). So are our most potent life stories. Our hearts and wombs are some of the strongest and hardest-working muscles in the body. At this layer, we begin to get to the heart of our stories, to the womb of our stories. Our story muscles—our thoughts, feelings, and relationships to the external—need a voice in our narratives so we don't atrophy in our growth. Without these underlying dynamic movers and coordinators, our skin is lackluster and lifeless.

The story muscles speak in adjectives; they love quality and nuance. The story muscles point toward the heart of our story: the emotional, mental, and relational realms.

In the context of storytelling, this layer correlates with character development and mood. To reveal the muscles of our story, we may use internal monologue, description, and even dialogue and beats (which may reveal non-verbal communication as clues to the interior). These enrich our story. At this second level, we are the agents of our story, acting upon inner desires, goals, values, and plans.

The story muscles are dynamic and changing. Some of them fall under our control, while others function outside of our intention—just as our thoughts and feelings may arise without our intending them but are essential to our survival. This layer is woven throughout the body of our story but can look different in different places and in different stories. In one place, the muscle is meaty and robust as a key driver of our action, while in another, the muscle is not as developed or relevant to the action in question. What is meaty and what is lean depends on the writer and her story. For a parent with a full-term, healthy baby, for example, a mention of the baby's length and weight in her birth story may not register much in her internal landscape, but for a parent whose child was born early or has trouble nursing, the baby's weight is of the utmost importance to her internal landscape.

How this inner landscape looks and how it is captured on paper is deeply personal and highly variable. Some people will feel at home in this layer and find ease in putting words to the inner world. Others may feel awkward or challenged by exploring this unseen but powerful level of experience. It can take courage to get to the heart (muscle) of our stories and bear the truth of this layer. But the benefits of this reflection can be tremendous.

Muscles and connective tissues are anything but static—they are fluid and dynamic and changeable. Our thoughts and feelings are also fluid and dynamic. Here we unearth the seeds of our liberation from victimhood, shame, and limiting beliefs, should they factor into our internal landscape. We may not be in charge of our skin layer (the external), but we can wrestle with, claim control over, gain compassion for, and even reinvent our second layer.

As the agents in our story, we get to create its shape and learn from what it reveals to us. We can discover how we felt and what we thought in the course of our actual experience. And then later, as often as necessary, we can rewrite our relationship to the skin of our stories, choosing to lean into how we feel now, cultivate new thoughts and feelings, make new meanings and connections, and draw new insights. Here, we can make our story our own.

Deepest Layer: Our Story Bones

At our deepest layer, we find our story bones. Our bones provide the solid frame that holds our bodies, our stories, and our lives together—they provide structure and form. Just as our body's bones are moved by the muscles, the story bones are driven by the emotional-cognitive-relational internal landscape that forms as we experience our life. In our body, the bones protect what is most vital—our brains, hearts, lungs, and wombs. In our story, the bones also protect and represent what is most vital—our sense of what our stories *mean* and why they *matter* to us.

Our story bones are where we make meaning from experience—what lessons we have learned, what wisdom we have earned, and what enduring truths we have gathered from the depth of our experience.

Clarissa Pinkola Estés asserts that, in archetypal symbology, the bones represent the indestructible force. "They are by their structure hard to burn, nearly impossible to pulverize. In myth and story, they represent the indestructible soul-spirit."[1] Our story bones reveal our soul.

In the context of story, this level offers the themes, morals, and messages—the wisdom and the truth found in story. We were mere actors at the skin level and agents at the muscle level. Now, we become the authors of our story. As the autobiographers or memoirists of our stories, we can take stock of life—past, present, and future—to craft a story that tells who we have been, who we are, and who we are becoming as a result of our experience.

The story bones are what our readers come seeking from our stories. They may make the same meaning we have made, or one entirely of their own, built to fit their own soul's journey at that moment in time. When we are able to reveal our story skin and story muscles with vulnerable accuracy—to be willing to share specifically and vividly what an experience was like for us—we help our readers make meaning of their own lives, in light of what is evoked in them from reading our stories. This is the power of storytelling. It's bone-building and soul-marrow-nourishing.

Ultimately, the story bones reside in a deep place of mystery, wordlessness, symbol, and archetype. They are brought to the light of consciousness as we work to put words to this level of our experience. While it may be challenging or feel approximate at best, working at this level is where we gain integration and deep healing for ourselves and most powerfully connect with our readers within our book-expressions.

If we are in need of healing, the story bones beckon us to deep work—to melt away all the details—the connective tissues, the muscles, the skin—to strip down to the skeleton, the bare bones, the essence of our truth. What in our experience is essential? What is true? And when we've gathered these jewels from the depths, we swim back to the surface, reconstructing our stories, re-weaving the skin, muscles, and connective tissues together once again to make new forms.

As clinical psychologist, Jungian analyst, shaman, and author Carl Greer writes in his book *Change Your Story, Change Your Life*:

> "Your life is more than a series of events that happen over the course of time. It is a story with themes and patterns. How you tell your story is up to you, but if you can tell it honestly and are willing to work with the energies that affect your personal energy field, you can write an entirely new story with new themes and new patterns of events. [...] Even though you will not change the facts, you will modify your interpretation of them, and your framing of them. The emotional charge of your wounds will be diminished."

He notes that through writing your story, you may cultivate new emotional energies, such as pride in having survived difficulties and joy in having created something positive out of suffering.

Recently, I was working on a project that included writing about my childhood backyard. Now, my default story about my childhood was that it was fraught with challenges and that the loving, wise presence I needed as a child wasn't available. As I was working on that backyard story, the first line that sprang forth was: "I grew up surrounded by wise teachers and wild kin. Elder teachers, medicines and sustenance in abundance," in reference to the trees and plants with whom I forged deep bonds as a child. That perspective, that alternative truth to my standard perspective, changed something profoundly in me within an instant. We can always expand our aperture to see more truth about our experiences.

Seeking ways to make meaning from our experiences is a vital part of our processing and expressing our most potent life stories. When we reflect upon the significance of our stories and the insights we've gleaned, we can reap great rewards of understanding, connection, strength, healing, and more. However, there is a certain flavor of meaning-making that is best left out of our story recipe. Harmful lines of inquiry can focus on blame, guilt, and shame.

Questions like: *Why did this happen to me? How did I invite this in?* and *What did I do to deserve this?* are not fruitful lines of inquiry that yield much benefit. I've also heard the line of reasoning that *Because x didn't go as I'd hoped, this means I am flawed, bad, or wrong* in some way. This kind of meaning-making does not serve us well, nor is our reasoning often true. More often, this line of reasoning is the result of painful emotions that have not yet been fully processed and can indicate that further exploration and healing support are warranted.

When you begin to identify the meaning you've created from your story, ask yourself, *Is this really true? Does my experience support this conclusion? Can I find evidence in my story or my life that complicates or contradicts the meaning I've constructed?* There can be liberation here if we know how to navigate these waters. And we must tread carefully, not to cause any harm to ourselves.

If you are struggling with intense emotions around the stories you seek to share in your book, I recommend working with a qualified care professional who is trained in supporting one's journey to uncover and shift core and key operating beliefs. I work with many clients through the telling of their most tender stories. I find that many are surprised at the pockets of emotion that are unlocked as they write about the past. While we certainly do not want to re-traumatize ourselves in our writing (something I talk more about in my program Heal a Story That Hurts), it is expected that we will revisit some of the emotions, thoughts, felt sensations, and energies we experienced in those past moments we choose to write about now. These can be healing opportunities. I recommend going slowly into these territories and taking exceptional care of yourself as you express these stories from the past. Having a witness, in the form of a friend, therapist, or coach, can be really helpful. Keep your present time well-being at the center of your writing decisions, take it slowly, and make sure you have all the support you need.

How to Weave the Story Layers Into Your Writing

There is no easy answer or set formula for how to weave these three layers into your writing. My recommendation is to take this exploration out of your manuscript and into a journal. Build out the "what happened"—the scene, the chronology of events, and the like—on a big sheet of paper (a roll of kids' art paper or a posterboard can be great for this). Determine the sequence of how the events unfolded. Get clarity on what happened, where, with whom, and everything you can recall from that time. Engage your sensory memory to gather back the felt sensations and sensory/environmental impressions you have from that time.

You might consider the following questions to help build out your story skin. (Anywhere it says "you" here, you can replace with a particular character, as needed):

1. What did you *see*?
2. What colors are visible? What was the quality of light?
3. What did you *smell*?
4. What did you *hear*?
5. What did you *taste* (may or may not be relevant)?
6. What did you *feel* (as in touch, including temperature)?
7. What was the weather like?
8. What time of day was it?
9. What features of your environment stand out or serve as relevant details to the "plot" or action?
10. What other details of the scene can you call forth?

From there, perhaps you want to track what was unfolding in your (or your book character's) internal landscape at the time. What were they thinking, feeling, sensing, wanting, fearing, hoping, and experiencing in and around those events? How might you reveal that through your storytelling?

What meaning are you making of all of this, that you want to reveal to your reader? What themes and threads of wisdom or truth are you wanting to reveal through this story? How will you do that?

As always, you can check out how other authors weave these layers into their stories (so long as you stop short of the comparison trap and come back into your own lane and your own voice).

While we are here talking about these three layers, let's dive into two more storytelling considerations: characterization and proportion.

Characterization

When you introduce a character in your stories, give your reader a few specific, concrete details about their physicality so they can picture him or her in their imagination (just a jumpstart, not a head-to-toe account). When it comes to revealing their personality, it is better to do this with action and reaction (i.e., beats), interior monologue, and dialogue (showing us) rather than straight descriptions (telling us).

Particularly in memoir, where there is more space to develop the characters in your stories, you want to introduce them to your reader in a natural way. When two people first meet, they don't instantly learn everything about each other. Rather, they get to know each other over time. Reveal your story's characters to your reader in this same way.

As mentioned before, only share as much information and detail as needed to serve your story and spark your reader's engagement with the storyline.

When you complete a scene, story, or chapter, you can look back to see if you've told us anything that you later showed us in dialogue or in some other way. You can reduce redundancies. You can also check to make sure you offer relevant character histories (what your readers need to understand) and nothing more.

While you may not put all the details of a character into your story, you may again want to take your process out of your book for a moment and create a character sketch. Write a few pages about this character in exposition style or in any way you like. You may want to use the questions from Chapter 6 about audience, but apply them to your character. From here, when you are tuned in, decide what you want to weave into the story in your book.

Proportion

In memoir or other nonfiction, how do we know what level of detail and how much to share about aspects of our experience within our storytelling? While we want to be specific and concrete in our writing, we don't want to over-explain, provide excess detail or description (especially for minor points), or be redundant (for example, showing and telling the same thing).

When you fill in all the details for your reader, you leave them little space to imagine with you, and this can feel patronizing. And boring.

What you spend your time focusing on in your storytelling will convey to your readers what is most important to your story. So, you want to make sure you're putting time and attention into the elements that are most essential to your messages, themes, and desired focus. If we go back to this notion that our stories have the purpose of illustrating the point we are making, we can keep this bigger point or purpose alive as we write and check that we are staying true to its illustration. Make sure you're taking your readers where you want to take them.

Proportion is a quality you can be aware of as you write your first draft and return your focus to it again during revision. For example, if you notice you've written three pages about your story's setting, and it doesn't leave any room for your reader to imagine nor does it carry the story forward by any real measure, then you might consider going back and editing to keep only what you really want to share to jumpstart your reader's imagination and get them to the action of the story.

For example, I recently read a client's chapter in which she is talking about a hospital experience that shook her to the core. In the early part of the chapter, she develops a full scene, several pages long, about how she was speeding and was pulled over by a police officer on the way to the hospital. But the freeway incident doesn't really do much to build character or contribute to the point of the chapter (this turning point in her experience at the hospital). As readers, we spend a good portion of the chapter reading about the traffic event, so we are led to believe that it is important to the story. But we don't come to discover its importance to the main narrative thread. If the speeding was meant to foreshadow what was to come or reveal the writer's anxiety prior to the event, it could still be shared, but perhaps not at the same level of detail. Proportionally, most of the detailed scene-building would want to focus on the hospital scene. We want to be intentional about where we focus our reader's attention and to what end.

CHAPTER 26

Dialogue and Beats

Whether you are writing memoir or telling stories within your nonfiction book, you may want to utilize dialogue and beats (defined and described in the following section) in your scene creation.

As Anne Lamott writes in *Bird by Bird*,[1] "Good dialogue is such a pleasure to come across while reading, a complete change of pace from description and exposition, and all that *writing*."

Unless you have a background in creative or fiction writing, crafting dialogue is not likely to be an oft-practiced skill for you. But that doesn't mean you have to avoid it or can't learn to do it well.

In what follows, you'll learn general best practices in the use of dialogue so you can intersperse it into your scenes with greater skill. We'll also cover *beats*, which are bits of action interspersed through a scene.

Dialogue in Nonfiction

Sometimes in nonfiction and always in memoir, we will want to use story as a way to transmit and share information with our audience. Humans are storytelling creatures, and stories are often what settle into our bones when we read something transformational (see the previous chapter for more about story bones).

Using dialogue is a powerful tool of storytelling that can convey a lot of information in an accessible and potent way to our readers. We can use dialogue to open a scene (or a chapter) and to hook or draw our readers in efficiently and powerfully. We can use dialogue (or direct quotes) to have an emotional impact on our reader, create immediacy, and inspire intimacy.

Dialogue and the Truth

If it's been twenty years (or even twenty days) since the scene you are writing actually happened, you can be fairly sure that you'll have to recreate the words spoken in an approximate manner in your dialogue. It's rare that dialogue is a reflection of the exact word-for-word spoken truth that transpired in the past.

Dialogue is an author's recreation, and as with all our writing, this comes with responsibility. While we may not be able to recreate the exact conversations of the past, we can capture the capital-T Truth in dialogue to the best of our ability. We can do our best to keep true to the *spirit* of the conversation and the characters—what they would have said and how. And we can use dialogue to move our agenda forward in our books and stories.

Dialogue is often more compressed, concentrated, focused, and purposeful than actual speech. Anne Lamott says that dialogue has a greater sense of action and is more interesting, concise, true, and dramatic than real speech. Yet our aim is to make it as natural as possible.

If you are considering incorporating dialogue into your book, I invite you to begin listening to people talking with an ear for how to capture natural spoken language in written form. You may even record and transcribe spoken conversations and learn about how to write natural dialogue.

I also encourage you to study dialogue in the books you love. Put your proverbial writer's glasses on and read with an eye for technique and style, what you find effective and enjoyable as a reader, what flows, and where you stumble.

Be sure to read your dialogue aloud to see how it sounds. This is imperative. If you find that you change words naturally as you read aloud, consider changing them in the text, too.

You want your dialogue to reflect your characters as accurately as possible. You can show so much about people by showing us the way they talk—the words they use, their grammar, their cadence, their emotions, their history, and their personality. Dialogue is a great way to *show* emotions and the inner landscape. From Lamott again: "Dialogue is *the* way to nail character."

> **Making dialogue sound natural**
> - Use contractions.
> - Use sentence fragments the way people do in speech (true to how your "character" would speak).
> - Connect two sentences using a comma instead of a period to reflect and capture the rhythm of real speech.
> - Don't pack information into dialogue for information's sake; characters should always have a reason for saying what they're saying.
> - Stick to shorter words people use in speech (avoid polysyllabic words, unless they reveal something about your character).
> - Don't make all your characters sound like you.

Resist the Urge to Explain

Newer writers of dialogue can get caught up by over-explaining, actually weakening their scenes. When creating a scene, don't *tell* your reader what you have just *shown* them in the dialogue. We have to trust our reader to get what we are conveying in the dialogue through the dialogue itself. For example:

"I won't stand here and listen to another minute of this garbage," Jonathan said *with exasperation*.

We can gather from his words that Jonathan is exasperated. Let the dialogue reveal it.

Another way we can over-explain in dialogue is through the use of *-ly* adverbs.

"I won't stand here and listen to another minute of this garbage," Jonathan said *angrily*.

The exception to this general guideline to avoid *-ly* adverbs is to clarify how something was said if the words themselves don't make it clear.

"I can't do this anymore," he said quietly; this is different from "I can't do this anymore," he screamed.

In general, you can write your scenes during drafting and go back during your self-editing process to review dialogue, checking to see if you've over-explained or used -ly adverbs to your scene's detriment.

Speaker Attributes: He Said, She Said

Some writers have the inclination to pepper creative and unique verbs throughout their dialogue—*Jane snapped, Carisa cooed, Ryan grunted, Daisy singsonged.*

The function of speaker attribution is primarily to indicate to your reader who is speaking. It is not usually the best place to pack in additional information about the scene or the character. It's better to write strong, revealing, and clear dialogue.

I encourage you to use the word *said* as your default verb in speaker attribution. In other words, use *said* most of the time. It may seem boring or less creative, but it serves your book and your reader.

How? Readers read the word *said* almost like a punctuation mark. It does its job without calling attention to itself. It is unobtrusive and allows your reader to focus on what is being expressed in the dialogue. Other verbs and the -ly adverbs call your reader away from the dialogue and call attention to your technique as a writer, which interrupts the flow and can weaken even strong dialogue writing. You can use them, for sure, but just use them sparingly and when doing so is essential to the dialogue you are creating.

It's important to ensure that you are using adequate speaker attribution so that your reader is crystal clear who is speaking at every moment in your dialogue. I find that lack of clarity in some client writing, and it causes a lot of confusion for the reader. Remember, whatever work you don't do for your reader, they need to do themselves. We want them doing the rich work of fluidly tracking and imagining our scenes within their minds, not laboring to understand who said what.

Beats

Beats are bits of action that you intersperse through a scene, such as a character's body language or behaviors. Beats usually involve physical gestures or a reference to a sensory element in the scene. They can reveal an emotion, an action, a realization, or a shift in tone or emotional state. These anchor our dialogue into a physical time and place (setting), help us build our characters, bring our scenes alive in a reader's mind, and can be used to shift the narrative forward.

SPEAKER ATTRIBUTION GUIDELINES

- The best arrangement is noun-verb: *Sarah said* instead of *said Sarah*.
- Put the *Sarah said* at the first natural pause after her dialogue begins: "I have to get this project done before Friday," Sarah said. Or "I was wondering," Sarah said, "do you have time to grab some tea together?"
- Keep the name of the speaker consistent at least through a scene. Don't call someone *Sarah* and then change it to *Ms. Grove* mid-scene.
- If it is clear who is speaking, you can omit speaker attributions.
- You can replace some "saids" with beats to give variety and avoid too much "he said, she said." (See the description of beats.) This can be especially helpful if you have a roomful of speakers in your scene.
- Use an em dash "—" to show that a speaker has been interrupted. Example:
  "I was just going t—"
  "I don't care what you were going to do. You need to empty the trash first," Betty said.
- When you introduce a new speaker's words, begin a new paragraph.

A beat can also be a short snippet of internal monologue, usually indicated by italics, not quotation marks. But avoid long sections of italic internal monologue, as they are difficult for your reader to read. It is better to use beats sparingly and to offer more hints for your reader—just enough so they can fill in the rest with their imagination. "Resisting the urge to explain" also applies here.

Here is an example from a fictional book by Sarah J Maas:[2]

> "I don't like it," Cassian growled.
>
> "You don't have to like it," Feyre said, head lifting, full of that High Lady's authority. "You just have to watch from the sidelines and not look like you want to rip his head off."
>
> Nesta cut in, "Tell Morrigan I'll meet with her for dancing lessons whenever she's available."
>
> Feyre and Cassian, still bristling at each other, silently turned toward her.
>
> Nesta approached the desk, laying Ataraxia there. "Here," she said to Rhys, "You can take it back."
>
> Rhys said nothing, but Feyre's brows rose. "Why don't you keep it?"
>
> Cassian's curious stare seared her like a brand, but Nesta only said, "I have no interest in more death."

We learn a lot from the beats here. First, in a scene involving at least four characters, it helps us to sense the dynamics between them. We can see the emotional tension and power dynamics between Cassian and Feyre, for example. We glimpse something of Nesta's character in her actions and words, and the absence of beats describing her non-verbal expressions provides intrigue and reveals something of her tone and character in itself.

If you are new to dialogue and beats, try it out and play. You don't have to be brilliant at it on your first try. Just play around with the various techniques of dialogue and beat use to find your own style.

SECTION THREE

SELF-EDITING SUPERSTAR

CHAPTER 27

OVERVIEW OF SELF-EDITING

"To write is human, to edit is divine."
— STEPHEN KING

I'd like to say that the drafting process is the hardest part and that everything gets easier after you've completed that first draft. It can be true, but it is not entirely true for most writers. One might say that drafting is to editing what raising a toddler is to raising a teenager. They are both intense, but in different ways. And, ultimately, both take deeply engaged effort, focus, and a ton of patience, grit, and grace.

While most writers would love to pop out a "perfect" first draft, it's about as rare as a unicorn sighting. Writers just want to be done after they first write something, but that's not how this writing game works. When I set out to write my first book, I reached out to a two-time author who was a leader in the yoga and personal growth field, thankful he was willing to answer some of my questions about authorship. I'll never forget the shock I felt when he said he'd written fifty versions of his introduction. Fifty! While you won't need to write fifty versions of your book, it would be supportive now to normalize the process of editing and revising your work.

Way back, I talked about the first draft as the Sketchy First Draft (SFD) or the Empty the Bag Draft—for many of us, we are getting the raw materials out of our minds and onto the pages with the first draft. It's not necessarily organized or in optimal form yet (especially if we haven't used a working outline or Table of Contents). Editing and refinement are absolutely essential. This is where so much of the magic—and hard work—happens.

While you may be tempted to pass your SFD off to a professional editor to sort through, it's a bit of a bypass. We need to do some refinement work on our own writing before it is ready to pass off to an editor. Editors don't have a magic wand to wave over your draft to bring it instantly into coherence. (We all wish.) That hard work needs to come from you. So, let's look at the self-editing process and what you can do to take your manuscript as far as you can before you hand it off to an editor to help you take it to the next level. (I mention the professional editorial process here but explore it more fully in Chapter 35.)

When to Self-Edit

DURING DRAFTING

The drafting phase is not the ideal time to edit your work. For some of us, the urge to edit during the drafting phase is more an inner drive for perfection and a discomfort with the holy hot messiness of first drafting than it is a valuable use of our time. Remember that the drafting phase is largely a "summer" activity of discovery, generation, and manifestation, whereas editing is more of a "fall" phase where you reflect on and refine that which you have cultivated in summer. (See Chapter 2 for a review of the creative seasons.)

That said, you may have a few fall-like elements in your drafting process. You may review what you have written to get back into the flow of your writing. You may read what you've written to get a better sense of where to go next. You may need to deepen an element of something already written to prepare yourself to share what comes next. Your Inner Genius (Chapter 4) will know when such efforts serve you and your process. You may also notice when it's more of a resistance activity or a perfectionist impulse to want to go back and clean up as you draft.

Resistance and perfectionism aside, some of us will still want to edit during draft time—we want to change words and reorder elements. A bit of this (maybe 5–10 percent of total drafting time) is okay when it feels in the flow of your process, but I suggest tracking your editing impulses rather than fully indulge them.

For example, if you know your first account of a topic will need to be deepened, use the track changes and marginal comments features in your word-processing program or select a specific color for "Editing Notes to Self," and note these impulses. You might write, for example, "Deepen the inner landscape here," or "Connect more explicitly to the previous idea," or "Unclear; return later." And then *keep going*.

When you're done with your drafting phase, you will have notes from yourself about what to focus on specifically as you go back into your manuscript during revision.

AFTER THE FIRST DRAFT

Once your first draft is complete and you have given it some space to breathe (which we'll cover in greater detail in the next chapter), you're ready to return to your draft with an eye for revision and editing. This is the ideal time to dive into the processes we'll outline in this section. Here is an overview of the four-phase process of self-editing, explored one by one in this section, and overall best practices for self-editing.

Self-Editing Process Overview

MACRO TO MICRO

With self-editing and professional editing, the best practice is to go from the macro level of your work to the micro level. We want to focus on the bigger view first—the ideas, concepts, ordering, and presentation of information—before we focus on the smaller details like the words, spelling, and punctuation. Some people may feel more comfortable with the details (hey, it's definitely easier to run spell-check than to rework and refine your main concept!), but don't skip the macro-level editorial phases. We must go from the broad focus down to the details. With this spirit in mind, I offer you a four-phase self-editing process.

PHASE ONE: Review and Appreciate (The Whole)
In this phase, we read over our entire manuscript, getting a feel for the whole as it exists in this moment and beginning with a solid appreciation for all we've accomplished and all that is strong in our current manuscript.

PHASE TWO: Revision (Concept, Idea, and Order)
In phase two, we look at the macro levels of our concepts, order, organization, and clarity. This is akin to developmental editing. We call it revision because

it is our opportunity to re-vision, or to see our work with new eyes, so we can shape it into what it needs and wants to become. We are at the section, chapter, and chapter-parts levels here. Our goal is to make sure we are clear and articulate in our ideas and present them in a method and order that best serves our readers. This phase is *huge*! Skip this stage to your book's peril.

PHASE THREE: Refinement (Paragraphs and Sentences)
In phase three, we are in the refinement stage, focusing on the paragraph and sentence levels of our book. This is akin to the copyedit or line editing phases of our editorial process. This is when we look at our paragraphs and sentences to make sure we are efficient, clear, and stylistically strong.

PHASE FOUR: Final Polishing (Words and Symbols)
In phase four, we are in the final polishing stages, akin to proofreading. This is where we are making sure we are accurate in our spelling, grammar, and punctuation and that we format our document appropriately.

Chapter 28

Self-Editing Best Practices

Schedule Editing Sessions

As I've suggested for the planning and drafting phases of your project, it is imperative to schedule time in your life and calendar for the editing process. For phases one and two of self-editing, I suggest working in two- to four-hour sessions, but adapt this suggestion to your own preferences. I suggest shorter bursts of time in phases three and four because this work is more micro-focused. The key here (and always) is not to burn yourself out.

Have Realistic Editing Expectations

Remember back when we first talked about ethos, the author's credibility? You can have amazing ideas, but if you don't convey them clearly and without error or obstruction, this will have a negative impact on how you are seen as an author (and how people receive your message). In other words, a solid and thorough editing process is absolutely paramount to producing a quality book that will serve your readers and your ethos.

Be realistic about how fast you expect to move through the editing process. Some newer authors believe that once they've written the first draft, they're just weeks away from publication and can breeze through the editing process.

I hate to burst anyone's balloon here, but I find, more often than not, that the editing process typically takes months, if not a year or more, depending on many factors. It's a significant process. Don't be too daunted, though; this is where so much goodness happens, and how great books get made. You can do this!

Save All Versions

Create a new version of your book for every major draft. This means cutting and pasting into a new file or choosing to "save as" your work with a clear version number each time you make substantial changes to your book. You never know when you may want to return to a chapter or idea you previously cut, go back to weave in an old idea into a new section, or the like. By creating a new version of your document each time, you can go back and find a history of your original draft and all the changes you've made.

In his book *Originals*,[1] Adam Grant offers research that reveals how creatives don't always know when they have a "hit" on their hands. Psychologist Dean Simonton has found that creatives often backtrack to older creative ideas or previous forms of their creation that they once discarded as inadequate in order to rework them into their pieces with great success. For example, Pablo Picasso made seventy-nine drawings to prepare for producing *Guernica*, and many final images in this painting were based on earlier, not later, sketches. Ludwig van Beethoven threw out the conclusion of his Fifth Symphony's first movement only to return and reincorporate it later.

This isn't to convey that you should second-guess your editing choices; rather, it is to suggest you preserve your older versions in case you want to return to an earlier draft idea later on.

Print It Out

This is the author's choice, but I am a strong advocate of printing your full manuscript on paper to do your self-editing work. I like to get my drafts spiral-bound at an office supply store (it's practical, useful, and rewarding). In this day and age, many people will prefer to work electronically with track changes and marginal comments, but I don't prefer this method myself. One, digital editing can be hard on the eyes and the brain. (I speak as a full-time professional editor, so I am a little biased.) Two, when you read it on paper, you can read it as your reader likely will and interface with your work in a more robust way.

Now, you'll want to bring your editing choices back into your document electronically to change your manuscript. And I understand that this may feel time-consuming, having both on-paper and then on-computer processes to undertake. But I still find that it works best for me and many writers I work with. That said, if you want to work only on the computer and that is working for you, get it with your paperless process!

> **EDITING IN SCRIVENER**
>
> I want to mention Scrivener here again. As of this writing, Scrivener has both limitations and benefits when we hit the editing phase.
>
> In terms of limitations, Scrivener documents are hard to share with editors. And Scrivener lacks good track changes and marginal comments features like Word. Some authors bring their manuscript into Word for part or all of the editing phase to use these features and work with editors.
>
> The benefit of using Scrivener during the editing phase is that you likely have your manuscript easily broken down into chapters or other segments already, so you can drag and drop a chapter to change the order of your manuscript. That's easier than going into a 300-page Word document and looking for pages 56 to 59 and moving them to page 79, for example. You can do it—heck, I'm doing it in this manuscript because I like working in Word best, to be honest—but it is cumbersome.

Read Out Loud or Listen

During your editing phase, read your book aloud or listen to it read to you (by a live person or via an audio application). You can read your story aloud to yourself, your pet, a tree, or another adult. Reading aloud can help you catch errors, run-on sentences, phrasing and ideas that make little sense, and wordiness. During phases three and four of self-editing, an effective way to edit for sentence-level accuracy is to read your writing backward, sentence by sentence. Doing this sounds strange, but it removes the content from your consciousness so you can focus on the structure of your sentences.

You may also have someone else read your story and clean up your sentence-level issues, which we will explore more in the section on professional editing.

Find the Middle Path

With editing, we must find the middle path between exhausting ourselves in an impossible quest for perfection and being too casual and careless about our editing work. My best analogy is to see our book like a garden—we want to pull as many weeds as we can and prune our chosen plants to allow them to be healthy and vibrant. But we don't want to pluck out too much of the garden or over-prune, as the plants will wither and die, and we'll have a sad garden.

There is this morbid phrase in the writing world: "Be willing to kill your darlings." It means we must be willing to cut what doesn't serve the whole, even if we hold that part dear in our sweet writer-hearts.

When I wrote my first book, my editor suggested I cut whole chapters from the book. *Whole chapters!* They weren't bad chapters, but they weren't fully in scope with the intentions of my book and what my reader actually needed from me. So onto the chopping block they went. Editing is good for the ego.

Know When to Get Help

As I stated in the last chapter, I definitely recommend doing some self-editing before you involve professional editors. I suggest at least one round of editing through phases one and two (if not a full round or two through phases one to four) before hiring professionals or sharing your book with beta readers. This will give you the space and time to shape and refine your ideas before bringing in outside support and opinions. This is true whether you are self-publishing or traditionally publishing.

That said, I do not recommend that you do all your editing yourself. We are super close to our manuscript, and being so close, we absolutely have blind spots. We need editorial support to catch these blind spots so we can address them prior to publication. We also tend to read our manuscripts as we meant to write them, not as they are actually written, so we don't always catch errors. We'll talk more about the professional editorial support you may seek in Chapter 35, but for now, just know that the editorial phase is best approached with a combination of DIY and professional editorial support.

Done Is Better Than Perfect
(NO WORK OF ART EVER FEELS COMPLETE)

No matter the medium—whether a song, poem, painting, or book—all creatives could tinker with and refine their work forever. We are ever-evolving creatures, continuing to adapt our perspectives, refine our ideas, and change how we look at and feel about something. Yet a book is like a fossil or a Polaroid—it can only capture a moment in time. While our stories and perspectives will continue to breathe and live on after publication, our book will stay the same (unless we write subsequent editions). Tension with this truth is unavoidable.

Creatives can get stuck in perpetual tinkering. Don't let this be you.

You don't have to get your book "perfect" for it to be ready to greet the world. At some point, we want to find that magical place of "good enough" (it's okay if your inner perfectionist cringes at this statement). I say wait for that "ejection impulse" moment in your writing process, where you are almost to the finish line and feel a fierce compulsion to just GET IT DONE. At some point, done is really better than perfect. When that phase of your process comes, trust it and take it as a sign that you're close to being ready to release this creation into the world. No one can stay pregnant forever (thank goodness). And it doesn't serve you, your book, or your readers to hold on longer than you need.

Give yourself permission to accept that you know what you know in this moment, and in the future, you may have a different (or even fuller) understanding of what you are sharing in your book. It's okay. This is what book editions are for. And if you self-publish, creating an updated manuscript is a breeze if you need to add or change something later. Give yourself permission to accept that there will be things you wish were different about your book after you publish it. Give yourself permission not to be perfect. Give yourself permission to be done. Give yourself permission to be good enough. In book writing. And in life.

Chapter 29

Review and Appreciate

So, you have completed the epic feat of writing your first draft. It was no small task, as you well know. Most would-be authors never make it to this point. The first step is to fully celebrate this major milestone. I am applauding you right now and honoring your determination and dedication to your book project. Take a moment to tap back into your original desire for this book and celebrate all it's taken to get to this point. Know that if you can get this far, you can absolutely meet success in your editing endeavors. But the work is not over yet.

Take Space

When you are done with your first draft, Elsa that thing and *let it go* (you parents of a certain generation get the reference). Close up your computer and let your manuscript be without looking at it for a couple of days, a week, or longer before you return to edit. Stephen King reports that he often waits six weeks before returning to a draft for editing.

Giving yourself some space from your draft will offer you a fresh perspective when you return to it, especially if you give yourself enough space so you can see it again and discover how you'd like to change it. It's almost as if we need space to forget what we wrote so that when we come back, we are looking at it with new eyes. Distance is key for our sanity and our editing.

Read Through It Completely for Content

Once you are ready to come back to your draft, I recommend printing it out (or pulling up your digital doc; you do you) and reading the whole thing from start to finish. Get the gestalt of the work you've been deeply engaged in for all these months. The purpose is to begin at this macro level to see the entire form as it exists today. I recommend that you don't take the proverbial or literal pen to your work just yet; rather, give yourself space to take it all in as a reader.

I'll never forget the first time I read a full draft of my book *Birth Your Story*. I sat in a coffee shop and cried. I was seeing my hard work with new eyes, and I was moved by it. I was proud. It was better than I imagined. I gave myself the gift of this bird's eye review of all my diligent effort. (Also, I can't read or hear birth stories without crying, so that was a big reason for all the tears through the draft.) I hope your manuscript makes you cry tears of joy and satisfaction.

Appreciate What You Love

Before you turn your attention to what needs to be changed, added, eliminated, and revised, take a moment to appreciate what is strong about your draft. Don't skip this phase; it matters. Truly. We need to acknowledge what is strong as well as what we want to improve. By appreciating what is good, we honor ourselves and our work, and we notice what works so we can create more of it in revision.

After you are done reading through your whole manuscript, journal for a page or two about your first high-level observations, ideas, and celebrations before you dive into editing. This makes for a strong foundation for this next phase of your work.

What are your first thoughts and impressions? Your high-level observations?

_____

_____

_____

_____

What did you discover in your drafting and in this initial review?

What major themes have emerged, anticipated or unanticipated?

What are you most proud of?

What moved you?

What did you capture that feels true and powerful?

What feels like the best approach you'd like to take from this point forward as you go into editing?

CHAPTER 30

Revision

Once you have gotten a gestalt picture of your current manuscript and appreciated and reflected on the macro-level view of your book, it's time to dive into phase two: Revision. This phase is akin to professional developmental editing. In revision, you will focus a layer deeper to address:

- Your writing structure: How are the sequencing and order of your ideas and major parts of your manuscript?
- The content and clarity of your writing: Are the ideas clear, and does the reader's journey flow?
- The focus of your work: Does it align with your original intent (regarding audience, purpose, project, and key messages)?
- Your level of detail: Where do you need to deepen? What can you cut?
- Your style: How are the voice and tone?

Be prepared to make *big* changes at this level. During this phase of your creative process, focus less on the nitty-gritty, sentence-level issues of grammar, spelling, and punctuation and more on the content and structure of your work.

Reverse Outlining

If you don't have an up-to-date and accurate Table of Contents for your manuscript, I suggest beginning here by updating your table or creating one now. We can call this reverse outlining because you will go into what you've written and create an outline of this existing material. This will give you important information about the overall structure and organization of your manuscript.

Spend some time here considering your current structure. Will this ordering of information and ideas best serve your audience? Are you missing anything important? At this view, what do you discover that is inessential?

Charting

Here's the deal: Charting is the freaking bomb. Geeky bomb, but bomb. Charting will help you get crystal clear about what you say in your book, how you say it, and the order in which you say it. Charting will give you a whole new understanding of your writing and what needs revision. I learned this skill in my master's program, and it is THE secret tool in my developmental editing toolbelt as a professional. It is the magic behind how I am able to suggest significant improvements to my author-clients, and it looks like magic. But, it's charting.

Charting is the act of going into your existing writing and tracking your "moves" and your "content" paragraph by paragraph. In one margin, you write what you are "doing," and in the other, what you are "saying." You can also make editorial notes to yourself. In my online program on editing, I offer an explanation of this process in greater detail. This tutorial will help you understand the value of this method: don't miss it.

This process shows you how to go through a single page and chart your text. You can do this for a whole chapter that you know needs reworking, or the whole darn book.

Charting also has a more easy-going cousin, called chunking. Chunking is when you draw a line between each major movement within a chapter. So let's say you have an intro story that takes five paragraphs, then in paragraph six, you shift to introducing the main idea of the chapter. You'd put a line between paragraphs five and six. Next to paragraph one, you might write, "intro story about {insert short description}," and next to chapter six, you might write, "main idea {short identifying phrase}." Do this for a whole chapter, and you'll be able to see the main moves and topics you cover in this chapter.

SAYING

HOW TO CHART YOUR DRAFT TO DEVISE

DOING

How is writing different from telling my story aloud?

unique effects & benefits of (W)
remember
process
ownership
heal
culture

① The telling of birth stories, to ourselves or others, through any medium— be it oral storytelling, art making, online media, computer typing, pen-to-paper writing—is powerful. However, **writing down your birth story has unique effects and benefits** that no other medium offers. At its simplest, writing down your birth story helps you (remember and record) what it was like to give birth (or witness your partner give birth)— capturing and preserving these life altering moments. Writing down the details of your birth can help you (process) what happened, (gaining ownership) and understanding of your experience. If necessary, it can also help you (heal and release) any traumatic aspects of the experience. Writing our stories can also be a courageous, even revolutionary, act that shakes the foundation on which our (culture of birth) and treatment of women currently sits.

main idea
overview

claiming

② Writing is an act of (**claiming**, **or reclaiming,** our stories as our own. Birth can be so intense and for some it can feel like something that happens *to us*. So much of our birth experience is beyond our control—being able to control the telling of our experience is paramount. When you write your story down, you are in complete control of how you tell the story. You claim it as your own, no matter how your birth unfolded. In this way, writing can be a very empowering and healing act.

subpoint support

engage thoughts & feelings

*claim

③ Telling our stories on paper is a way to (engage with the thoughts and feelings) we have about our birth experiences in a meaningful and valuable way. Writing our stories allows us a window into our thoughts—both conscious and unconscious—and can tap us into our true feelings in a way that other forms of expression cannot. Exploring what we think and how we feel about our births is important because these weave together to from the stories of our lives. Our very identity is the accumulation of stories we tell ourselves about who we are. Writing gives us a space to tell our stories with intentionality, reflection and purpose—enabling us to have agency over who we are. Claim your stories, claim your life, claim who you really are.

subpoint support

relationship to past

④ We can actually (change our relationship) to our past and to ourselves, dramatically by writing. "Through writing, we revisit our past and review and rewrite it. What we thought happened, what we believe happened to us, shifts and changes as we discover deeper and more complex truths. It isn't that we use our writing to deny what we've experienced, but we use it to shift our perspective." Writing has the power to help us discover and choose what meaning and power our stories hold.

subpoint support quote?

⑤ Writing down your story offers you (a space of your own) that doesn't need to be shared, with anyone. Writing does not require a social context and is unaffected by listeners. You don't have to edit or filter depending on an audience, which we all do to some degree when we speak with another person. When we write our stories, no one is there to comment, criticize or curtail the way we tell our stories. This makes writing a safe and free place for us to be as we truly are. Our defenses can come down. We can say what we truly want to say. We can be as we are. Our stories can be ours.

REVISION EDITS: #1 - rework subpoints

#2 · consider ⊕ evidence

current

unique benefits of writing
/ remember
/ process
/ ownership
/ heal
/ culture
/ claiming
/ engaging thoughts & feelings
/ past ownership
/ space of own

→

suggested revision

unique benefits of writing story
remember
process
claiming ownership
healing
culture
thoughts & feeling
space own
relationship to past & self

229

Revision Considerations

CONSIDER RELEVANCE (ELIMINATING ALL THAT DOESN'T SERVE)

Go back and connect with your anchors:
- Why are you writing this book?
- Who is it for?
- What is the main message of your book?
- What is your project (the work you are setting out to do)?
- What is in scope for your project and what is not?
- What's your overall purpose for writing (what you want your reader to know, believe, feel, or do because of reading your book)?

With this in mind, work through your draft with an eye for relevance. With each section, chapter, or idea, ask yourself: Does this serve my overall concept with this book? Is it relevant?

For example, one of my books is about writing your birth story. In an early draft, I devoted a whole chapter to my personal ideas about why birth is so powerful and matters so much. This chapter felt so important to me. But I cut it. Why? Because it was not about *writing* your birth story. It didn't help my readers understand the value of *writing* their birth stories and how to do it. As such, it didn't serve *this* book. It was good but inessential to my purpose and project.

You can't be afraid to cut large passages, even whole chapters, from your book if they're not essential. While it can be painful and tough on the ego to cut big parts from your book, if the book is stronger for it, you must make this sacrifice.

It is common and normal for most authors to cut about 10 percent or more of their word count from their first manuscript. Sometimes, we find we need to work something out for ourselves in our first draft process, and it doesn't need to go in our book after all. Sometimes, we explain something in two chapters when we only need to make it a subsection of a single chapter so we can carry on with other key messages. Sometimes, we have something that we needed to write and express, but we don't need to share it with the world.

This is also where you can consider proportion (see Chapter 25). Did you invest too much of your book's "airtime" on something that needed less time?

Here's a bit of good news: Often, we can repurpose the passages we cut.

They can become a blog article for our related business or a resource for the launch and promotion of our book. They can become bonus content. They can be material for our next book. They can become articles we pitch to the media during our book marketing campaign. And even if we can't repurpose it, we can almost always find the reason why we needed to write it.

CONSIDER REDUNDANCY[1]

Charting can help in this area, too. Do you say one thing many times? Do you give eight examples when you only need two? Do you repeat the same idea, giving it a different name each time? Go through your manuscript, section by section, and find where you say the same thing more than once. Now, there are no hard rules for this. Sometimes, we need to repeat a point more than once for our readers to understand our concept. But we need to repeat ourselves *with a difference*. In other words, our repetition needs to add something new that we didn't share before. It needs to build on itself. Otherwise, we have the effect of insulting our readers by assuming they need us to tell them the same thing many times.

CONSIDER ORDER

Even if you had a clear working outline or Table of Contents before you wrote, you'll want to return to the order of your ideas and your structure now. Bring in your reader here and decide if this is *the* most effective ordering of ideas, sections, and chapters for them to receive in your book.

Often, restructuring and reordering can make a *significant* difference in strengthening your book. You can improve flow, reading comprehension, and the impact of your message.

Don't be afraid to play with your structure and order. This is not an easy feat to remix your draft. I know firsthand from my own book-writing experience and the experiences of many of my authors (which is why we offer editorial coaching to support authors during the revision stages). While developmental revisions can stretch us, they are often necessary and super valuable. The order and sequencing of your content matter.

CONSIDER YOUR AUDIENCE

This is where you give attention to your audience's anticipated reception of your manuscript. While I suggest that a writer consider their readership at the outset of their book-planning process, I also urge writers to write for themselves first (especially with memoir) and be chiefly concerned about getting down their most potent and true version of their stories and messages as possible. This step is crucial.

As we turn our attention to editing, we must consider our audience and what from our first draft we actually want to share with them. Brené Brown encourages us to ask ourselves who has earned the right to hear our stories, which she considers a privilege. She reminds us that not all our stories are meant for everyone. Writing a book and publishing it answers this question with "I am making the conscious, self-empowered choice to share my stories with the world." And that is no small thing. I encourage you to be your own gatekeeper and choose the stories you're ready to share. Just because you wrote something doesn't mean you have to publish it.

I encourage you to be exceedingly brave. This is your chance to take a risk and to bare your soul, your heart, and your mind. What we are most scared to share often becomes the most powerful, impactful, and life-altering elements of our books for our readers. Be bold. Be as fearless as you can. But also, be discerning. You hold the power to decide what you keep in your manuscript and what you leave out.

For memoir writers, especially, the question often comes up, "What about the impact of my book on those I speak about in my book?" I explore this in Chapter 6 and Appendix A, but on a high level, I'll share that you must first accept that someone may not like how you have represented them or their actions in your book. I like what one famous author said: "If they didn't want their actions known, they shouldn't have done them in the first place." As I suggested in Chapter 6, it can be helpful to practice the line: "Yes, I understand that is not your memory of what happened, but it is my memory of what happened, and it's okay we don't agree on this."

I also invite you to reflect on your intent. If you have malicious or vengeful intentions in sharing a detail, or you just needed to vent or express something that might cause unnecessary insult or injury when certain people see it in print, you might take these elements out of your book.

You don't have to be responsible for the responses of others to your book, but I encourage you to care about the potential impact and to consider this carefully when revising your book. You can know the truth, you can tell the truth, and you also get to decide what stays in the book and what does not.

Aside from brave writing, considering your audience here is about making sure you are meeting and serving your audience well in every part of your book. I suggest going back to Chapter 6 and recalling what you expressed about your audience. Having beta readers (more in Chapter 31) who are in your intended primary audience is also quite useful, as we can only anticipate so much.

CONSIDER CLARITY

Go through your book, section by section, chapter by chapter, even paragraph by paragraph, with an eye for clarity. Does what you say make sense? Is it expressed as clearly as possible? In what ways can you make what you say even clearer? Do you adequately define and explain new words or concepts upon introducing them? Are there any parts where your reader may get confused? Or object to your ideas? These may be places to clarify or add explanations that will meet your reader exactly where they are.
When evaluating your manuscript for clarity, it can be tremendously helpful to get the input of beta readers or professional editors. You know your content better than anyone, and you likely understand what you've written. But we need to make sure your readers will find your writing clear.

CONSIDER CONNECTIONS

This phase offers an opportunity to consider where you can make connections between your ideas, connections you perhaps didn't see before or haven't fully developed. Often, it is through reading our writing that we come to see the connections between our ideas. So, this is a great time to consider the connections between your ideas and stories and how to articulate these explicitly in your book.

CONSIDER DEEPENING

This is also the perfect time to locate the places in your manuscript where you want to deepen what you wrote. Often, our first draft is our first pass at trying to explain or describe something. It's our first venture into the layers of a story (described in Chapter 25), and we are now ready to get to deeper layers of our truth and the meaning we are making about our experiences. This is a time to deepen, add detail, fill in gaps, and write about what you think is missing. You may also add evidence for your points or to round out a story.

CONSIDER VOICE AND TONE

Last, you'll want to consider your voice and tone throughout your manuscript. Voice is the unique quality and style of your writing and how you say things in the way only you can. You'll want to check the consistency of your voice throughout your work. There is no hard and fast quantitative way to do this; it's more qualitative. As for tone, this is your attitude toward your topic and your reader throughout the book. You'll also want to check for consistency here.

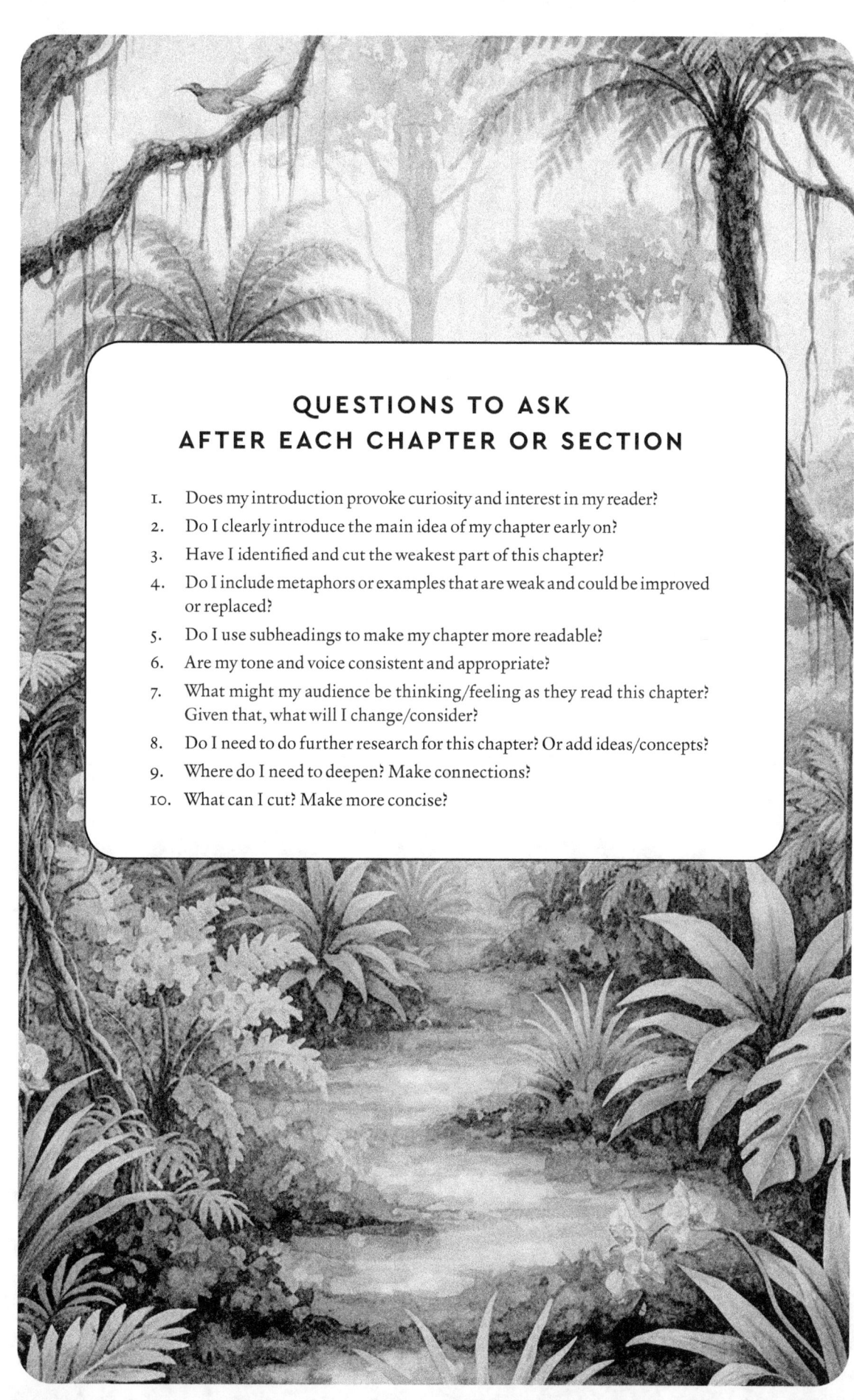

QUESTIONS TO ASK
AFTER EACH CHAPTER OR SECTION

1. Does my introduction provoke curiosity and interest in my reader?
2. Do I clearly introduce the main idea of my chapter early on?
3. Have I identified and cut the weakest part of this chapter?
4. Do I include metaphors or examples that are weak and could be improved or replaced?
5. Do I use subheadings to make my chapter more readable?
6. Are my tone and voice consistent and appropriate?
7. What might my audience be thinking/feeling as they read this chapter? Given that, what will I change/consider?
8. Do I need to do further research for this chapter? Or add ideas/concepts?
9. Where do I need to deepen? Make connections?
10. What can I cut? Make more concise?

CHAPTER 31

Beta Readers

This chapter is a bit of an interlude to your four-part process of self-editing. But I include it here because this is the stage at which you may want to consider seeking beta readers for your book.

Having a round of beta readers and gathering their feedback is an incredibly useful process during the editorial phase of your book project. This chapter goes into detail about how to find beta readers and how to set everyone up for success so you can get what you need from this process.

What is a Beta Reader?

Beta readers are people whom you know or connect with for the purpose of reading and offering feedback about your book prior to publication. They are not professional editors, per se, but will review your book to offer you feedback on the content. Beta readers are often unpaid.

When to seek Beta Readers

I recommend considering beta readers after you've completed your first draft, but before you get to the line editing stage. This is because your beta reader process may compel you to change some of your content, and you'll want to do that before you get into the refinement stage of your writing process.

How to Select Beta Readers

You want to be careful and considerate when choosing beta readers for your book. You may want to start by returning to your work in Chapter 6, where we uncovered your book's ideal readership. Consider finding beta readers who are in your ideal readership category.

I recommend you look for people who will offer different points of view on your book and those poised to provide additional insight or help you find blind spots in your content or perspective.

Make sure your readers are willing to give you *honest* and *constructive* feedback. Pure cheerleading may make you feel good, but it's not nearly as valuable as authentic, meaningful suggestions about how to make your manuscript stronger.

I suggest asking at least two to five people to review your book as beta readers. Having a single beta reader is not likely to provide enough audience diversity for a well-rounded, robust readership reaction to your book. More than five is too many cooks in the kitchen.

FRIENDS AND FAMILY

Only you can make the call here. Sometimes, having a dear loved one read our manuscript feels like a necessity before we launch it to the public. For others, we are wise to complete our process before we share our work with loved ones. Consider what is truly in service to you and your project when it comes to inviting friends and family to be your beta readers.

OTHER WRITERS

If you have other writers in your life, they may also make good beta readers because they can give you an eye for the structure, tone, and other writerly aspects of your manuscript beyond content. I offer the same advice here as I did regarding loved ones: consider if sharing your manuscript with other writers is truly in service to you and your project.

IDEAL AUDIENCE AND BLIND SPOT SEEKERS

You'll want to ask people to be beta readers if you think they will help provide constructive feedback and check for perspective blind spots. After all, you are only one person, and you may miss a consideration or a point that a beta reader may highlight for you. Beta readers can also share their reactions to parts of your manuscript so you can get real feedback about the impact your work has on diverse readers.

When I wrote my book *Birth Your Story*, I asked a few of my colleagues to read it. I chose doulas, midwives, mothers of multiple children, mothers who'd lost children, a social worker, and a father to read my book. I wanted to get perspectives that I myself did not have (because I was not in any of these roles with the exception of being a doula). I specifically wanted to get their reactions to how certain ideas landed and to learn if there were points or perspectives I had failed to previously consider. I gained valuable insight from this beta reader process, not only about the content but also about readers' emotional reactions to my content, which was super helpful and did influence the way I shaped my draft in the next round of edits. This insight was essential to my process.

Questions to Ask Beta Readers

I strongly recommend providing parameters to your beta readers about what you do and do not want them to offer feedback on and how. Here are some prompts to provide your beta readers.

- What is missing? Where are the holes in my manuscript, idea-wise? Where are the lapses in logic and narrative? Where do you get lost or confused or lose interest? What objections, thoughts, or emotional responses do you have as you read?
- Can you articulate what my big idea is?
- Where does my writing move, inspire, surprise, or delight you? Does it change how you think, feel, or take action around my subject area, and in what way?
- What is your biggest takeaway from the book?

- What would you tell a friend (who is my ideal reader) about the book?
- If you could make one to three suggestions for overall improvement, what would they be?

Tips for Working with Your Beta Readers

Ask them upfront if they would like a paper copy or a digital copy of your manuscript.

Give them a deadline for completing the manuscript review. Personally, I think four to six weeks is fair for a 250- to 300-page book. If it is shorter, maybe two to four weeks. You want to honor their busy lives and realize that not everyone will be able to devote loads of time to your manuscript.

Schedule a follow-up call. You might consider asking for email feedback to the questions listed earlier *and* book time to talk through it. You can get so much insight on a call. I recommend getting the email feedback first and then following up to talk about one or two specific topics.

Receiving Feedback
"THANK YOU" AND "THANKS, BUT NO THANKS"

Remember, *you* are the author of your book. You are the gatekeeper. You have full authority to consider every suggested change made by anyone and determine whether you will allow it to influence how you perceive your book and how you revise it. You owe no one the duty of editing your book to serve their suggestion if it doesn't feel completely resonant with you.

It's like a romantic relationship, to some degree. Others can see from the outside and sometimes provide the exact, wise insight we need (things we might not be able to see) to help us make decisions about our relationship. It's the same with your book. Ultimately, no one really knows your vision and the interior of your deep relationship with this book and its consciousness. You do. Have a strong gatekeeper and make sure she checks the IDs of every edit suggestion that comes through the gates. Have permeable boundaries, not walls, and not an unchecked gate where anyone can crash your party and make the rules in your castle. Like my mixed metaphors?

Chapter 32

Refinement

Once you have worked through your developmental editing and revision process (major congrats for completing that process), it's time to turn to refinement. With its different set of skills, this stage is akin to line editing or copyediting, and it often begins with the second draft or later in your process. At this phase, you will focus on reworking paragraphs and sentences and adding or eliminating smaller sections. Here, little tweaks can make big improvements to the quality of your manuscript. This is the activity most people associate with "editing."

Paragraph Level

As I mentioned in Chapter 18, the paragraph is to the book what the cell is to the body; these are independent units of the whole. As such, you want to stick to one major idea per paragraph. When working at the paragraph level, the activity of charting (Chapter 30) will help you identify what you need to address. I suggest taking your paragraph editing focus chapter by chapter or section by section. You'll want to make sure your paragraphs introduce the topic and then support it, staying focused, clear, and concise. Make sure everything serves a purpose, and you eliminate unnecessary sentences.

At the paragraph level, you'll also want to check for transitions between paragraphs, sections, and chapters. You'll want to make sure you introduce and frame all your quotes (see Chapter 23). Be sure you have adequate and effective introductions and conclusions for each section and chapter.

WORD EFFICIENCY

Rigorous, quality writing is concise. Go sentence by sentence in each section and eliminate all unnecessary words. This doesn't mean that every sentence must be short—ideally, you'll vary your sentence length and complexity—but that every word serves a function. Don't say in ten words what you can say well in five. Don't use a sesquipedalian word when you can say it straight.

Cut out phrases and words that add nothing or are repetitive. Anything that is not pulling its weight gets cut. Look for strong verbs and specific, concrete words that say exactly what you mean. Watch for the overuse of adjectives and adverbs.

Here are examples of wordy phrases and their corrections:
- He is a man who is > He is.
- Her story is an odd one > Her story is odd.
- The reason why is that > Because.
- There is no doubt but that > No doubt.
- In spite of the fact that > Though/although.
- She nodded her head in agreement. > She nodded.
- He clapped his hands. > He clapped.
- She shrugged her shoulders > She shrugged.
- He heard the sound of the dog barking > He heard the dog barking.

WORD FREQUENCY

Everyone has words they prefer and use often, both in speech and in writing. Let's call these *word besties*. While it is normal to have word besties—they can contribute to our overall voice and style—we want to be sure we are not overusing them.

There are a few ways to discover your word besties. Scrivener allows you to check word frequency, and you can also load your manuscript into programs like TextFixer, WriteWords, and ProWritingAid, to discover your most used words.

Once you discover your word besties, you can determine whether it's best to remove or replace some of them.

Refinement

FACTS AND CITATIONS

In this stage of your editing process, you'll want to ensure all the facts, quotes, and other information you share are correct and properly cited. (I talk in detail about citations in Appendix C.) You'll also want to check your cross-references at this point.

Style at the Sentence Level

1. **Check for tense and POV consistency.** You'll want to make sure each scene and section keeps the same tense (e.g., past tense, present tense) and point of view (first, second, or third person).

2. **Change passive voice to active voice.** Examples:
   - The statue is visited by hundreds of tourists every year. > Hundreds of tourists visit the statue every year.
   - My books were stolen by someone yesterday. > Yesterday, someone stole my books.
   - The house had been broken into by a burglar while the owners were on vacation. > A burglar broke into the house while the owners were on vacation.

3. **Put statements in positive form.** A reader wishes to be told what is, not what is not. Look for places where you put something in the negative and change it to the positive. An exception to this rule, however, is using negative and positive in opposition to make a strong statement.

4. **Use definite, specific, and concrete language.** For all language, and especially your verbs and adjectives, be direct, specific, and concrete, and use the best word for the job. This may require the use of an online thesaurus or time spent clarifying your point so you can say what you mean clearly. Use the best verbs—replace *to be* verbs (am, is, are) where possible. You might go through and highlight "to be" verbs and look for more precise verbs. And with another color, you might highlight your adjectives and be sure they are appropriate and specific.

5. **Avoid a succession of loose sentences.** This is in the realm of run-ons. You risk watering down your writing. Loose sentences have two clauses, the second of which is introduced by a conjunction.

   Coordinating conjunctions: and, but, or, nor, for, so, and yet

   Subordinating conjunctions: after, although, as, because, before, how, if, once, since, than, that, though, till, until, when, where, whether, and while

   Aim for sentence variation. Mix up simple sentences with those that are more complex (such as sentences joined by a semicolon or sentences that contain a series of elements, like a list).

6. **Parallel construction.** Express coordinate ideas in a similar form. Example:
   - To complain is easy, but finding solutions is difficult. > To complain is easy; to find solutions is difficult.

   Here's a trick with successive clauses: Identify the root to which all clauses apply and check each one alone. Examples:
   - The accountant in this department has the responsibility for the formation of budget procedures, maintenance of related records, rendering financial information, and submitting special reports. > The accountant in this department forms budget procedures, maintains related records, renders financial information, and submits special reports.
   - The success of a television program depends on how well the program has been advertised, the actors taking part, and is it a comedy or a serious drama. > A television program's success depends on how well it's been advertised, the fame and skill of the actors, and whether it's a comedy or serious drama.

7. **Keep related words together (e.g., subject and verb).** In minor cases, this creates weak sentences; at its extreme, this creates unintended meaning. Consider the following examples of misplaced modifiers, where the details are separated from that which they are modifying.

    - I brought my dog to the veterinarian with fleas. > I brought my flea-ridden dog to the veterinarian.
    - He kept a black book of all the girls he had dated in his desk. > In his desk, he kept a black book of all the girls he had dated.
    - He kept all his medicine in the medicine cabinet that had been prescribed for him. > He kept all his prescribed medications in the medicine cabinet.
    - The man was stopped for speeding in the blue sweater. > The man in the blue sweater was stopped for speeding.

8. **Place emphatic words at the end of a sentence.** Put the element of the sentence you want to emphasize at the end of the sentence for greater effect.

ONLINE TOOLS TO SUPPORT YOUR EDITING[1]

Wow, there are a lot of cool programs available online these days that can help you improve your sentence-level issues. Here are a few programs to check out:

- **Grammarly**: Chrome extension you can find at app.grammarly.com; the Premium version has the ability to run a plagiarism check (at the time of this writing)
- **Hemingway App**: found at hemingwayapp.com
- **ProWritingAid**: found at prowritingaid.com
- **PerfectIt**: found at intelligentediting.com

Please note that these don't take the place of an actual human being reading your writing.

CHAPTER 33

Final Polishing

After you've completed the first three phases of the editing process, we come to the final polishing, which is akin to the proofing process in editorial parlance. At this phase, the focus is on the words and symbols (punctuation), as well as on formatting. We focus here on grammar, spelling, punctuation, fixing typos, and making sure everything is as accurate as possible, down to the periods.

Best practices for this stage are to work in short bursts (this phase can feel tedious to some of us), read out loud, read backward sentence by sentence, print and edit on paper, and hire fresh eyes to do your final proofing (because fresh eyes on your work will see more). I also recommend using the apps mentioned in the last chapter, though this is not a substitute for your own or another human's proofreading.

Spelling and Grammar

Spelling is a pretty simple one—we have spell-check and autocorrect (though imperfect) on nearly all word-processing applications. And yet, we still should read for spelling.

Most often, what gets missed are words that are spelled wrong, but they spell another word (so they don't get flagged). For example, you meant to write *said* but you typed *sad*, and the word is not flagged. This is why we still need humans. To read. To edit. In general.

Another common way that words are misspelled is when the writer uses the wrong form of the word. For example, *their* instead of *there*. Here are some of the most troubling words you'll want to be on the lookout for:

- a lot/alot
- affect/effect
- can/may
- further/farther
- good/well
- i.e. (means *in other words* or *that is*) / e.g. (means *for example*)
- into/in to
- it's/its
- lay/lie
- less/fewer
- that/who
- their/they're/there
- then/than
- who/whom
- your/you're

If you want to go deep with it, I suggest checking out *The Elements of Style*[1] by Strunk and White and the other resources listed in Notes at the end of this book. *The Elements of Style* has a whole chapter about commonly misused words and expressions. These include:

- aggravate/irritate
- illusion/allusion
- allude/elude
- alternate/alternative

Format

Here's the deal: if you're self-publishing, you'll need to have your manuscript professionally formatted (I highly recommend this), and if you're traditionally publishing, your publisher will format the interior of your book. But you'll still want to do a little formatting before you hand your manuscript over to beta readers, editors, agents, and publishers. This shows professionalism and enhances the readability of your document. Here are the basics:
- Save your manuscript as a Word document (.doc or .docx) or a PDF.
- Use double spacing between your lines of text.
- Use a single space following periods (like me, you may have been well trained to put two spaces between sentences, so I get it: world

rocked). To replace all double spaces with a single, do a find-and-replace search. Type two spaces in "find" and one space in "replace" and hit enter. Bam. And hallelujah.

- Use black, twelve-point, Times New Roman (or similar) as the font.
- Use regular one-inch margins.
- Don't hit tab to indent paragraphs.
- Don't indent the first paragraph of any chapter, or after a subhead, or following a bulleted or numbered list. (As an interior book designer, I prefer that an author doesn't indent *at all*. But if you are formatting it yourself, indent away.)
- Use page breaks between chapters.
- Number your pages.

You may also want to consider consulting with The Chicago Manual of Style (online or in print) for more formatting guidelines (including rules on how to cite works referenced). Do you feel like you're in college again?

Please see the Notes for this chapter for more resources on editing.

CHAPTER 34

Comma Police
FASCINATING GRAMMAR TIDBITS

I know, I know. You've waited this whole book for me to teach you about commas and semicolons. I get it. Let's nerd out together.

Commas

1. **Set off, or enclose, parenthetical nonrestrictive expressions.**
    A parenthetical phrase or clause is like a side comment, a part of a sentence that adds information but is not essential in making the sentence complete.

    How do you decide if a clause or phrase is essential to the sentence? One way is to take out the expression and see if the sentence is complete without it.

    Example:
    The play at Metropolitan State University, *where I am a student*, was exceptionally funny.

    One could remove the phrase "where I am a student," and the sentence would be complete without altering the essential meaning (because it is about the play). If you can add the words "by the way" to the phrase or clause inserted into the essential part of the sentence, chances are it is parenthetical.

    Strunk and White refer to parenthetical phrases as **nonrestrictive clauses**. "Clauses introduced by *which, when,* or *where* are nonrestrictive; they do not limit or define, they merely add something."

    By contrast, **restrictive clauses** are essential because they add a

crucial piece of information to the sentence.
Example:
People who live in glass houses shouldn't throw stones.

You would *not* write: "People, who live in glass houses, shouldn't throw stones" because the "who live in glass houses" defines the type of people who should not throw stones. You can test this sentence by taking out the clause:

"People shouldn't throw stones." Then determine whether the new sentence has the same meaning as the original.

People shouldn't throw stones ≠ People who live in glass houses shouldn't throw stones.

2. **Separate a series of three or more terms.**
   The **serial comma**, also known as the Oxford comma, is a comma between every term in a series of three or more. An exception to this rule is with business names (Little, Brown and Company)
   - Stop, drop, and roll.
   - Eat, drink, and be merry.

3. **Are used before a conjunction introducing an independent clause.**

   Before a *what* introducing a *what*? Let's define terms essential to this rule:

   A **conjunction** connects phrases or clauses. Conjunctions include:

and	but	since	though
as	if	so	unless
because	or	than	while

   An **independent clause** has a subject and verb and forms a complete thought. (Example: Adam goes to Fiji every year.)

Case 1: Use a comma to **connect two independent clauses** separated by a conjunction.
- Adam goes to Fiji every year, unless he is flat broke.
- Adam goes to Fiji every year, and he always brings his friend.
- Adam goes to Fiji every year, since he loves to travel to tropical climates.

Case 2: You also need a comma after a **dependent** introductory phrase. A *dependent clause* lacks either a verb or a subject and does not form a complete thought.
- *Even though he should have been working,* Adam booked his flight to Fiji.
- *While the boss was out to lunch,* Adam scheduled his annual trip to Fiji.
- *During his important work meeting,* Adam was daydreaming about Fiji.
- *If he is not careful,* Adam will lose his job.

Commas set off other elements of speech:
- Dates (Tuesday, November 11, 2025)
- Name or title in a direct address (Thank you, Professor Fleres, for finally teaching me how to use commas properly.)
- Abbreviations
    - etc. (add a comma before "etc.," which means "and other things" or "and so on")
    - i.e., (which means "that is" or "in other words"—used to clarify or specify)
    - e.g., (which means "for example")
- Professional degrees and titles (Marshall Greenburg, PhD, discusses the importance of not chewing gum and walking at the same time.)

Semicolons

1. **Join two independent clauses.**

As you recall from earlier, an independent clause has a subject and a verb and forms a complete thought. You can join two of them together with a semicolon:

- <u>Adam</u> <u>goes</u> to Fiji every year; <u>he</u> <u>is</u> flat broke.
- <u>Adam</u> <u>goes</u> to Fiji every year; <u>he</u> always <u>brings</u> his friend.
- <u>Adam</u> <u>goes</u> to Fiji every year; <u>he</u> <u>loves</u> to travel to tropical climates.

However, you can also use a period to separate two independent clauses. You would use the semicolon to express to your reader that these ideas are so closely linked that you just couldn't bear to keep them apart via such halting punctuation as the period. Really, either is considered correct.

An exception to this rule is when the clauses are short and similar in form.
- Sit down, be quiet.
- Here today, gone tomorrow.

2. **Separate a list of items that already includes commas.**
   - On his vacation, Adam will go to London, England; Sydney, Australia; and Suva, Fiji.

Colons

1. Use after an independent clause to introduce a list of particulars, an amplification, or an illustrative quotation.

List of particulars—a colon can mark the beginning of a list after an independent clause.
- Smokey Bear asks you to do three things: stop, drop, and roll.

However, if the leading clause is not independent, you *do not* use the colon—
- Smokey Bear asks you to stop, drop, and roll.

An amplification—when the second independent clause interprets or amplifies the first independent clause in a sentence.
- Mary asked Jason for a divorce: she does not want to be married to a drunk.

An illustrative quotation—a colon can introduce a quotation that supports or contributes to the preceding independent clause.
- Aung San Suu Kyi believes that fear, not power, lies at the root of all corruption: "It is not power that corrupts but fear. Fear of losing power corrupts those who wield it and fear of the scourge of power corrupts those who are subject to it."

Dashes

A dash is a mark of separation stronger than a comma, less formal than a colon, and more relaxed than parentheses. The punctuation you choose tells your audience how to interpret the relatedness of your ideas.

comma   dash   parentheses
More relaxed and less separation ⟷ More formal and more separation

Two types of dashes exist: "em" dashes and "en" dashes.

"Em" dashes (—) are the width of the letter *m*. They are used to set off phrases in sentences.
- o His first thought on getting out of bed—if he had any thought at all—was to get back in again.

You can make this dash by making two "en" dashes between the desired words without any separation between the letters. Microsoft Word will automatically generate an "em" dash.

"En" dashes (–) are the width of the letter *n*. They are used with numbers, ranges, and between dates.
- pages 159–267
- The Civil War, 1861–1865
- 11 p.m.–1 p.m.

You use the hyphen to connect parts of words in compound phrases, such as:
- the six-year-old
- the well-worn path
- mid-1980s
- ex-girlfriend
- fifty-five bananas
- well-known
- two-way street

Who or Whom?

These words—who and whom—are often mixed up because writers do not know the difference between their meanings.

>**Who**—is a pronoun that always refers to a *subject* (I, you, he, she, it, they)
>
>**Whom**—is a pronoun that always refers to the *object* of the verb or of a preposition (me, you, us, him, her, them)

To test which one is appropriate for your sentence, check your statement or question by substituting one of the nouns to which the "who or whom" refers.

- Who/Whom did you call?
  I called **HIM**—so "Whom did you call?" is the appropriate way to ask this question.
- To who/whom should I write this million-dollar check?
  Write it to **ME!**—so "To whom should I write this million-dollar check?" is correct.
- Who/Whom ordered the ton of dynamite?
  I ordered the ton of dynamite—so "Who ordered …" is correct.
- Who/Whom wrote this amazing chapter on grammar?
  Jaime did! **SHE** wrote this amazing chapter—so "Who made …" is correct.

A Few Important Notes on Verb-Subject Agreement

Use the **singular verb** form after these words (to check your verb-subject agreement, substitute *s/he* for each word):
- each
- either
- everyone
- everybody
- neither
- nobody
- someone

Each of the doctors wants to be in charge.
Everybody in the room notices the huge stain on his shirt.
Either of the ideas you suggested works for me.

A singular subject remains **singular** even if other nouns are connected to it by:
- with
- as well as
- in addition to
- except
- together with
- no less than

*Her style, together with her attitude, **makes** her a real winner.*
*His speech, as well as his manner, **is** objectionable.*

Dangling and Misplaced Modifiers

Modifiers are words or phrases that describe or give more information about other words or phrases in a sentence.

A **misplaced modifier** ends up adding a description to the wrong element of a sentence because it is incorrectly placed within the sentence.

Wrong: *Linda saw the White House flying over Washington, DC.* (The White House was flying?!)
Right: *Flying over Washington, DC, Linda saw the White House.*
Wrong: *I went outside to get the paper wearing my bathrobe.* (The paper is wearing a robe!?)
Right: *Wearing my bathrobe, I went outside to get the paper.*

A **dangling modifier** is a descriptive element intended to modify a sentence element that is missing or implicit.
Wrong: *Rushing to class, the books fell out of my bag.* (The books are rushing to class!?)
Right: *While rushing to class, I dropped my books.*
Wrong: *Trying to text a friend, my car swerved into a ditch.* (Your car was texting?!)
Right: *While I was trying to text a friend, my car swerved into a ditch.*
Or: *Trying to text message a friend, I lost control of my car and swerved into a ditch.*

CHAPTER 35

Professional Editing

Once you have completed the first round of self-edits on your manuscript and gotten your work as far as you can alone, it is time to consider editorial support. Everyone's editorial journey looks a bit different depending on the state of your manuscript, your budget, your preferences, your resources (coaches and other writers in your life), and more.

If you are indie/self-publishing, you will go through the editorial stages with the help of one or more professional editors whom you will hire directly. For traditional publishing, you may not hire any editorial support, as it is handled in-house by the publishing company. However, this is still the process they will take you through, and you will still be involved in the revision process, so it is good to familiarize yourself with it. Some traditionally published authors do go through a round of developmental editing on their books (and sometimes a round of copy editing, too) before they begin to pitch it to publishers, to ensure that their ideas, content, and organization are as strong as they can be before pursuing a book deal. I highly recommend that step!

As I have mentioned about self-editing, the editorial phase is important and takes time to do well. I don't recommend trying to publish your book without comprehensive professional support. Your ethos and the success of your book really depend on your commitment to doing this phase thoroughly and effectively. Here are some of the options for professional editing and what each may mean for you and your book.

Manuscript Evaluation

A manuscript evaluation can be an economical way to have your work reviewed by a professional editor. You'll want to make sure you've taken your manuscript as far as you can in self-editing to avoid getting revision suggestions you already know you have to make. A manuscript evaluation looks at high-level structural and content issues like a developmental edit, but it is *much less* detailed and specific. A manuscript evaluation gives you a high-level overview of what works and what doesn't. I personally recommend a manuscript evaluation to Whale Song clients when they are just looking to get a pulse check on their progress or an eye on a working draft to ensure they are on the right track. It can be great for those who feel stuck midway through a draft and need some help. This may be the most appropriate option for those who have significant budget restraints, though it will still not take the place of a developmental edit.

Developmental or Structural Edit

A developmental editor will give you high-level feedback on your entire book. For nonfiction, developmental editors (also called content or structural editors) focus on clarity, flow, tone, and voice, what could be added or eliminated, and how to most effectively organize the book, its chapters, and its sections. This is the most intensive level of editing. You may do one, two, or even more rounds of developmental editing on your own and/or with your editor before you feel complete with the structural revisions of your book.

A developmental editor will not make changes to your manuscript for you; rather, they will suggest changes that you can implement or choose not to implement. You are always at the helm of your creation—a developmental editor's suggestions are simply that: suggestions. A developmental editor will typically make marginal comments on your draft and offer an editorial report or letter on what they suggest to improve your manuscript. At Whale Song, we offer a thorough manuscript review, editorial comments and suggestions throughout your manuscript, a five- to seven-page editorial letter, and a follow-up call to ensure you understand the suggestions and feel confident about your next steps.

Be sure to get clarity about what a developmental edit will and won't include before you hire anyone for developmental editing. I also recommend asking for testimonials from other clients and learning more about the editor's experience. Developmental editing is a complex task that requires a skilled and experienced editor. It is also very time-intensive. For both of these reasons, developmental editing is not cheap (and you definitely get what you pay for), but it is totally essential to producing an excellent book.

A Copy or Line Editor

When you are fully through your developmental revision stage and it's time to polish your writing, a line or copy editor will comb through your manuscript paragraph by paragraph, sentence by sentence, to smooth out your prose and make sure each word reads beautifully. They may also address formatting issues (such as chapter headings, subheadings, bullets, examples, callout boxes, and more) and stylistic consistency.

A copy editor will typically use Word Track Changes, or the like, to offer or make suggested changes in your manuscript. And you can expect a lot of line suggestions on this round of editing. You get to choose whether you accept or reject a suggestion an editor makes.

Once your manuscript has been well-combed and edited at the paragraph and sentence levels, it will likely feel 99 percent, if not 100 percent, complete to you. Yet, there is still one more stage of editing, and it is an important one.

Proofreading

Proofreading is the final and essential phase of your editing responsibilities. While you may feel tempted to skip this stage, don't. It is likely you've made many revisions in the editing stage. Your book needs one final pass to ensure that it is error-free. You don't want little missed errors to detract from your credibility.

Proofreading can happen before your book goes into design or after. You'll want to be absolutely sure that your draft is 99.9 percent complete, with a commitment to NO major changes, if you are going to have a book designer design the interior of the book before you proof it. The benefit of proofing before design is that you can fully complete editing and move definitively out of this stage before you move into design. The benefit of proofing after design is that you can catch things in their final form in the book. For the latter, you'll want to make sure you have an agreement and plan with your book designers about when proofing will take place and how necessary adjustments will be conveyed to them and implemented.

A proofreader will examine each word, letter, and punctuation mark to ensure there are no typos, misspellings, punctuation errors, or inconsistencies in your book. I recommend getting at least one, if not two or three, sets of eyeballs proofreading your manuscript. It can be difficult for a writer to proof their own book because they've seen the content a bajillion times, but it can be done. I get a little squeamish as a book publisher when a writer insists they've proofed their own book, only because I've seen many errors persist after such a declaration has been made!

Finding the Right Editors

You'll want to do your homework when it comes to hiring your editorial team. I'd suggest finding someone with interest and experience working with authors in your genre and topic area. You may ask writers in your genre for recommendations. You may look at the acknowledgment pages of your favorite books and see if they mention who their editors were. You may look at an editor's website or blog to get a feel for them, or have a discovery call to get to know more about their work. Some editors will offer a sample editorial letter from a past project or testimonials from past clients.

When you find someone, make sure you receive a clear contract with the timeline and scope for the work. This should include the price, the deliverables (e.g., an editorial letter, marginal notes, in-text suggested changes), and the date by which they will be delivered. You'll want to make sure that you are clear on what the process involves, what is inside and outside the scope of their work, communicate expectations and needs upfront, and ensure you feel good about everything.

Remember, you are paying them for constructive, critical feedback on your work. That said, you don't have to take every suggestion they make. I find most authors take 80–90 percent of the editorial feedback they receive (higher for proofreading, of course). You want to work through each change they suggest and resist the urge to "Accept All" on the suggested changes.

Editing is a major investment of time, energy, and money. The average time in the editing phase of a project can be anywhere from five to twelve months or more for a full-length manuscript. But this process is absolutely worth it.

CHAPTER 36

Anatomy of a Book

Once you have completed your manuscript and it is in the editing process, it's a good time to consider developing and building the other parts of your book. These include:

Front Matter (Before the Main Text)

Every book varies slightly in the inclusion and order of the following parts, so I suggest looking at this list to include what is relevant and desired for your book. You may also want to look at a few books you love to get a feel for what they include, and in what order, in their front matter.

- **Title Page:** Announces the title, subtitle, author, and publisher of the book. Other information that may be found on the title page includes the publisher's location, the year of publication, and descriptive text about the book and illustrations.

- **Copyright Page:** This page carries the copyright notice, edition information, publication information, printing history, cataloging data, legal notices, and the book's ISBN or identification number. In addition, rows of numbers are sometimes printed at the bottom of the page to indicate the year and number of the printing. Credits for design, production, editing, and illustration also go here.

- **Dedication:** Not every book carries a dedication, but for those that do, it typically follows the copyright page.

- **Blurbs/Endorsements:** This section may come at different places in the front matter, but many contemporary authors put it on the very first page or after the title page. These are quotes from others offering praise for your book. These can help sell your book to browsers and establish your ethos right away. Please see Appendix E for more about endorsements.

- **Epigraph**—An author may wish to include an epigraph—a quotation—near the front of the book. The epigraph may also appear facing the Table of Contents or the first page of text. Epigraphs can also appear at the heads of each chapter.

- **Table of Contents:** Also known as the Contents page, this page lists all the major divisions of the book, including parts and chapters. Depending on the length of the book, a greater level of detail may be provided to help the reader navigate the book. You may also have a list of figures/illustrations and a list of tables, if relevant.

- **Foreword:** This is usually a short piece written by someone other than the author, usually someone well-known in a field related to the book's topic or genre. The Foreword may provide a context for the main work, share another expert's framing of the topic in a way that is supportive and introductory to the book itself, and serve as a bit of an extended endorsement of your work. This contribution is meant to be supportive of your book, and that is where the spotlight should stay (and on the topic of the work itself). If you don't like the Foreword someone offers you, you have the right to suggest edits or politely decline its inclusion in your book. It's your book. The Foreword usually ends with the Foreword-writer's name, credentials, location, and date.

- **Preface:** Written by the author, the Preface often tells how the book came into being; it offers contextual background information as a prelude to the introduction.

- **Acknowledgments:** The author expresses gratitude for help in the creation of the book or the ideas that informed or inspired it. (This may go before the main content of the book or after.)

BODY OR MIDDLE (THE MAIN CONTENT OF YOUR BOOK)

- **Introduction:** The author explains the purposes and the goals of the work and may place the work in a context, as well as spell out the organization and scope of the book. Please see Chapter 20 for what to include in your book introduction.

- **Sections or Parts:** Both fiction and nonfiction books are often divided into parts or sections when there is a large conceptual, historical, or structural logic that suggests these divisions and when the author believes that the reader will benefit from this meta-organization.

- **Chapters:** Most fiction and almost all nonfiction books are divided into chapters for the sake of organizing the material to be covered.

- **Chapter Sections:** Chapters may have subheadings that delineate sections of the content within. These are intended to help the reader follow along and keep track of the main ideas. Section titles are bits of metadiscourse that alert your reader that a new main idea will be introduced next.

- **Callout boxes:** You may have content that you want to give special callout treatment to, such as lists, exercises, activities, or reflection opportunities that you want to stand out from your main body text.

- **Calls to Action/Exercises/Applications:** These often come at the end of each chapter and give your reader a conclusion, summary, or invitation to interface with your ideas and material in some practical way.

- **Conclusion or Epilogue:** A brief summary of the salient arguments of the main work, or a conclusion of the narrative, that gives a sense of completeness to the work. See Section One's "Structural Support" resources for more ideas on your conclusion.

BACK MATTER (CONTENT AFTER THE MAIN TEXT)

- **Afterword:** This post-conclusion content, written by the author or another person, may offer additional commentary, reflection, or insights on the work itself. It may explore the book's context, reception, or influence. What is the difference between the afterword and the conclusion? The latter is part of the main arc of the book itself, while the former is distinct. In memoir, an afterword is distinct from the main storyline, and may account for the time since the memoir story's conclusion, add concluding thoughts for the reader to consider, reflect on the personal impact of the events described in the book, offer some future perspective on the memoir's contents, and so on.

- **Acknowledgments:** These may be placed in the front matter or back matter; see earlier for details.

- **List of Contributors:** A work by many authors may require a list of contributors, which should appear immediately before the index, although it is sometimes moved to the front matter. Contributors' names should be listed alphabetically by last name, yet appear in the form "First Name Last Name." Information about each contributor may include brief biographical notes, academic affiliations, or previous publications.

- **Index:** An alphabetical listing of people, places, events, concepts, and works cited, along with page numbers indicating where they can be found within the main body of the work. (You will likely want to hire out this work for your book, if you feel it is needed.)

- **Appendices + Additional Content:** A supplement to the main work.
    - Exercises
    - Processes
    - Checklists
    - Images
    - Illustrations
    - Additional information
    - Poems
    - Summaries of other work

- **Glossary:** An alphabetical list of terms and their definitions.

- **Author Bio:** This is a paragraph or two, often accompanied by an author photo, that states your credentials, qualifications, background, and a bit of personal information. We covered these in Chapter 8, you might remember, but you can also pull a few books off your shelf to see what to include and how to format this page.

- **Notes:** Endnotes come after any appendices and before the bibliography or list of references. The notes are typically divided by chapter to make them easier to locate. This may be the same section an author lists their references.

- **Resources:** This can be a list of further resources you want to offer your reader to give them more support and information on your topic or related topics.

- **References (Works Cited and Works Consulted):** A systematic list of books or other works, such as website content and articles in periodicals, that have been cited in the main body of the work.

- **Call to Action:** Many nonfiction books, especially business books, include a note from the author inviting the reader to engage with them or their larger work in the world in some way—it may invite readers to follow them on social media, sign up for their newsletter, or download information about programs and events the author offers.

CHAPTER 37

Explore Your Publishing Options

WHEN TO MAKE PUBLISHING CONSIDERATIONS

Some people must write a book first before they can even think about where and how they want to publish. Other folks won't even consider writing the draft of a book unless they have a book deal in hand. Some writers know with 100 percent certainty that they either want to traditionally publish or indie (independently) publish or self-publish. Others aren't so sure. Before you go listening to everyone you know about their experiences of book publishing, let's start with you. Let's examine your big considerations as you explore your publishing options.

Overview of Your Publishing Options

While we'll get into greater depth with each of these in our coming chapters, let's lay out your options here. For our purposes, we are going to divide your publishing options into three categories: traditional publishing, indie or independent publishing (including hybrid or partnered publishing), and self-publishing.

Traditional Publishing is when you seek representation from a literary agent with the intention of procuring a book-publishing deal with a traditional publisher *or* approach traditional publishers directly (for those that permit this) with your book proposal and/or manuscript in seeking a traditional publishing book deal. With a book deal, the publishing house buys the rights to the book, may offer an advance against your royalties, and will handle all or most costs associated with editing, permissions, design, production, and some aspects of marketing.

Indie Publishing (short for Independent Publishing) includes collaboration with a smaller-sized publisher or a publishing partner that supports you in bringing your book through the development, editing, design, production, and marketing stages of the book process. This type of publishing also includes hybrid publishing and supported publishing models. This is a middle path approach to publishing—in this approach, authors retain creative control and direction, yet have the support of publishing industry experts who can help the author through all stages of book publication. While the author assumes most or all of the financial costs associated with bringing their book to market, they retain all rights to their books and receive 100 percent of all royalties. Crowdfunding is an excellent strategy for indie authors. Whale Song uses an indie publishing partnership or supported publishing model.

Self-Publishing, sometimes considered a subset of indie publishing, is when the author assumes all responsibility for the development, editing, design, production, and marketing stages of their book. They may hire independent contractors for different aspects of their project, but they serve as the project manager and assume full responsibility for all aspects of the publishing process. We'll include self-publishing under indie publishing moving forward but will differentiate between the two when needed.

Busting Publishing Myths
Traditional Publishing Myths

MYTH 1

TRADITIONAL PUBLISHING WILL GUARANTEE MY BOOK GREATER SUCCESS IN THE MARKETPLACE.

Truth: Successful book sales depend on many factors, many of which have more to do with author marketing efforts than the benefits of having a publishing team. It also depends on how you are defining success, which we'll explore more in the next chapter.

MYTH 2

A PUBLISHER WILL DO EVERYTHING FOR ME.

Truth: Most publishers do not have the resources to walk an author through their drafting process and provide early editorial support (hence the advent of the book coach). They expect authors to come with a complete and polished manuscript. They will offer editorial support during the revision process but not likely during drafting. Yes, a publisher will have a team to design and produce your book. And they will work for a short time on your book's distribution. But note that publishers' book marketing efforts are primarily focused on bookselling channels (distribution), *NOT* on reaching your target audience directly (marketing). Some will offer a level of marketing support, but it is often not comprehensive or sustained support. Which leads us to Myth 3.

MYTH 3

A PUBLISHER WILL MARKET MY BOOK TO MY IDEAL READERSHIP AND BUILD MY AUTHOR PLATFORM FOR ME.

Most publishers expect you to come with an established platform and a clear plan for marketing your book. In fact, they will make decisions about taking on your book based on these factors and how much selling power *you* bring to the table, not the other way around. They want your proposal to show what your current following is (social media, email lists), who your connections are, and whether you have a website. They will *not* build your platform for you; they want you to come with one.

Further, it is a major myth that your publisher will spend weeks or months promoting your book after it is released. Publishers focus more on distribution than marketing, as mentioned. They will not spend weeks or months promoting your book; they will expect *you* to do this. This is not to say they don't do anything—they are in the business of selling books, and many times, they will set the stage for opportunities such as traditional media engagement or extended distribution of your book. Don't expect, as a first-time author, to land a fully paid-for book tour or a full calendar of speaking or media engagements courtesy of your publisher.

In reality, publishers are busy and are pumping out many books annually. It is more common for them to spotlight your book for a short time around publication—days or weeks—and then move on to the next title in their wheelhouse. Some authors, even those who publish with big publishing houses, are shocked to find that their books disappear from bookstore shelves three to six months after publication.

Indie Publishing Myths

MYTH 1
I CAN START WITH SELF-PUBLISHING AND THEN PITCH MY BOOK TO PUBLISHERS.

Truth: While there are some unicorns out there that started with indie publishing and crossed over easily and successfully to traditional publishing, it is not the norm. For example, *The Martian* by Andy Weir was self-published, then picked up by a traditional publisher, and then made into a blockbuster movie. Same for E. L. James's *Fifty Shades of Grey*. But these are outliers.

If you are going to write a series, it is not likely that a publisher will pick up your whole series after you self-publish book one. Efforts to use indie publishing as a stepping stone to traditional publishing of that same book down the road often aren't successful either.

This all said, if you indie publish, are well received by your readership, and build a strong platform and track record of success with your book, you can use this in your pitch to a traditional publisher for your *next* project, often with success.

MYTH 2
I WILL EARN MORE MONEY IF I SELF-PUBLISH.

Truth: Yes, by and large, you will keep a significantly higher percentage of your earnings per book if you indie publish. With indie publishing, you aren't dividing your earnings between you, your publisher, their team, and potentially an agent. Royalties for indie publishing can range from 60-90 percent, while royalties for traditional publishing are between 5-25 percent.[1] That said, you have to consider 1) sales volume, 2) the extent to which you can recoup your upfront investment as an indie author (anywhere from $3,000 to $20,000), and 3) a potential advance from a traditional publisher (between $5,000-$15,000 on average, and you have to earn out your advance—sell that much in books *at your royalty rate of 5–25 percent* before additional revenue from royalties can be earned).

MYTH 3

I CAN EASILY AND QUICKLY PUBLISH A HIGH-QUALITY BOOK ON MY OWN OVERNIGHT WITHOUT MUCH ENERGY AND EFFORT. YOU JUST HIT THE PUBLISH BUTTON ON AMAZON, RIGHT?

Truth: Indie publishing—*when done well*, and this phrase is *key*—takes a substantial amount of time, energy, money, and dedication. You have to commit fully to a lengthy process of book writing, book editing, book design, book production, and learning the business of book publishing, distribution, and promotion. Yes, you can technically pump out a book in a few weeks or months, plug it into a design template, and launch it on Amazon in a few weeks—but to do a good job and bring your book to the standards of quality we expect in traditionally published books, it takes time and money. You need to find quality professionals to design a beautiful book interior and book cover. You need to learn about the book-publishing world and determine your strategy. You need a plan to build a platform and launch your book. You need a long-term marketing strategy. And much more. Yes, you may be able to do it quickly, but the quality of your work and the success of your book often take a hit in this rush. (This is why we love support models of indie publishing!)

Weighing Your Options

TRADITIONAL PUBLISHING

Pros of traditional publishing:

- You gain the credibility that comes with publishing with a larger house. Traditional publishers have long acted as book quality gatekeepers; thus, the traditional process can lend instant legitimacy to your work.
- You get to work with an experienced, professional team of editors, designers, formatters, and digital and print sales and marketing experts, who all share the same goal of making your book a success.
- Print distribution into bookstores is much more likely and will be more extensive.
- You have fewer upfront financial costs of producing your book. You don't have to pay for the production expenses. You may also be given an advance.
- Literary prizes and critical acclaim are often easier to come by with traditional marketing.
- While traditional publishers don't do all of your marketing for you, traditionally published books often have greater exposure to a wider audience.
- Publishers and agents also offer access to an international market and professional translators (Amazon does offer extended distribution to international markets for self-published authors, too, FYI).

Cons of traditional publishing:

- Traditional publishing can be slow. It can take a while (years, even) to secure a publishing deal, and after that, it can take anywhere from six months to over two years for your book to be published.
- Writers often face rejection. Your book may be rejected many times before you land a book deal. Approximately 90–99 percent of all book proposals are rejected by publishers.
- The publisher has creative control and gets to make the final decisions about your book, including content and organization, book

cover, pricing, publication date, and title.
- You don't get to choose your editor. With a publisher, you will get the editors assigned to you, and they may or may not align with your vision for your book.
- The publishing house owns the rights to your book; you do not. That means you can't share samples of your work in other contexts without permission.
- Royalty rates (the amount of money you receive for the sale of your book) are much lower than with indie publishing. These rates average between 10 and 15 percent[1] and vary depending on factors like the format and your contract. Often, first-time authors receive the lower end of this range. And this percentage may also be the net, after book production costs, which lowers the royalty further.
- Royalty reports and payouts may only come every six months, with some exceptions.
- Competition for publishing-house attention.
- Limited marketing support. As covered, publishers expect you to come with a platform and a marketing plan and to shoulder the bulk of the marketing work yourself.

INDIE PUBLISHING

Pros of indie publishing:

- The stigma around indie publishing has greatly diminished. While some self-published books are AI-written and lack quality (don't be that person!), indie-published books can be indistinguishable from traditional books in terms of quality. If a book is well-written and designed, most readers won't know the difference between your book and a traditionally published book.
- You have total creative control over your content, format, organization, title, cover design, interior design, publication date, and more. You also get to control who you work with, and if you don't align with someone, you can work with someone else.
- If you want to change anything about your book (the cover, the title,

a rebrand, new information, or a new edition), it is much easier to do.
- You are often able to get your book published much more quickly.
- You get to determine the price of your book.
- You retain the rights to your book.
- You receive much higher royalties (there is less of the "pie" to share). As of this writing, Amazon paperback royalties are 60 percent minus production costs (40 percent for expanded distribution). For a $20 book with a $4.10 production cost, the author would receive $9.54 per book in royalties. If you purchase books to sell directly on your website or at events, you just pay the cost of production and shipping, making your "royalty" per book $15.90 in our example (minus shipping, which will vary). eBook royalties at Amazon are 30 to 70 percent.
- If you self-publish successfully, you may attract the interest of an agent or traditional publisher for future books (not a guarantee or a motivating factor, however).
- With companies like Amazon dominating the book sales market, you have the same chances online as traditionally published books in getting visibility and sales. Often, a reader cannot tell how your book has been published. Traditionally published books don't have an advantage in this marketplace over indie books.
- Print-on-demand options make it quick, easy, and affordable to sell and distribute your print books (you often only have to pay printing/materials and shipping costs).
- With supported indie publishing, you get the benefits of having a professional publishing team and get to enjoy all the perks above.

Cons of indie publishing:

- For DIY self-publishing, you bear the responsibility for the entire project. You have to hire your own editors, designers, marketers, etc., and ensure these professionals offer high-quality service. You essentially become a project manager, navigating and managing all aspects of your project yourself. It is a lot more work in an unknown territory with a steep learning curve.
- You have to pay upfront for your editing and production costs.

- You're not as likely to be eligible for literary awards and other prestige or opportunities that come with publishing houses.
- It can be harder to get your books distributed to bookstores.
- You are responsible for all of your marketing and distribution and will likely have to invest your own financial resources and considerable time, energy, and attention toward these efforts.
- It is more difficult to get mainstream reviews and media attention.

In the next chapter, we'll dive into the key factors you'll want to consider when choosing your publishing path.

Chapter 38

Publishing: Key Factors to Consider

While I'm sure the last chapter provided clarifying information that will help you make a decision, I want to shift over to you and your book now, and give you a chance to consider the key factors that will likely go into your publishing decisions.

What are Your Values?

What are your **top three values** when it comes to your book-publishing journey?

This is an important question for you to answer for yourself.

Publishing a book is like planning a wedding—there are so many choices and factors to consider, and no single right or wrong way to plan one (though your in-laws may disagree!). *Do you want the five-hundred-person wedding in your mom's backyard, or do you want to elope with a few of your best friends as witnesses? What really matters to you? The music, the food, the DJ, the location, gathering everyone you've ever met, pleasing your parents, or having an adventure?* You're likely to be more satisfied if you know what matters most to you and build your wedding accordingly.

Book publishing is the same. Whether traditional or indie publishing, there is no right or wrong way to publish—one is not better or worse than the other. It depends on what matters to you. So, what matters to you the most? The considerations we'll explore in this chapter will help you determine what is most important to you. You may come back to this question after you've read through the chapter, or make a first pass now.

What are your three top values for book publishing? What is most important to you?

_____

_____

_____

_____

_____

_____

Your Goals for Your Book and Personal Views on Publishing

You first want to get clear about your specific personal (and possibly professional) goals for this particular book and use that information to make a wise choice about your publishing options.

Furthermore, get clear on your personal views of your publishing options. Even though the stigma of indie publishing is a relic of the past—authors can produce excellent books to the same professional standards of traditional publishing, and readers don't care as much these days who published a book—it is useful to ask yourself what *you* perceive and what is most important to you.

If you've always dreamed of getting a traditional publisher and won't feel satisfied unless you do, honor that (while checking where that perspective is coming from). There is no reason to convince yourself to indie publish for other reasons if you know in your heart that landing a traditional publisher is your goal. If you are craving the support, guidance, and validation of a publisher, I'd recommend exploring this option thoroughly at first. Keep reading, though, so we can bring you more clarity on what traditional publishing does and doesn't provide.

Key Factors to Consider

CREATIVE CONTROL

Creative control is a major issue to consider when looking at your publishing options. With indie publishing, you will be in control of your content, organization/structure, and the expression of your ideas. You'll also be in charge of your book's title, the cover, how it is formatted, and all other aspects of the production process. You'll also decide when it is published and how you'll promote and market it.

With traditional publishing, your publisher will make all these decisions. You will likely be consulted to some degree, but it is ultimately their choice. It is important to recognize that decisions made at varying stages of the process may or may not align with your creative vision or preferences.

LEVEL OF DESIRED SUPPORT

On the flip side, how much support do you want during your process? Do you want someone to hold your hand and take care of everything without you having to invest your time into learning the publishing world? If so, traditional or indie publishing might be better aligned than self-publishing. Traditional publishing will take the lead, creatively and financially, in most or all of the publication stages; while indie publishing partnership teams will partner with, support, and guide you through all the stages, keeping you in the creative and financial driver's seat. With self-publishing, you can still gather all the support you need, but you must hire it out and dedicate considerable time to learning the publishing process and finding the right support professionals to assist you. You bear all the responsibility for getting the support you need.

YOUR CURRENT PLATFORM

What are the benefits of each option in terms of your current platform and connection with your book's intended audience?

What can a publisher realistically do for you, given the extent of your established connections? For example, if you are a fitness coach with a following of thousands of loyal fans, a traditional publisher may not do much more than you can do yourself to promote and sell your book. This one is tricky because book publishers don't typically do a comprehensive marketing campaign for their books. Rather, they rely on and expect authors to come with their own platforms and actively market to them. Traditional publishers do not build your platform or readership for you. They expect you to bring yours to them. This is really important to know!

Also consider your marketing goals, how you are positioned, and how you want to be positioned in your market with the help of this book.

Related to your readership, you'll also want to consider whether your audience is more primed to purchase media digitally, through online channels, or at a physical bookstore. Certain genres sell better digitally than in brick-and-mortar bookstores. Some genres see better success with traditional representation. I suggest doing research on your genre. Given that my focus is on authors of transformational nonfiction, I will say that there are pros and cons to traditional and indie publishing.

At the time of this writing in 2025, Amazon digital book sales (of either print or eBooks) account for 50 to 80 percent of the market share. They control approximately 80 percent of all book distribution and 50 percent of all book sales in the US. Amazon's eBook sales and distribution is above 80 percent in the US and nearly 70 percent worldwide. According to early 2020s research, print books still account for 80 percent of sales (versus 20 percent eBook sales), whether through Amazon or any other book retailer, digital or brick-and-mortar.

The industry is changing quickly, so feel free to do a search for the latest trends in the industry.

YOUR ENTREPRENEURIAL EXPERIENCE

How entrepreneurial are you? Are you willing to learn the business of publishing? Do you have the time, energy, and desire to be the project manager for your book during the production, distribution, sales, and marketing phases?

For people who are more entrepreneurial-minded, indie publishing is often a familiar process, much like launching a course, product, or program.

Entrepreneurs are often comfortable with the processes of hiring freelancers and support pros, have a degree of proficiency and comfort being active online and in social media, have some degree of comfort and knowledge of marketing, and are used to managing big launch efforts. Entrepreneurs are also used to having creative control over their work and may not want to give up too much to a traditional publisher.

If you are comfortable in the entrepreneurial realm, many of the skills you already possess will parlay well into the world of producing and promoting your book. You will still need to learn about marketing books, specifically, and there is a lot of learning to do in this realm, but it may be somewhat familiar territory to you.

If, on the other hand, you want an established team of people to work with or you want to have someone else project-manage your book process, then traditional publishing might be more up your alley (whether or not you're an entrepreneur). Indie publishing partners, such as Whale Song, can also provide this support.

YOUR TIMELINE

What is your desired timeline for getting your book into the market, and *why*?

It is wise to be clear about the varying timelines for different publishing options. Most of the time, the traditional publishing route takes longer, approximately 18 to 24 months from book deal to publication. This doesn't account for the time you are shopping your book around to agents and publishers seeking a book deal (which can take anywhere from weeks to over a year), nor does it account for the time it takes to write your book.

In my years of experience, I find that once a book is through all the editing stages, authors can bring their books to market via indie publishing within three to six months, on the longer end for those fully self-publishing and on the shorter end for those in a supported indie publishing process.

Most authors would prefer their books to be out as soon as possible, but don't let impatience deter you from considering traditional publishing if you have a lot of alignment with this option for other reasons. We want to be honest about our reasons for a desired timeline—sometimes, we don't have one to two years to get our book to market, but we also want to keep our eyes on the long game.

BOOK AVAILABILITY

Where do you expect your book to be available? Only online? In brick-and-mortar bookstores around the country? Internationally?

Generally speaking, a traditional publisher will more widely distribute your book in print. For indie publishing, you can get into physical bookstores using IngramSpark and some alternative platforms. However, most indie-published books are sold online, both in print and eBook format. Brick-and-mortar book stores will never purchase your book from Amazon, so you have to use a platform that bookstores use to purchase books.

Remember, more than half of all books are sold on Amazon, regardless of format. But it is wise to know that most indie books only sell online or through direct sales (at speaking gigs, events, or via the author's website, for example), and you'll need a traditional publisher if you want to be stocked in bookstores nationally. Traditional publishing is also a better choice if you want to increase your chances of international print book sales and translations.

FINANCES

What are your financial needs and goals?

Indie publishing requires a higher financial investment upfront—anywhere from a few hundred to several thousand dollars. That said, you get more money in your pocket per book sale (think anywhere from $5–10 or more per book sold). Traditional publishing may offer an advance, and you won't have to cover the upfront book production costs, but royalties are often small (like under a dollar per book), and you have to earn out your advance first before seeing any additional revenue from book sales.

MEDIA GOALS

Are you hoping to get major media attention?

If so, go traditional publishing. It is more difficult for indie authors to get major media attention for their books. This is *not* to say it is easy or automatic for traditionally published authors to get media attention, however.

DO BOOKS MAKE YOU MONEY?

This is a big question—and the answer, of course, is different for every author. Some authors make loads of money directly from book sales, starting with the first book of their career. The majority of writers do not make a living off their first book. Some writers are shocked to learn how little money they make from direct sales of their books.

If you are serious about making a living off selling the books you write, you will find that this requires steady commitment and consistent production and promotion of your books over *years*. You have to learn the business of book writing and selling and make it your *business*. You have to dedicate yourself to building a following/readership and connecting with and nurturing this audience.

Many professional full-time authors find they gain traction in direct book sales as a steady income-generator after years of commitment and after writing several books (four to five).

Here's an important consideration when it comes to making money off your book. Many of the clients I work with are entrepreneurs, and their books are tied to their other income-generating activities. This raises the important matter of what doors (financial and otherwise) a book will open for you. And this is where we start to see that even if you don't make piles of money from *direct sales* of your book, a book can make you a lot of money and bring a *ton* of value to your work or career.

According to the indie publishing company Grammar Factory,[1]

34 percent of entrepreneurs *double* their rates after writing a book
63 percent are featured in the media
72 percent land speaking gigs (about 33 percent are paid)
74 percent land new referral partners
86 percent experience significant growth in their business

A book sets you apart in your field and establishes you as an authority. It acts like a supercharged business card, bringing you qualified leads who already know and love your work when they come to you. A book brings visibility and opportunities to speak with, write for, and connect with wider circles in your field, including colleagues, partners, clients, and customers.

I recommend you consider the overall value of your book as being more than what your direct monthly revenue from direct book sales will be. Books are often vehicles that amplify other income-generating streams of work.

Indie-published authors may have a harder time garnering mainstream media attention, but there is no stopping you from getting guest posts for blogs and articles, being a guest on a podcast, and using social media to gain visibility.

BESTSELLER STATUS

How important is The New York Times bestseller list?

While an indie book will be unlikely to hit The New York Times bestseller list, you can make The New York Times eBook bestseller list and Amazon's bestseller lists as an indie publisher. I will say in short that Amazon bestseller lists have more to do with utilizing a specific strategy to get on that list, than high volume sales happening organically based on the merit of your book. You can study strategies for making these lists, and even hire experts to help get you there. I suggest doing your due diligence on this topic if it is a high priority for you.

Chapter 39

The Traditional Publishing Path

If you're ready to pursue traditional publishing, let's explore your path ahead a bit further. The first step is to determine whether you'll seek agent representation or submit your work only to publishers that do not require agented submissions. In your exploration of traditional publishing, I suggest you first do research to determine the kinds of presses/publishers you are interested in approaching and learn what they want, when, and whether they accept direct submissions from authors.

Overview of Agents and Publishers

AGENTS

If you desire to explore the traditional publishing route, there can be major advantages to seeking out a book agent. These include:

- Agents often have strong working relationships with main publishing houses and know who's looking for what.
- Publishers appreciate working with agents, who have already filtered out books they don't feel 100 percent confident in.
- An agent knows your market and can make sure your book is a good fit.
- Agents may help you shape your book or your proposal before you approach publishers to make sure your pitch and book are strong and aligned.
- Agents know the ins and outs of publishing contracts and can ensure you are signing an agreement that is advantageous to you—they can help you negotiate deals, ensure you are paid as promised and fairly, and run interference between you and the publisher when needed.
- For bigger publishers, you will need to have an agent.

PUBLISHING WITH THE BIG FIVE

The Big Five are the top five publishers in the US and beyond. They are:

1. Penguin Random House
2. HarperCollins Publishers
3. Simon & Schuster
4. Macmillan Publishers
5. Hachette Book Group

Each of these also has dozens of imprints, trade names, or divisions under which they publish books. Examples are *Avery* and *Vintage* of Penguin Random House, and *Atria* of Simon & Schuster.

These houses often work with books that appeal to the mainstream and large national or international audiences. Many of these authors have celebrity status, are known authors, or are established industry leaders. Nonfiction authors with a large established platform also appeal to larger houses. The Big Five won't take a book unless they anticipate being able to sell at least ten thousand to twenty thousand copies, which requires a strong hook/book concept and a solid, established author platform. Not all books and authors are a good fit for the Big Five, which doesn't mean your work is of any less value. Authors without a strong platform, memoirs with common storylines, and essay collections often have a difficult time finding a place with the Big Five.

All of these houses require submissions to be made by agents and don't take proposals from authors directly.

PUBLISHING WITH A LARGE- OR MEDIUM-SIZED PRESS

These publishers include large presses (but not at the Big Five level), including:
- Houghton Mifflin Harcourt (agented)
- Scholastic (agented)
- W.W. Norton (agented)
- Sourcebooks (agented and unagented)
- Cambridge, Oxford, and other university presses

Prominent large- to mid-sized publishers in the self-development genre include:
- Hay House Publishing (agented only)
- Sounds True (agented and unagented)
- Shambhala Publishers (agented and unagented)
- North Atlantic Books (unagented)
- New World Library (agented and unagented)
- Red Wheel/Weiser (unagented)
- Findhorn Press (unagented)

These publishers also publish books with mainstream and broad audience appeal, as well as those with a more specific niche or special-interest appeal. Some of these are agented and some are not, as noted. Advances and royalties are often smaller compared to the Big Five. Some offer more flexible or progressive agreements that feel more collaborative compared to Big Five contracts. Note that university presses often pay a low advance and have small print runs, often with a focus on academic or library markets.

TRADITIONAL SMALL PRESSES

Small press is a catch-all term for publishers that can range from well-established and esteemed, such as Graywolf Press, to established and credible indie publishing partners, to pop-up publishers without established credibility. The distinction between traditional and indie publishing can get a little blurred here. Some small presses operate like traditional publishers, while others operate as indie publishers, supporting authors to publish their own books. Let's talk about the former here.

Small publishing presses often accept unagented submissions. They often work with emerging, first-time authors. They are also more friendly toward experimental or less commercial types of books. An attractive feature is the more collaborative, personal working relationships but with the support of a publisher in production and marketing.

Do your homework when it comes to the credibility and capabilities of a small press. Legitimate small presses will not ask authors to pay for publication (note that indie publishing presses work on a different model). Also pay attention to the contract and how they term your rights to your work and your royalties/advance. With small presses, you may or may not receive an advance. And they may or may not distribute print books to physical retailers. In short, do your homework!

When to Seek an Agent or Publisher

Authors seek agents and publishers at different points in their process, and it is wise to be aware of what agents and publishers want from you when you query. Some agents and publishers are open to simple query letters, where you pitch your project at the early stages of your drafting process. Most will want a book proposal, which includes a list of detailed chapter summaries and at least two to three sample chapters of your book. For memoir and fiction, they sometimes want to see a complete manuscript. Some agents and publishers would like you to wait to query until you have a finished manuscript.

How to Find Agents and Publishers

One great place to begin looking for agents or publishers is the *Writer's Market* book, which is published annually online. They also publish the *Guide to Literary Agents*. This book includes listings for agents and publishers, as well as consumer magazines, trade journals, and contests and awards. Each listing in this book will give the pertinent details you need, such as contact information, what types of books this publisher/agent is looking for, how to submit your proposal and when, how many books they represent/publish per year (and often the percent of first-time authors), and their royalty and advance details. This book also has an index of book publishers by subject so you can narrow down your search easily.

To find aligned agents and publishers, you may also leverage your social and professional networks. You can look at the acknowledgment pages of books in your genre and books you love, and see who these authors worked with. See the Notes section of this book for more ideas on how to find your agent or publisher.[1]

In regard to agents, please note that becoming an agent does not require any certification or training, so be sure to do your homework as you find potential book agents, and be clear about their background and experience before you agree to work with them. You may want to consider finding someone who is a member of the Association of Authors' Representatives (AAR), which means they do not charge for reading, critiquing, or editing.

I suggest finding five to fifteen agents or publishers you think would be a good fit for your work.

ONCE YOU'VE GOT YOUR SHORT LIST:

1. Check out their websites and make sure they're taking submissions.
2. Make sure they are taking books in your genre; study their list of published or represented books. How do you and your book fit into that?
3. Check out their submission guidelines (and be sure to follow their instructions to a T).
4. Develop whatever materials you'll need to approach them, which may include a query letter, chapter samples, a book proposal, a full manuscript, and other examples of your writing.

Remember, you are pitching to them, making an argument for why they should want your book. Make sure you've done your research. See the next chapter for more about book proposals.

The Common Path to Traditional Publishing

1. Write: You write some or all of your book. At a minimum, two to three chapters prior to seeking an agent or publisher.

2. Research: You research agents and publishers looking for manuscripts in your genre.

3. Approach: You submit to agents or publishers your query letter, a book proposal, or a full manuscript, based on what each one specifically asks for. *Most nonfiction requires a full book proposal. Most memoirs require a full manuscript.*

4. Receive: You wait to hear back from agents or publishers. Some will not reply at all, some will decline your submission, and some may ask for a full manuscript or inquiry, further moving toward accepting your book. The submission process can take months or even years. Some books are never picked up because there isn't a market for them or a way to revise the work successfully. Some books are amazing and are still not picked up.

    For example, J. K. Rowling, the author of *Harry Potter*, was rejected numerous times before any of her titles were picked up, and it took years for her work to become popular.

    If an agent agrees to represent you, they will begin to shop your book to publishers.

5. Agreement: You receive a book deal offer from a publisher and begin to hash out a contract.

6. Production: The publisher takes your manuscript through the editing and production process. They have creative control over the ultimate content and aesthetic of your book. *It typically takes six to twenty-four months for a publisher to publish your book once they've accepted it.*

7. Publication and Promotion: The publisher determines a publication date and may offer a degree of distribution and marketing support around launch promotions.

HOW AGENTS TYPICALLY GET PAID

Most agents do not get paid anything upfront and only receive payment when a work has been sold. Agents typically receive an average of 15 percent commission on everything the author gets paid, including the advance and the royalties. Avoid agents who charge upfront and who charge additional fees to you. Agents are motivated based on the size of the advance they think they can negotiate for your book. If they don't feel your book could garner a sizable advance, they may not choose to represent you, regardless of the quality or merit of your work.

Tips for Navigating the Traditional Publishing World

1. Publishing is a business; they are looking for books that will make money and provide a good return on investment. You are in the business of making a super compelling case for why your book will sell and is a good ROI for your publisher/agent.
2. Professionalism and respect are key attributes of a successful author in the traditional publishing world.
3. You *will* get rejected. The submission process takes dedication, persistence, and tough skin.
4. Don't call an agent or publisher and query by phone or just to chat.
5. Don't visit agents/publishers at their offices. If you want to interact with agents and publishers directly, consider attending a writer's conference, pitch conference, or similar event.
6. Know that you will likely be asked to make changes to your work that you do not want to make. Remember that the publisher has creative power and control over your book. They own it. To be successful, you have to approach this with professionalism and flexibility.
7. You'll be far more attractive to agents and publishers if you are actively marketing and promoting your book and if you come with an established platform. Remember, your publisher will expect *you* to bring the audience for your book, not the other way around.

CHAPTER 40

BOOK PROPOSALS

WHAT IS A BOOK PROPOSAL?

A book proposal is a 20 to 60-page document that you, the author, write to convince an agent to represent you or compel a book publisher to offer you a book deal. You may think of the proposal as the business plan for your book.

While writing a book proposal is generally a stage in the process of traditionally publishing your book, a book proposal can also serve as a self-publishing plan for those who wish to independently publish their books, because a proposal will outline what your book is about and how you plan to promote it. It will also convey a strong case for why your book is valuable and needed in the market, which will give you compelling, concise language to use when marketing your book.

Writing a book proposal can help you:
- Get crystal clear on your *why*—why you, why now, why this book
- Get clear on your concept for the book
- Focus your ideas and make sure you have a viable, sellable idea
- Get clear on the commitment required of you to complete the book (time and energy)
- Be certain you want to commit to this book project

Publishers will make their decision on how much to pay an author based on the details offered in the book proposal. They will also consider how many copies of your book they think they can sell in the first year based on researching the sales of similar titles.

Proposals are also used by publishers to generate enthusiasm, interest, and engagement within their internal teams, as well as with retailers.

Proposals are fairly standard, though each publisher or agent will have specific submission instructions. I usually recommend that you write a template proposal that you can adapt for each specific publisher or agent you are submitting to. Usually, there are a few somewhat minor changes or additions required.

When Should I Write a Book Proposal?

There is no set answer to this question, but let's explore.

WRITING THE PROPOSAL BEFORE YOU WRITE THE MANUSCRIPT

On the one hand, the benefit of writing a proposal earlier in your authorship journey is that you can use it to determine whether you can secure a book deal without having to write the whole book first. In this case, you can save time and test your idea in the publishing world before committing months or even years to the first-draft writing process. I have known some authors who are not willing to invest the time and energy into writing their full manuscript until they have sold it. If that is the case for you, you'll want to consider writing the proposal earlier in your process.

Here's the thing: You need to know a lot about your book before you're able to write a strong proposal. That's why I recommend writing your proposal after you've completed a thorough planning and visioning process. (Section One of this book should help you get there!) You not only need to have a clear concept, but you also need to know the book's structure and sequence of material, be able to summarize each chapter, and complete a few sample chapters. You'll also need to be able to articulate who the book is for and why they will want to read it. Further, you'll need to be able to talk about your current audience reach and how you plan to promote the book.

WRITING THE PROPOSAL AFTER YOU WRITE THE MANUSCRIPT

You can also choose to write the proposal after you've written your first draft. By writing the book first, you can gain valuable feedback from editors and beta readers before presenting your book idea to publishers. You will have refined your ideas and honed your organization to the point that you are fairly confident *this* is the book you want to deliver to the world. You will also have an entire manuscript from which to select the sample chapters (and chapter summaries) required in a proposal. The publication process can go faster when you have a ready manuscript at the time of a book deal.

I find that authors with a ready draft can write a proposal more easily than those who haven't written it yet. While I am happy to help those who haven't written their books yet, I find the process goes a lot more smoothly when the first draft is complete. Part of this is because writing is a process of *discovery*, meaning you find out what the book is actually about only by writing it. What you think you're going to write is bound to change, and that makes the "guess work" of writing a proposal for an unwritten book a bit more challenging.

Getting Started on a Book Proposal

I am a big advocate of planning, both for your book and for your proposal. I believe in the value of strategic visioning and planning for your book's concept before you write your book proposal or first draft. I also suggest looking into your publishing options before you begin writing a proposal. (See the earlier chapters in this section for more support with that.)

When it comes to the proposal itself, a little planning can go a long way in saving you time, energy, and frustration. Structure creates freedom.

DON'T WRITE THE PROPOSAL IN ORDER

Just as I recommend that people leave the introduction of their book for last in the drafting process, I also recommend that people leave the introduction of their proposal for last.

Furthermore, I don't recommend that you write your proposal in the exact order in which the information will appear in the final form. Often, authors move between sections of the book proposal as they craft it. We often begin each section with a high-level "sketch" or concept and then work to fill in the details.

With that in mind, we want to create a system and structure for writing the book proposal that will serve your process.

GOOD SYSTEMS ARE *GOLD*

If you use Scrivener, I recommend creating a separate project for your proposal, just as you would for your book itself. Here, instead of having folders or files for the chapters of your book, you'll have folders or files for each section of your proposal. You may also have folders/files for Notes, Inspiration/Ideas, Research, and the full final draft.

You can also simply use a Microsoft Word document to write your proposal. You may wish to create a folder on your desktop (or wherever, author's choice) and create individual Word docs within the folder for each section of the proposal. You can do the same thing in any other word-processing or file management system.

If all these files and folders overwhelm you, just stick with a single word-processing document. If you use Word, you may want to consider using the heading function—if you stay consistent with your use of heading 1, for example, for the name of each section of the proposal, you can create a Table of Contents at the beginning and jump to sections from there.

CREATING YOUR SYSTEM BY PROPOSAL COMPONENTS

I recommend that you create a folder or file for each section of the proposal. These are in the order in which they usually (but not always) *appear in your proposal*:

1. Overview/introduction
2. Author bio + platform (note sometimes these are separate sections of a proposal)
3. Market/audience
4. Promotion and marketing plan
5. Competitive titles
6. Book Table of Contents
7. Chapter summaries
8. Sample chapter(s)

This is the order I *recommend you write them* (though you can choose your own adventure):
1. Book Table of Contents
2. Chapter summaries
3. Sample chapter(s)
4. *Competitive titles***
5. *Author bio + platform*
6. *Market/audience*
7. *Promotion and marketing plan*
8. Overview/introduction

The ones in italics can go in any order that feels best to you.
** Some experts recommend starting here.

You can determine whether you want to sequence your files in proposal order or drafting order, author's choice. Just stick to one and know what it is. Also note that you will likely go back and forth between sections as you write, so you won't necessarily go step-by-step through each one, no matter your filing sequence.

Once you feel like you have a completed section, you may wish to move that content into a *Full Draft* folder or file so you can keep track of what feels finished and what is still in progress. Once every section is in the Full Draft folder/file, you can print it out as a whole and begin the editing and refinement process. (You can use Section Three of this book to help you edit your proposal.)

COMMIT TO A PLAN

Once you have your systems set up, commit to a plan for your proposal writing. Consider what is doable in your life (i.e., how many hours per week, when, and for how long) in terms of the time you can commit to this proposal. It doesn't matter if it's twenty hours or two, just commit to something doable—any regular plan *you actually show up for* will move your project forward.

You might consider focusing on a section per week, for example. Or you may just commit to a certain number of hours of engagement per week and allow the journey to be more organic. Set yourself up for success. Know the power of scheduling your proposal-writing time into your schedule. This is not research time or book concept exploration time, but actual proposal-writing time.

If it's not in your schedule to write your proposal, you'll find it difficult to get it done. Period. It depends on your process, but most authors I've worked with need a few months to write a book proposal, more if they need book concept clarification and development, and less if they have a completed manuscript and a good amount of time to dedicate to the process.

I find that proposal writing goes better with support, so consider hiring an editor (and possibly even a coach) while you are writing your book proposal.

Sections of a Book Proposal

OVERVIEW

This is your chance to hook your proposal reader with a high-level, compelling argument about why the publisher should publish your book. Why does your book matter, and what needs does it meet in your audience? Why do we need this book in the world now? What are the highlights and strengths of your book specifically? How can you engage the interest and emotions of your reader to make them want to keep reading the rest of your proposal? Consider the angles you might take here: what will be most compelling for this specific publisher or agent?

The overview is to your proposal what your introduction is to your book. I recommend writing it last because writing the rest of your proposal will inform what you want to say here.

ABOUT THE AUTHOR

This is a page or two about you, showcasing your strongest and most relevant experience and background. You don't need to tell us everything you've ever done, but only what is most relevant to showcasing you as an experienced and qualified author for this book. Show your proposal reader how your experience and background have yielded a strong platform from which to connect with your readership. Highlight strengths that will build credibility with your readers and/or help sell books. These can include connections to other authors or influencers (those with a network), your online following or email list, and your previous success in marketing yourself and your work.

MARKET ANALYSIS

This section talks about your primary audience and makes the case that there is a large, hungry audience waiting for a book like yours to buy. You may want to look back at Chapter 6 to help you flesh out this part of the proposal. You don't want to make generic comments here, such as: "This book is for women aged 20 to 60." That is way too broad of an audience. You don't need to talk about the population of book buyers either, but drill down closer to data you can find about books in your genre and even on your topic. This is a section of your proposal where you need to back up your audience information with qualitative data that reveals market insight.

For example, (I am making some of this up),

> "Eight of the ten top The New York Times best sellers for the last two years have been books written about healing trauma, revealing that readers are hungry for books on this topic. *The Body Keeps the Score* by Bessel van der Kolk, has been a The New York Times best seller for more than 245 weeks, ranked at #1 for 27 of those weeks. Readers of this book will appreciate my book for its complementary approach to trauma healing, as I weave in more personal insight and offer less professional and academic prose, which makes my book more accessible to my ideal readership."

PROMOTION

This is where you explain in detail how you will promote your book. If separate from your About the Author section, the promotions section is where you will talk about your current platform, such as your web traffic, mailing list subscribers, social media followers, and the like. Do you have any contacts for speaking gigs, promotion, or Foreword and endorsement writers? Do you belong to any associations or networks you can successfully leverage to bring visibility to this book? Talk numbers here. For example, write, "I have 5,180 current followers on YouTube where I am actively engaged in providing weekly content to my ideal readership. My videos receive at least 20-30 comments, indicating active engagement with them" instead of "I have YouTube, Facebook, and Instagram accounts."

Elements of your platform you may account for, as relevant:
- Previous book publications
- Website, blog, podcast, newsletter; include URLs and visit/subscriber numbers
- Media coverage of you or your work
- Awards, fellowships, grants, or other recognition
- Articles and posts on other platforms
- Video content on your or another's platform
- Active social media accounts, links to profiles, and follower numbers
- Professional or relevant group or community engagement and level of reach that would afford you and your book
- Past and current speaking engagements, presentations, workshops, conferences, and retreats
- Notable contacts, relationships, or affiliations you can leverage to sell books

Further, when you talk about what you will do to promote your book, be confident, accurate, and clear. Instead of talking about what you might do or hope to do, talk about what you are going to do, how, and when. Make sure you are only sharing what you are actually capable of and willing to do to promote your book. Example: "I have hired a book marketing team for six months. We are devoted to generating consistent content across my strongest channels of digital social engagement. We will post daily on my LinkedIn account, as my post engagement there averages 40-50 comments per post, and 20 reshares, reaching an estimated 10,000 to 12,000 people per share." [Continue to share plans at this level of specificity as possible.]

COMPETITIVE ANALYSIS

Here, you showcase other books that are similar yet different from yours, making the case for the niche your book fits into and how your book is different from what is already out there. Remember compare and contrast essays from school? This section is a lot like those essays.

Hot tip: You do not need to read all the competitive and complementary books on your topic. For goodness' sake, spare yourself (especially as you are writing your book—too many cooks in the kitchen and voices in your head!). Here is my inside trick. Go to Amazon and look for books in your genre, then on your topic. Find ones that are recent (ideally in the last five years), by reputable authors, and have sold well. When you find one, go to the description of the book and see how it is the same and different from your book. If you can find something about the book in each category (same and different), green light. Then go to the "Look Inside" feature and go to the book's Table of Contents. Here, you are looking to get a sense of the book's structure and what they say and in what way. That should give you more compare/contrast fodder. Then you might read the intro content to get a feel for the tone and learn more about the book. You might also do a little research on the book's reception and sales (if data is available). If all this still makes you think this is a good comp for your book, bring it into this section of the proposal.

Here are possible domains of your compare/contrast work:
- Author (how the author's position, reputation, or perspective is the same or different from yours)
- Main message (is the message the same or different, if different, how and why does that matter to your readership)
- Their project (i.e., the work they are doing in their book) and how they are carrying out that project (structure, approach)
- Contents/structure of the book
- Inclusion or exclusion of a particular angle or perspective
- Tone or style of the book
- Intended audience for the book

In this section, account for the book at a summary level (think back-of-book description sentence or two), then explain how this book is like yours, and how it is different. The point is to show that there is an existing audience for your book, "People already buy and read books like mine," but some aspect of your book is unique and not yet contributed to the larger conversation *and* is something your readership wants and will benefit from: "My book is unique because…readers will benefit from this because…" You don't have to make your book look better than the comp book. Instead, think of this as niche work: you are showing that your book has a unique niche in the ecosystem of your topic and genre.

BOOK TABLE OF CONTENTS

This is just what it sounds like, the planned chapters of your book in order, as best you know them. This is a short section and pretty straightforward.

CHAPTER ABSTRACTS OR CHAPTER SUMMARIES

This section goes chapter by chapter, giving a brief, high-level summary of what you will do and say in each chapter and how that will benefit the reader. Don't get into the content of the chapter itself; you need to stay at a high level and "meta" here. Don't include parts of the chapter; rather, talk about the chapter. Say what the chapter is going to cover (content), how it will cover that content (structure), and how that is going to contribute to the book and the reader's experience (the why).

SAMPLE CHAPTERS

You'll likely choose two or three chapters (5000 to 10,000 words total) you want to write and showcase in your book proposal. They are often the first chapter (not the introduction) and a middle chapter. You'll want to share your strongest writing while giving your proposal reviewers a good glimpse into what they can expect in your book. Show that you can deliver on the proposal's promise and showcase your best work.

Hopefully, this chapter has provided you with a much clearer picture of what book proposals require and more about what agents and publishers are looking for. If this all feels daunting, remember that proposal writing is new territory: none of us has practice in writing something like this (unless you are already a traditionally published author or work in grant writing or something similar). Go slow, get the help you need, and just present the strongest case you honestly can for you and your book. Be confident and believe in yourself and your book.

CHAPTER 41

The Indie Publishing Path

As we have covered in earlier chapters, the indie publishing path presents a range of options—from fully supported author services to a complete DIY approach to self-publishing your book yourself.

Types of Indie Publishing

FULL-SERVICE INDIE PUBLISHING AGENCIES

Individuals and companies can do the work of getting your manuscript through production, publication, and distribution for you. They will typically have an in-house team of designers, editors, and marketers who can get your book published without you having to take the time and energy to hire your own team and learn the industry. For many busy professionals, these services respond wisely to a need in the market. If you have the money to invest in your project and don't have an interest in learning the ins and outs of the publishing world, this can be an attractive option.

Do your homework, as many of these services vary widely in the marketplace. You want to look for a service that charges a clearly articulated upfront fee for a clearly articulated set of services, doesn't take any rights to your work, and doesn't take a cut of your book sales (meaning they pass 100 percent of net sales to you as the author). Know that with some of these options, there is no guarantee your book will be stocked in bookstores. (Whale Song Creative is my agency that offers this type of publishing support.)

HYBRID PUBLISHING OPTIONS

Hybrid publishers offer a blend of traditional and self-publishing services. These can be a tricky option to navigate because there are different levels and models of services (with differing levels of benefit to authors).

One kind of hybrid publisher is editorially curated, which means they are somewhat selective in the titles they choose. In these models, authors pay upfront for some portion of the production costs, the company takes a portion of the sales/royalties, and they may do some work to get your book into physical bookstores.

Another hybrid option is crowdfunding-driven, where the author must raise a portion of funds from their audience before they are given a book deal or are published, and once that money is raised, the company will offer services akin to a traditional publisher. Examples are Unbound and Inkshares.

Some hybrid publishers, such as certain traditional publishers with a self-publishing arm, can have the most questionable value for authors. (I shall not name names here.) One of the biggest warnings with these types of publishers is that they don't offer the value of a traditional publisher in exchange for your upfront cost, share of royalties, and so on. In other words, you pay a lot for not much in return.

A good hybrid publisher will have a method of curating the titles they publish, evaluating the market potential of prospective books, and considering their chances of success. These hybrids should also offer to market and distribute your book into physical bookstores beyond what you can do (which is to list your book on IngramSpark). Hybrids should also offer pre- and post-publication support and a clear marketing plan. Make sure you consider what they are offering you that you cannot do alone. And if you go with one of these options, do your research thoroughly and know exactly what you are getting and giving with this publishing option.

DIY SELF-PUBLISHING

Do-It-Yourself (DIY) self-publishing is where you are the creative director and project manager for your book's editorial, production, publication, distribution, and marketing efforts. Most people understandably feel overwhelmed by this list, but self-publishing can be learned and mastered, even by busy professionals. Like book writing, you take one step at a time and seek qualified support along the way.

CROWDFUNDING YOUR BOOK

Raising funds for your book editing, design, production, and marketing efforts through Kickstarter, Indiegogo, or a similar crowdfunding platform can be a fabulous way to offset self-publishing costs, promote your book, and create strong pre-sale momentum for your book. I personally ran a successful Kickstarter campaign for my book *Birth Your Story*. I'd definitely recommend considering this option if you want to go the indie publishing path. It takes some effort to put together and promote a successful campaign, but it can really help indie authors offset the costs of book publishing while building an engaged readership.

The Self-Publishing Process

STEP ONE: WRITE

First, you finish your first draft of your manuscript. Pretty straightforward.

STEP TWO: EDIT

Second, you move into the *editorial* phase. In this phase, you work with developmental editors, copyeditors or line editors, and proofreaders to shape your book into its final form (see Chapter 35 for details about each of these phases of the professional editing process). This is also a good time to start seeking beta readers, book endorsements, and a Foreword author (more about those in the next section).

I will emphasize again: the editorial phase is important and takes time to do well. I don't recommend trying to publish your book without comprehensive professional support. No, sorry, your slick editing software or the latest AI does not replace the careful work of an actual human being. Your ethos and the success of your book depend on your commitment to doing this phase thoroughly and effectively.

This is also the phase where you will want to complete all the front and back materials for your book (see Chapter 36) and seek endorsements (see Appendix E).

STEP THREE: DESIGN AND PRODUCTION

Interior formatting: When all the proverbial I's have been dotted and T's crossed, the next step is to have the interior of your book formatted (or designed) for both print and digital (eBook) formats. You can DIY this, but I don't recommend it. At the minimum, I'd use a professional book design software program, such as Vellum, which is great but does have design limitations (and is not appropriate for workbooks and those with special design features, such as callout boxes). If you want the best quality and most ease, hire a professional. Again, if you skimp on this stage, it will show, and you risk losing credibility in the eyes of your readers.

Outside Cover: You'll also need to have your book cover designed. In addition to the cost of your book cover, factor in the cost of any art or photography for the front cover, as well as a professional author photo for the back. Don't skimp on the book cover; it is your book's first impression and must be done *well* by a professional who understands cover design best practices. Don't just hire any graphic designer, but find someone who specializes in book covers specifically. There are specific conventions and technical details a designer must have a good handle on to create a strong book cover design.

ISBNs: You'll need to purchase an ISBN (International Standard Book Number) from Bowker at myindentifiers.com.

Copyright Permissions: If you need to get permission from other publishers to use any quoted material in your book, I recommend doing so early in the production process or even late in the editing process. This can take weeks if not months, and you don't want to be held up waiting for permissions when you are ready to publish your book. See Appendix D for more about permissions.

Indexing: Most indie-published books do not require an index. However, if your subject matter lends itself to the inclusion of this resource, you can definitely find a professional indexer. Note that this will likely be a print book-only index, as a hyperlinked eBook index is a separate service. Be sure to factor into your publication timeline the time it takes to create an index, which can be one to two additional months.

STEP FOUR: DISTRIBUTION

You have many options at this point, but I will simplify this realm and share what I recommend. You are welcome and encouraged to do your own research to determine how you would like to handle distribution. Things are changing in the industry all the time; so, this is subject to change, but this has been my approach for many years.

Print Books: Here is what I consider the optimal approach for most authors when it comes to distribution platforms. There are other great options you might consider, depending on your print and distribution needs, but these are the most common.

1. You publish your book to **Amazon's KDP** for sales on Amazon.com and its international affiliates. You may also choose to put your book on Amazon as an eBook, or just the print version.
2. You also publish your book to **IngramSpark**. Ingram is the world's largest wholesale distributor to bookstores. If you want to make your book available for print retailers, you want to use Ingram. This won't guarantee distribution in brick-and-mortar stores, but it is the way in for indie publishers. You can approach bookstores with your Ingram-published book, and they will consider it. I've never met or heard of a bookstore that will buy your book from Amazon to carry in their stores.

Both of these are print-on-demand distributors, which means you pay little to no money for publishing on these platforms, and they only print books when they are sold, which means you don't pay for a large upfront print run or warehousing your stock of books. They earn money through royalties when you sell your books.

These services are also at-will (meaning you can take your book off their platform at any time) and non-exclusive (meaning they don't own any rights to your book, and you are not hindered in what other platforms you distribute your book through). Their print quality is akin to that of traditional publishers, and readers can rarely tell the difference between a self-published and traditionally published book in terms of print quality. Your design and formatting will also obviously have the biggest effect on readers' perceptions of quality.

eBooks: I recommend distributing your eBook on a platform that channels your book to multiple sources. For example, Draft2Digital, a company I recommend, distributes your book to numerous eBook platforms at once. You can also use Amazon KDP and IngramSpark.

Pricing: At the time of this writing, I recommend pricing your eBook between $2.99 and $9.99 USD. I recommend pricing your print book wherever you want it. The standard for paperback books is between $12 and $25 per book, with hardback pricing between $20 and $30.

Print Proofs: During this step, you will also want to get printed proofs of your books from Amazon and IngramSpark. You want to make sure the spine alignment, colors, and other design features come out as desired. I had to go back and forth several times with Amazon to get the colors correct on the printing of one of my books. Note that it does cost money and time to review proofs, so factor this into your timeline. If you delayed proofreading until this stage, you'll also want to carefully comb through the book now and ensure all writing and formatting is error-free.

Audiobooks: Audiobooks are another option to consider. Essentially, you can record your book yourself or hire a professional narrator to narrate your book. Companies I work with also have excellent options for at-home audiobook narration, although it will require that you purchase equipment. The landscape of audiobooks is changing all the time, so I will refrain from making any specific mentions here, but know that Whale Song is happy to make more specific recommendations.

Publication Date and Pre-Sales: During this phase, you will also set a publication date and have the opportunity to do pre-sales. If you are ready to launch right away, it typically takes Amazon about two to three days to make your book available, and Ingram can take a couple of weeks.

STEP FIVE: BOOK AMBASSADORSHIP

At some point, we shift from being just the writers of our books to also being their ambassadors in the world. I recommend that you begin to consider building an engaged readership well before you plan to publish your book. The sooner the better, but at least aim for several months prior to launch. Generally speaking, you will absolutely want to create a marketing plan that begins before your release date and continues for at least the first three months of your book's life. It is better to consider a yearlong or multi-year plan to build awareness and interest in your book and your related work (if relevant). More about this in the next chapter, onward!

CHAPTER 42

Book Marketing and Promotion

Maybe you're someone who *loves* marketing and feels passionate about building an audience and selling your products and services. Or perhaps, you're like a lot of writers I've worked with—you *love* the process of writing your book, but the idea of marketing and promoting your work feels overwhelming, or even downright repulsive. You started writing to share your message, not to become a marketing pro!

Trust me, you're not alone. Many writers feel uncertain about where to start, resistant to the process, or overwhelmed at yet another to-do on the list. Often, people hope for a quick fix or shortcut—some marketing expert to come along, wave a magic wand, and grant you immediate, easy book bestselling success.

But here's the truth: author platforms aren't built overnight. Nor are they handed to us. They grow through time, care, and consistency.

The good news is you don't have to figure it all out on your own! Here, I will give some high-level information about book marketing, platform-building, and promotion. Note that you'll need to be at the helm of your marketing efforts, whether you publish traditionally or independently.

In best practice, it is wise to look at book marketing as being less about you and your book and more about your readership. You want to consistently convey the value you are providing through your book and larger work. To market effectively, get crystal clear about whom you are marketing to (which you likely articulated for yourself back in Chapter 6) and how best to reach them.

Author Platform

Whether you traditionally or independently publish, you'll want to have a way to reach your readers directly and sell your books. This is your *author platform*, an umbrella of all your author marketing strategies.

Author outreach is anything you do that takes people from not knowing you exist to knowing you exist, and it can be a crucial part of developing your author platform. Put simply, you want to get clear on your ideal intended audiences—who you want to be talking to and who is likely to buy your book and enjoy your work. (Again, see Chapter 6.)

Next, you want to identify where those people are in person and online and how you might show up in those places and deliver presence and value. You may also identify those who already have an influence on these people and where they hang out. With influencers, you can discover how to offer each other mutual benefits by collaborating. Reach out to those folks and see what might be possible. For example, can you do an interview, a podcast, or offer a guest post of content they can share? Sometimes, it's wise to offer value before you ask for support; find ways to offer mutual benefit to one another.

Author content is what you offer to the world through written, audio, visual, and video/multimedia that helps people know, like, and value you and the work you are creating and sharing in the world. Content can be used across multiple channels.

There's no one-size-fits-all strategy when it comes to building your author platform—and that's a good thing! You can create a platform that feels authentic and sustainable for you. Start by considering your strengths and preferences.

Do you love writing but dread video content? Focus on blogging, email newsletters, and guest articles.

Do you thrive in talking about your topic to others? Leaning into podcasts, webinars, and live events could feel more rewarding for you.

As your book evolves, your platform can, too. You might start with one channel and expand into others as your confidence and audience grow. Remember, your platform is not just about selling books; it's about building a community, sparking conversations, and sharing your unique voice with the world.

Think of your platform like planting seeds in different places (but not everywhere!) so readers can find and engage with your work. All of this makes it easier when it is time to promote your book.

Author platform-building is not a one-time effort or something to consider only a week before you launch your book. It's wise to begin building these connections with your potential readers as early in the process as possible.

> ## NOTE ABOUT DIGITAL PLATFORM-BUILDING
>
> One thing to note, when it comes to digital platforms, is the difference between an author-owned platform and a platform owned by someone else. An author-owned platform is one that you build for yourself and that belongs to you. Examples include: your website, your email marketing list, your podcast, your videos, your in-person contact list, and so on. Platforms like Facebook, Instagram, and so on *are not yours*. If they change their algorithms, go dark one day, or decide to put you in their proverbial purgatory for some likely unfair reason, you lose access to the people you were connecting with on that platform. No bueno.
>
> Be smart. If you find your people on a platform you do not own, do your best to encourage them to connect with you on a platform you do own. Invite them onto your email list, to listen to your podcast, or visit your website. Bring them into a space that you manage, not Zuckerberg. Just sayin'.

Author Website

Your author website is the digital "home" for your book. While an author website is just one strategy you can use to build an author platform, we are going to talk about it first, since it is one that I do recommend you have. See the box about Digital Platform-Building for just some of those reasons.

You'll have to make the call about whether you'll create a website just for your book or add it to an existing website, if you have one. Many book marketing professionals suggest you make your web presence platform-centric (going beyond this single book) rather than book-centric (focusing only on this book). For the former, you would make your URL your name (not your book title) and focus on you primarily and you as an author secondarily. It's up to you how you want to do this.

I suggest working with a web designer to build or design your website. The following is a high-level list of important areas to include in your author website:

- **Opt-in/lead magnet/freebie:** This should be the number-one call to action on your website. You offer something of value to people for free in exchange for their email address and permission to contact them again by email. Your opt-in can be a sample of your book or related content that provides immediate value to your potential reader, connects you to them, and allows you to continue nurturing the relationship with them through additional content.

- **Bonus content:** Any additional resources you want to offer your readers besides the content of your book. It can be for public consumption or just for purchasers of your book.

- **Author bio:** Tell people who you are and why they should buy your book.

- **Book sales page:** This is the place where you tell your reader about your book and its value. You may want to include endorsements/social proof, an enticing description of your book, your book's unique value, who the book is for, why they will love it, a video trailer, and images. Be sure to have direct links to where they can purchase your book.

- **Author speaker's page:** (if relevant) Here, you will share that you are available for speaking opportunities (and be specific on what topics), and include previous speaking engagements and upcoming opportunities to see you or work with you.

- **Related blog content:** You can establish more credibility on your topic with content that shows your expertise in your topic area. A blog is a great way to increase your SEO and drive traffic (visitors) to your website.

- **Audio and video content:** Consider adding videos by connecting your YouTube channel (if you have one) to your website. You can add any videos that tie in with your messaging, such as your author introduction video and videos featuring you as a speaker or podcast guest. Only add your YouTube channel if the content is supportive of your author ethos and your book.

- **Featured publications:** Link to podcasts, blogs, and other publications where you have been a featured writer, interviewee, or host.

Book Marketing and Platform-Building Strategies

The good news is that you don't have to be everywhere and do everything. In fact, trying to do so can be a major factor in an author's struggle with book marketing. Instead, focus on where your readers are and what feels natural to you.

Analytics can help you be more targeted. The key is to choose the methods you enjoy and can commit to consistently—showing up meaningfully in a few places is far more effective than spreading yourself thin across every platform.

These are all places that you can begin to build your author presence and relationships with your ideal readers as you write, edit, and publish your book…and beyond.

- **Social Media:** Pick one to three platforms where your readers gather—YouTube, LinkedIn, Instagram, or Facebook—and engage meaningfully.
- **Email Marketing:** Build a nurture sequence and show up consistently—once a month at a minimum—to provide value.
- **Podcasting:** Be a guest or start your own show.
- **Live Events:** Speak at workshops, book talks, retreats, or conferences.
- **Collaborations:** Partner with influencers, businesses, organizations, associations, churches, universities, and so on (and around launch, bookstores).
- **Guest Articles:** Write for print or digital publications.
- **Guest Teaching** in another person's paid program or group.

Before, during, and after your book launch phase, these additional strategies can be helpful to get the word out about your book:

- **Amazon:** Create an author's page and presence, and explore options to get on the best sellers list.
- **Book Clubs:** Offer virtual or in-person visits.
- **Book Tour:** This can be a physical tour where you go to different geographic locations to speak about your book or offer related workshops and events. You can also do a podcast or blog tour from the comfort of your home.
- **Live Events:** Book talks, speeches on your topic, workshops, classes, and retreats.
- **Conferences and Expos:** Give talks. Network. Have a table in the vendor area where you can promote your book.
- **Book Trailer** on YouTube or similar.
- **Affiliate or Influencer Marketing:** Partner with influencers who can share your book with their audiences in exchange for commissions or collaborations.
- **Paid Ads:** Amplify your reach selectively. You may want to hire a professional to help.
- **Traditional Media PR:** Pitch your book to secure interviews and media coverage.
- **Book Giveaways or Sales:** Run limited-time promotions or contests to encourage reviews and attract new readers.
- **Strategic Book Donations:** Donate copies to libraries, schools, or community centers to increase visibility and gain new readers.
- **Related Services/Your Book Ecosystem:** Develop related digital products and professional services to offer to your ideal client base.

What other ways can you think of to promote, share, and raise awareness about your book?

_____

_____

_____

_____

CONCLUSION

And so, we come to the end of this book, which may or may not be the end of your own author adventure. Whether you've journeyed through this book and still have your own adventure to undertake, or you find yourself at the summit of a book project, I want to congratulate you for getting this far and for all the ways you've shown up for yourself, your soul, your creativity, your voice, and your book project so far. Keep going. And don't forget to pause regularly and celebrate all the milestones along your path. (Even the seemingly tiny ones.)

No matter where you are, I encourage you here, at this book's end, to remember your why. *Why do you care to learn the art and craft of writing a book? Why is it worth all your time, energy, and attention to write in the first place? What is at stake for you here? What matters to you?*

For me and the many authors I work with, we write because it is our soul's deepest longing to do so. We write to explore and articulate our experiences, to liberate our voices, to find freedom and self-empowerment through authentic expression, to dare to take up space, to claim that our ideas and stories matter, to offer our deepest service to the world, to share with others what has helped us so profoundly on the journey of being human, to leave a legacy for our families and communities, and so much more.

Through all the twists and turns of your author adventure, keep coming back to the pulse of your own creativity, to your why, to the wise heart inside your very own chest. This journey is long but it is profoundly rich. I can almost guarantee that when you get to the end of your days, you will not regret a single moment you devoted to your own creative expression. I deeply honor and bow to you for your courage to keep on navigating this path, through easy segments and more challenging passes.

I encourage you to return to this book whenever you are needing a refresher on any aspect of the author adventure. Of course, this book is not conclusive nor fully comprehensive. I could add to this book for ages, but then you'd never hold it in your hands. Your book will be the same. You'll know there is more to say, you'll know there are gaps, you'll know the story of your life and/or your understanding of your topic will continue to grow and evolve beyond the snapshot moment when you hit "publish." Book writing is a bit of a paradox—the book ends but the actual journey never does. We have to make peace with that. We have to say, this is good enough.

In that spirit, I find myself ready enough to say, *this is good enough*. I hope you'll stay connected to my work and the work of Whale Song, as there is more to be said and so much more to be shared.

When we seek to write a meaningful book from our soul, it is never just about getting the words on the page, it is about our unfolding experience of ourselves and the world, as we write and as a result of writing. It is my most profound honor to companion courageous creatives like you on this journey of personal transformation we call book writing. As I said at the outset, this book covers much of the nuts-and-bolts information you need to write a book—yet, the journey of your soul through the process is a whole other rich layer of inquiry. No matter what your author adventure looks like, I hope you are able to deeply honor the personal transformations underway and that you feel abundantly supported, seen and celebrated as you navigate the adventure of becoming an author. Your voice matters, your stories and ideas matter, and you matter. Never forget that. And if you do forget, find a creative companion to remind you.

It has been a pleasure to companion you in this way, and I look forward to when our paths meet again.

APPENDICES

APPENDIX A

Audience Awareness
(Originally published as a blog article)

What happens when your truth offends your reader?
As authors, how do we deal with audience consideration while maintaining alignment with our truth and purpose for expression?

These are some of the questions that arise regularly in my book coaching work with authors.

One of my current clients is working on a memoir. We're deep in workshopping mode, which means that biweekly, she sends me a chapter of her book-in-progress, I review it, and we hop on a call to dive deeper.

A few passages in this chapter gave me pause. When I read for a book coaching client, I am present to and monitoring many elements of their writing. One thing I do is read as if I'm the author's intended audience and consider the objections, agreements, emotions, and other reactions they may have as they read.

In this chapter, my client was exposing her vulnerable inner landscape around an experience that challenged her fundamental beliefs and ideas. She was also bravely entering tender and highly politicized territory—around gender identity—expressing values and opinions that may not align with those of her intended audience.

Getting to the truth of your experiences and sharing them with others is about the most vulnerable thing you can do, and it's what makes memoir rich and engaging. It's essential, yet no small task for any human daring to bare their soul on paper.

While this authentic truth-telling is so incredibly valuable, we also must balance it with a consideration of our audiences. Because we aren't writing in a vacuum—the effects we have through our writing are real, and they matter.

How do you stay authentic and aligned with your perspective, purpose, and truth while also considering others' reactions to your writing? And the consequences of that reaction?

I love this quote by Nonviolent Communication teacher Miki Kashtan:

> "It's not my job to prevent others from reacting to me.
> It's only my job to act with integrity,
> which also includes caring for the impact."

I like how Kashtan distinguishes between responsibility and care. We're not responsible for managing our audience's reaction to our truths, but we should act with integrity and care about the *impact* our words might have. It's a subtle but important distinction. I call this act of caring about and considering the impact of your message *knowing the field*.

Knowing the Field

"Knowing the field" is the process of becoming *aware* of our message's potential effects on our reader and making grounded decisions about how and what we express. These decisions are grounded in our consideration of three elements:

- What we imagine our audience's reaction could be, or what our audience's reaction actually is (if we have beta readers, for example, who read our drafts prior to publishing)
- Our intended purpose in a section
- Our alignment with our own creativity, truth, and integrity

Let me give you two examples of how this might look: one from my client and one from my experience writing *Birth Your Story*.

Client Story

When my client and I spoke, I genuinely acknowledged and honored her honesty in this chapter. I also noted my concern that some passages might have an undesirable effect on some readers, causing them to disagree with her opinions and get distracted away from the storyline. At worst, I worried they might stop reading before they got to the point of better understanding her perspective.

We had a paradox on our hands. On the one hand, it was vital that she express what was true for her in the story she was recounting. On the other hand, we needed to be sensitive to potential audience objections because having readers turn off and stop reading is not our desired impact as authors.

We talked about how to align with her truth *and* maintain good graces with her audience. Our solution was to add more detail about the contributing factors to her perspective so her audience could have a better understanding of where she was coming from—to be able to empathize with her point of view (even if they didn't share her sentiments). We also explored how she could strengthen the end of the chapter to show how she grew in a challenging and affronting situation, because that was relatable and showed character growth, which is good for the ethos.

In making these minor but important adjustments, she was able to maintain the expression of her personal truth *and* mitigate the chances of offending her audience to the point of turning them off.

The point of "knowing the field" isn't to make sure you never offend or evoke strong emotions in your audience. It's about carefully considering the potential impact of your writing so you can make wise decisions about how you want to express yourself and what effect that may have.

And you might decide to keep more provocative or controversial elements of expression in your writing. You might be willing to offend for the sake of aligning with your truth. This, by the way, is what makes so many truth-tellers total badasses: they dare to speak their honest truth, regardless of the outcome.

Writing a book is not meant to be a please-all-people endeavor as much as it is a tell-my-truth-with-integrity sort of mission. Telling our truth *with integrity* requires that we consider all possible factors and outcomes as we navigate our narrative boats into a potential storm.

This brings me to my next example, an experience I had with my book.

Birth Your Story

In *Birth Your Story*, I write about the cultural narrative of birth: the ideas and perspectives about birth that are imposed on us through our media, culture, and kin and that invariably influence our expectations and experiences of birth-giving.

In the original draft, I very cheekily set forth what I believed was the cultural narrative of birth. Things like "You're *supposed* to breastfeed and have that go easily," and "You're *supposed* to labor with the support of your partner, who took the classes and knows all the things to support you perfectly," and "You're *supposed* to be able to birth according to your birth plan." I believed I was offering an accurate snapshot of what our dominant culture tells us about birth, though I neither agreed with nor wanted to perpetuate this dominant narrative.

Every one of my beta readers—mostly birth professionals who have dedicated their careers to dismantling disempowering aspects of the dominant birth narrative—had an intense emotional reaction to the snapshot I'd presented.

Each reader came to me wanting to debate the veracity of my claims and the politics of birth. So, I had to check myself. I still held true to the picture I'd painted. And I wasn't afraid to challenge my readers. But I had to consider my impact. The effects of my writing did not match my purpose for the section.

My purpose in the section was to invite readers to consider how the dominant birth narrative—however they defined it—influenced *their* birth experience. My purpose was not to wade into birth politics to advocate for my specific views and values.

In fact, I'd written my book in an intentionally apolitical way because my overall purpose was to make the book inclusive to all parents, regardless of their beliefs, births, or backgrounds.

If I were writing a treatise on the way birth *should* be in our culture, I'd be willing to make politicized arguments about the dominant messaging around birth. But it was neither the time nor the place for that.

Through coming to "know the field" more completely, I realized it wasn't important that my reader know or agree with *my* perspective on the cultural birth narrative but rather that they become clearly aware of their *own* perspectives.

I replaced my view of the cultural narrative with a series of reflection questions that would help my audience locate, acknowledge, and clarify their views. And I double-checked with myself to make sure I was still in integrity with my own truth in this section, which I was. I felt good about the changes I'd made.

In Summary

This is "knowing the field." You take all factors into consideration and use your deep knowledge of context to make conscious decisions around your expression. You load up the scales—on one side, your truth, desired message, integrity, and purpose; on the other side, your audience's potential responses—and you do your best to navigate it all with the utmost awareness and integrity. It isn't about pitting one side against the other but about seeing how they all play together so you can consciously direct the course of action.

I encourage writers to express their unadulterated truths first and consider the impact of their truths on others second. We must have safe places to tell the truth about our lives—and writing is one of the most sacred of these places. So often, simply telling the truth about our experiences *to ourselves* is a radical, world-wobbling act. But it is so vital to our souls. And we must protect it with the fierceness of a mammal mama.

And yet, our communication through books is interpersonal, so we ripple out from our experience to the experience of others, we come to care about our impact, and we make wise choices based on deep and careful consideration. We don't have to barter our souls away in the process. We get to find that place where our truth, our purpose, and our care for others work in harmony. That is the sweet spot.

APPENDIX B

SKETCHY FIRST DRAFTS
ORIGINALLY A BLOG ARTICLE

"When I write, I feel like an armless, legless man with a crayon in his mouth."
— KURT VONNEGUT

There is something you must know about the writers you love. It's 90 percent likely that the words you so cherish, in their polished form, are not at all the words that first landed on the page directly from your beloved writer's mind.

That is not how this writing game works.

Sometimes, we do, in fact, write something so brilliant and beautiful and perfect on the very first go, but *much* more often, we need to work at it.

It is a huge myth—and a huge disservice to all those with a book or story that longs to be written—to believe that the first draft has to be *good*.

Your first draft is not about making it *good*; it's about getting it *out*.

Let that sink in: **Your first draft is *not* about making it *good*; it's about getting it *out*.**

It's your vomit draft. It's where you empty out the purse or bag to see what it contains. It's *sketchy*.

I know this can be both a huge relief and a major pain in the ass. A huge relief because this truth lets us off the hook for perfection (or even decent) out of the gate. (By the way, there is no perfection ever anyway, so we might as well get over that one, too.) And this is a major pain in the ass because it means work for us. It means doing the hard work of getting it—whatever the hell "it" is—out on paper, however awkward or messy.

It's about facing all that will arise inside of us when we do—the judgments, comparisons, discouragement, and critical assessments of our creativity—and that is *hard*. (But also totally doable.)

It means that we also need to work with this first draft patiently and carefully to shape it into the most potent expression of what is inside of us. And that takes time, and that takes effort.

Don't just take my word for it; many of the greatest authors have my back on this one. Anne Lamott, in her book *Bird by Bird: Some Instructions on Writing and Life*, covers this very topic in a whole chapter, which she calls "Shitty First Drafts."

She writes:

> *"All good writers write [shitty first drafts]. This is how they end up with the good second drafts and terrific third drafts.*
>
> *People tend to look at successful writers [...] and think that they sit down at their desks every morning [...] feeling great about who they are and how much talent they have and what a great story they have to tell [...] but this is just fantasy of the uninitiated.*
>
> *[Of the very great writers I know,] not one of them sits down routinely feeling wildly enthusiastic and confident. Not one of them writes elegant first drafts.*
>
> *The only way I can get anything written at all is to write really, really shitty first drafts. [...] Just get it all down on paper."*

I quote her extensively (and really, you should just go buy her book because it is phenomenal) to make the point: First drafts are meant to be shitty. Stormy. Sketchy. Messy. No good. All over the place.

Your job is to get the words down on paper.

Your job is to excavate your insides for the truth and let it come out: wild, messy, and uncensored.

It doesn't matter whether you hate what you write or think it totally sucks. It doesn't matter.

It only matters that you allow yourself to become a clear channel for what wants to come through, and you don't stop until you're done.

That you get out of the way of the creativity that wants to come through you.

That you trust that you will have time and space to shape it later.

That you trust what you are doing is absolutely the "way" to write.

This takes great courage and grit. And you've got it.

So let your first drafts be shitty (or sketchy), even if that kills you a little inside. (It's not actually a killing sensation you are registering, but an initiating, molding, transforming, creative, and generative one.)

APPENDIX C

Research

Whether it's simply locating a street or restaurant name for your memoir; finding an epigraph quote for each chapter; or extensively compiling data, interviews, and stories to solidly support your ideas, virtually all nonfiction works, including memoir, require at least some research.

A Book as a Conversation

We can think of every book as a voice within a larger collective conversation. As such, we are speaking to and with others through our book. Part of how we do so is by bringing in others' ideas and voices into our books. This builds credibility because it shows we are well-informed about our area of exploration. It also helps us build a solid case for our way of seeing things. To bring in others' ideas and voices in a way that serves our project, we need to conduct some kind of research.

Research as Resistance

For some authors, the research stage of their project is a place for their resistance to rear up and prevent them from writing. These are often people who feel most comfortable and familiar with referring to others' work and folks who fear they don't have enough authority or knowledge to speak on their subject (hello, Inner Critic, here you are again!).

The thing about writing your book is that *you* are the authority and the main speaker. (The only exceptions might be an interview book or anthology, but even with these, your framework is the glue that holds it together.)

We must work with our Inner Critic to align with this concept. Your ideas, stories, and voice will and must take center stage in your book. We use others' voices and our research *to serve our own work*. Let's keep this in mind as we think of research.

Here are a few clues that you may be stuck down a research rabbit hole that is adding resistance to your creative momentum:

- You're accumulating books on a subject that will only get a passing mention in your book.
- You're convinced you must read everything ever written about your topic before you can begin.
- A single hour of scheduled research regularly turns into an entire day.
- You're stuck in the research-as-comparison trap.
- The world of information you find yourself in is minimally related to the work of your book.

I suggest giving yourself clarity and boundaries around your research process, which we are about to discuss further.

Research as Part of the Creative Cycle

Just like any creative project, book writing has four clear *seasons*:

1. Spring: the research, planning, organizing, and idea development stages
2. Summer: the phase of producing your work—of actually writing your draft
3. Fall: a time for reflection and assessment, also a time of revision, editing, and review
4. Winter: a fruitful darkness where it doesn't seem like much is happening, yet this is the place from which all creation is sourced. It could be time spent in a quiet state or seemingly not working on your book

So, while spring often feels great and energizing for many of us—and this is the research phase, remember—it is important not to get stuck here.

What Kind of Research Does Your Project Require?

First, you will want to decide what kind of research your book project warrants. To determine this, consider the kind of *evidence* you plan to present to support your claims/ideas/concepts in your book. (If you've already clarified what kind of evidence you plan to have, this is a good time to review that list.)

- Do you want to include case studies? How will you gather that information?
- Do you need to interview your past clients? Experts? Members of your target market?
- Do you plan to share the results of academic studies? Where will you find these?
- Will you reference the work of other authors in your field?
- What other questions are important to answer about your research project?

Another kind of research activity that may be appropriate to your project is to mine your existing content (journals, blogs, articles, and social media posts) for the information and content you plan to incorporate into your book.

What kind of research does your project require?

_____
_____
_____
_____
_____
_____
_____

DISCOVER SHORTCUTS

While much of the book-*writing* process must be done by the author, research is one of those areas that is outsourceable. Do you have anyone on your team who could put some time into executing your research plan? Could you hire a local college student to help you conduct your research?

In most cases, we are not the first to be researching our book subjects. What resources can you tap into that have already compiled research on your topic? For example, is there a professor at your local university you could speak with? Is there an expert on one of your topic areas that you could interview? Are there literature reviews, meta-analyses, or book reviews on your subject area? Can you look at the bibliographies and works cited pages of relevant articles and books to find good source material for your project?

What kind of shortcuts can you use in your research process?

_____
_____
_____
_____

Develop a Clear, Concrete + Actionable Research Plan

The more concrete, clear, specific, and actionable your research plan, the more likely you will be successful in this phase of your writing project. Use these questions to craft your research plan.

When will you do your research? Specifically, what dates and times will you devote to your research process? What amount of time (i.e., how many hours?) will you give yourself on these dates for your research process? (You'll want to be as realistic as possible about how long this research activity will take.)

___

How will you do your research on these days? What specific activities will you carry out on your planned research days? Will you visit the library database and search for academic articles? Will you hop on a recorded call to interview someone? Will you be reviewing a book?

___

Where will you do this research? In what specific location will you carry out this research? At home? The library? A coffee shop? Another location?

___

Next, and this is critical, put your research time *in your calendar*. If it's not on your calendar, it's unlikely you will follow through on your research plan. Never, ever, underestimate the power of scheduling your research time into your calendar. It's a powerful motivator and a necessary container of self-accountability. Take out your calendar and schedule your research time now.

DETERMINE AN END DATE

Next, you'll want to set a clear end date for your research process. This is the date by which, no matter how far you've come in your research process, you will switch gears—moving from spring to summer—and begin your writing.

What is the date by which you will complete your research? What are the research goals you would like to meet by this date?

Your research end date: _____

Goals: _____

Ways to Track and Manage Your Research

Make sure you keep track of your resources and references as you go. There are many ways of doing this, and determining yours will be a personal process. However, here are three suggestions.

USE COLOR AS AN ORGANIZING ALLY

Consider getting a stack of sticky notes, highlighters, folders, or other organizational supplies in all different colors. Next, determine what each color will represent for you in your research process. There are different ways to use this representation system.

1: By (sub) *topic*

You may choose a color for each subtopic of your book. For example, green represents step one of my five-step process. Blue represents step two.

For example, if you get an idea for something you want to ensure you say in step one of your book, jot down that note on a green Post-it, in your green folder, or in the "Green" document on your computer.

2: By *research* type

You may organize your research by the type of research it is.

For example, all green might represent interview materials you'll use for case studies. Blue might be expert testimony. Red might be personal stories from your existing content.

3: By *intended use*

Another way is to organize your research by how you intend to use it.

For example, pink might be my color code for all material I want to quote directly in my book. Purple means I plan to summarize or paraphrase this material. Blue means that these are work/ideas I want to question and pose a counterargument to in my own writing. Red is a fact or statistic I want to include.

You can use this color-coding system in your organization and outlining process and in your note-taking and idea-documenting process.

USE TECHNOLOGY AS AN ALLY

Elsewhere, we've explored using tools like Scrivener and Evernote to track your research, ideas, and organization. You may also wish to harness the power of these tools in your research process. Perhaps in Evernote or Scrivener, you make separate folders for resources, by topic, research type, or intended use.

WHAT MATTERS

The important thing is to come up with a system that will work for you and to actually implement the system, tweaking where needed to make it a success.

What kind of system do you feel will help you create success in organizing and tracking your research?

_____
_____
_____
_____

Organization is essential and will set you up for research success. That said, if you've already done a ton of research, don't get yourself stuck by trying to go backward and implementing a system that will be labor-intensive to execute to the full extent. In other words, you don't want to get bogged down with organizing your past research. You might consider how you can implement *some* organization of your old research so it plays nicely with the new system you are implementing, without getting mired in a process that doesn't carry you forward.

Using Your Research

Release the idea that you will use all the amazing information you compiled during your research. In fact, much of our research may never work itself into our final drafts. Sometimes, we have something important, a key concept or idea, that won't fit into our main manuscript, but we feel it is really important to share or mention. In this case, you might consider releasing this material as a bonus on your website/newsletter/blog, or put it in the appendix. This is good to be aware of but will likely not become a present consideration until well into your writing process or during revision. I suggest returning to this later.

HOW TO DOCUMENT YOUR SOURCES

You'll essentially have two kinds of source materials: 1) sources you have directly referenced (e.g., quoted, paraphrased, summarized) in your book, and 2) sources you have consulted (perhaps they have shaped or influenced your material and you want to give them credit), even though you never directly mention them in your book.

An example of the latter in my book *Birth Your Story* would be my appendix section, where I take people through a process fundamental to the practice of Nonviolent Communication. The original work was created by Marshall Rosenberg, but I never actually quote him in my book. I may list him as a "work consulted" at the end of my book to honor his influence on my source material for the ideas I present.

With that said, you may not know at the outset what you'll actually cite and what you'll consult. I suggest you come up with a system of documenting all possible sources at the outset. You can do this in a few ways.

The minimum: Create a new "Works Cited and Consulted" document on your computer. Each time you locate a new reference source, at the very least, go into this document and list the **title** of the publication, the **name** of the creator or author, and any other important details that will *help you easily find* the source again (a URL, for example).

For example, if it's a podcast, note the title, episode number, creator, guest, date, and URL. Tracking these key elements for each source is beneficial because you are noting the minimum so you can find the source again, but you don't have to distract yourself by looking up the exact way to create a citation for it at the outset.

Full citations from the start: Second, you can commit to a style of citation right now, such as Chicago Manual of Style, which is most commonly used in non-fiction books. Create a new "Works Cited and Consulted" document on your computer, and make a full citation for every new source you are seriously considering using in your book. This is beneficial because you won't have to go back and scour the bookshelves or the internet for your source information later on.

APPENDIX D

Fair Use and Permissions

We could argue that "permissions" is a topic best considered during the post-drafting phase of your writing process, but it is good to be aware of these matters early on. This resource is intended to give you a basic understanding of what you are allowed to share from another's work so you can avoid problems like: 1) heavily leaning on and quoting another's work only to have to take it all out later because you can't get permissions, and 2) weaving beautiful song lyrics into your book that you'll also have to omit because of permissions issues. Here are the basics about fair use.

If a work is in the public domain (i.e., it was published before 1923), you do not need permission to cite. You also don't need permission if you are merely mentioning the title or author of a work, which is considered a statement of fact. Linking to someone else's work, like a blog or a website, also doesn't require permission. Generally, if you quote a sentence or two from another book, this is often considered fair use, and you don't need to get permission to quote the author.

Fair use is not a solid, clearly distinguished line, so this is where it gets a little tricky. I am not an intellectual property attorney, so I can't advise you with certainty about the fair use of any source materials. Some attorneys would tell you that no amount of quoting from another source guarantees fair use. I don't want to get too weedy here, though this is important. There are many good sources of additional information available on the internet if you want to explore this further.[1]

Note that the copyright for traditionally published books is held most often by the publisher (sometimes the agent), and not the author. So, if you do seek permission, you have to make your request (most often) of the *publisher*, not the author of the book. So even if your best friend published a book with Penguin, for example, it doesn't matter if your friend gives you their wholehearted permission: you have to get it from Penguin.

I ran into this author/publisher issue with my book. I wanted to quote five birth stories from a birth story anthology (i.e., many authors' stories were in a single book). I was thinking the whole time that I was quoting five different authors, so five different sources. But the copyright to all their stories was held by the anthology's publisher, so I was quoting more extensively from a single source. I determined, based on the total word count I was quoting divided by the total word count in the anthology, that I was using more than what is often considered fair use[2] (again, being a totally gray area). So, I did two things: I reduced how much I quoted the book, and I reached out and asked for permission from the publisher to use the quotes I chose. Publishers often want to know what you are quoting, how many words, and how you are using them. Be aware that they often charge a fee for use of their copyrighted materials. And they can take a while to get back to you (be aware of how it may impact your publishing deadlines).

In general, it is safer to summarize another's ideas in your work (giving credit) than to quote them word-for-word. Please note that sufficiently citing someone (giving them credit) is not the same as having *permission* to share their words or ideas in your book. (In other words, citation doesn't automatically establish fair use.) All said, don't let this scare you away from quotes altogether. Note that you have to get permission for self-published books, too.

A Note About Music Lyrics and Images

Music lyrics are notoriously difficult to get permission to include in your book unless they are in the public domain. Generally, it is best to avoid using lyrics in your writing. The same goes for quoting poetry written by another person. *I know.*

If you want to use photos, diagrams, cartoons, or other images in your book (including the cover) that you don't explicitly own, then you need to ensure you have licensed the image for the specific purpose, or that it is in the public domain.

APPENDIX E

How to Get Endorsements

Endorsements of your book are like social proof from reputable fellow authors who speak to the value and qualities of your book. They help to provide compelling evidence to your reader that your book is worth reading. Endorsements are ethos turbo-chargers.

Endorsements are also called blurbs or testimonials. These are generally placed on the front or back cover of a book, inside the book in the front matter, or on your author website. You can also use them in social media and other forms of marketing.

Another related but different request you may make of a fellow author is asking someone to write your Foreword. This is a shorter essay or chapter that comes before your body text (front matter) and is written by someone else who essentially endorses your book and adds value and perspective to its content.

Whom to Ask

This is a good time to send your Inner Critic out to grab coffee or an avocado toast for you. When it comes to endorsements, I invite you to think big: who are the biggest-name authors in your genre? Who do you really respect for their work in your topic area? Reach out to them.

You can also think about who is in your web—who do you know who has written a book in your genre that you could ask for an endorsement? Who is a friend of a friend that you may be connected to? Can your friend make an introduction for you (recommended!)?

While you may think someone like Brené Brown, Glennon Doyle, or Oprah (or fill in the blank with your big-timer) is totally out of your league, I'll tell you what: it *never* hurts to ask. At the very least, you have a reason to contact them to share what you are positively contributing in an area they are passionate about. You have an opportunity to connect and genuinely share your gratitude for their work, as well. This is a no-lose situation. But we need to keep the Inner Critic busy with her tasks.

Generally speaking, authors who've been on The New York Times bestseller list in the past year are in high demand and will be less likely to respond. Authors who were on the list many years ago, or who are top in your genre but never made the list, will likely be more accessible.

Just like with college applications, I suggest you select three to six people from whom you think securing an endorsement will be easy—these are people you know or are one-off from those you know. Then I suggest you select three to six people in the mid-range—well-known authors but not the celebrity status ones. Then I suggest you select three to six people who feel like the biggest and best names you can imagine gracing your pages with praise for your book. You can never have too many endorsements, so go higher on these numbers if you desire.

Believe it or not, when you ask professionally and respectfully, you'll likely receive positive responses from most authors you solicit. They have been where you are, they know how hard you have worked, and they appreciate your contributions to this topic area. You may receive nos because of timing, but it's unlikely that anyone will be annoyed that you ask (again, you have to ask well, which we'll cover soon).

When I wrote my book, I went out of my comfort zone and asked a midwife, herbalist, and multi-book bestseller (Aviva Romm) to not only write an endorsement but also my Foreword. And she said yes. And was super kind and gracious with me the whole time. She even invited me on her podcast.

The thing to remember is that endorsing your book is also a marketing strategy for them. They get exposure to your book audience by writing you an endorsement. So, it's a gift that gives back. They also have likely received endorsements from others, so it's about reciprocity, where all authors give and get back. Amen to reciprocity.

How to Contact Them

Contact information is nearly always available online for even the biggest authors. I suggest visiting their websites or social media pages and seeking contact information. You'd be surprised how many authors you can reach directly via direct social media messages or email (be professional and respectful of their space, of course). Even if you can't reach the author directly, you may reach their team members who are there to handle inquiries like this. I have worked with Aviva Romm and Brené Brown's teams, and they were all great experiences.

When to Contact Them

Begin to reach out to potential endorsers months before your book's publication date. Ideally, you'll have your manuscript through all developmental and copyediting, and if you can, all the way through the proofreading process. But it's okay to send out a manuscript that still needs minor edits. Just share the status of your manuscript with your endorser prospect.

Some authors want to wait until they have a designed, book-form copy in hand before soliciting endorsers. I did this with my book. But I found I needed to give my endorsers more time than I would have had if I had waited for galley copies to arrive. All the endorsers I solicited were totally fine receiving a Staples-bound, at-home printed copy of my book or an electronic PDF for review. The key is to give them enough time to review your manuscript.

It almost goes without saying that people are busy, so the more lead time you can give them, the better. That said, you can also give too much time. I'd say the sweet spot is anywhere from four to eight weeks, depending on the length of your manuscript and your timing needs.

I would definitely give more time than that for anyone you are soliciting to write your Foreword.

What to Say

It is super key for you to show up as a pro as you reach out to fellow authors for endorsements. You want to show up in a professional way (avoid spilling your life story or pleading for assistance). You also don't need to go into detail about how this is your first book and you're not sure how it's going to sell, etc. Put your most confident foot forward, remember all your hard work to get to this place, and embrace the author-with-a-valuable-book that you are. As much as you can, see yourself as equal to this person you're soliciting and honor yourself fully.

WHAT YOU APPRECIATE, APPRECIATES

There is great value in appreciation, in book endorsement requests, and in life. I'd begin any correspondence with a brief (you don't have to gush) appreciation for this author and how they have positively contributed value to your life in some way. You may mention their books or places you've seen them speak. You may talk about how their work has benefited you in some way. Appreciation works every time, and it's a way of giving before you ask for something.

NOTE PERSONAL CONNECTIONS

If you have a mutual friend or have met them in some capacity or attended their events, mention it. Personal connections can take you far, even in (and especially in) this digital age.

INTRODUCE YOUR BOOK IN A COMPELLING WAY

Next, clearly and succinctly state that you have a new book coming out, when it's due for release (approximate is fine; you can give the month or even the season), the title (if you have one), and a brief and compelling two to three sentences about your book.

MAKE THE ASK + MAKE IT EASY

Then, you make a clear and simple request for a testimonial, give your timeline for feedback, and ask for all the details you need to make this easy for your endorser. You may ask if they'd prefer to see the whole manuscript or just the Table of Contents and a sample. (Most endorsers will not read your book cover to cover.) Ask if they prefer to receive your book in hard or electronic copy. You may ask if there is anything else you can do to make this endorsement an easy and delightful experience for them. You can share what this endorsement would mean to you (be heartfelt and authentic, and also professional).

BONUS POINTS

You may also add any other big-name endorsements you've already secured ("You'll be in good company because Deepak Chopra has also agreed to provide an endorsement.") If you have a large following or strong platform, you may also mention this. ("My social media and mailing list combined reach over ten thousand people each week, we've built a solid marketing campaign for this book, and you're sure to gain some great exposure.") If you don't have this, no worries, just omit it.

WARM SIGN-OFF

You can sign off with your name, contact information, and web address (it shows you're a pro).

ACKNOWLEDGMENTS

I want to thank all of the authors, writers, creatives, and mentors I've been blessed to work with over my twenty-plus-year career in the writing field. Truly, it is one of my great joys of this lifetime to be able to walk with you as you usher your brave, creative voice into the world.

I want to thank all my clients from the early days of Whale Song—you were the reason this book was created. Thanks for helping me learn and gather all this wisdom together for the readers of this book, in this form.

I want to thank Jennifer Jas for her stellar proofreading support. Thank you to the Book Designers—it is an incredible joy to partner with you on this and many other books!

A special thank you to Adam Hardt—thank you for reaching across the veil, suggesting the last-minute title change, showing me this book cover, and championing my creativity as I had the brief blessing of championing yours. You are missed here. My hope is that your book is next. Thank you for writing it.

Thank you to my daughter and my dear kin—Kelsey, Quinn, Harmony, Emilie, Angharad, Caroline, Nikole, Lauren, Pete, Alex, Nick, Yvette, Darren, Paul, Mom, Dan, Mike—for inspiring me every day to express what I came here to express and to make an impact in my little corner of existence.

Thank you to my incredible team at Whale Song, Grace and Rachel (and perhaps more I haven't met yet!). I am so inspired by you and am so very grateful you are on team Whale Song. It is a tremendous joy and honor to work with you.

Thank you to the trees that make books possible; I love you, trees, thanks for sharing your bodies with us to make reading possible. You are a gift in infinite ways. (Yes, I am a person who thanks trees.)

Thank you to all those I forgot to thank but who live in my heart in infinite gratitude.

ABOUT THE AUTHOR

Jaime Fleres founded Whale Song Creative in 2017, two decades into a long career as a professional writer, author, and college professor of writing. She has been coaching, mentoring, editing, ghostwriting, offering book proposal support, guiding creatives, publishing books, and helping writers professionally since 2003.

She's worked with hundreds of writers of memoir, self-help and personal development, spiritual, and other nonfiction works.

Jaime is the author of *Birth Your Story: Why Writing About Your Birth Matters* (2017) and *Honor the Whole Planner* (2019, 2020, 2021, 2025), and has several works forthcoming. She has taught workshops on creativity online and around the world. She holds a bachelor's degree in Women's Studies and English and a master's degree in Rhetoric and Writing Studies, specializing in Teaching Writing, all from San Diego State University, where she graduated at the top of her class with honors.

In addition to her great love of books and authors, she is also a healer and deep diver into personal growth and spirituality. She is certified as an Integrative Somatic Trauma Practitioner, Shamanic Healing and Energy Medicine Practitioner, Shamanic Astrologer, sound healer, and certified Qoya and Yoga teacher. She guides others in narrative therapy processes, including her signature Heal a Story That Hurts program (book forthcoming). She has studied Internal Family Systems, herbalism and flower essences, ancestral healing, Nonviolent Communication, healthy relationships, deep imagery, Jungian psychology, soul-based depth counseling, and much, much more.

When she is not writing, helping others write, or practicing healing arts, she can be found with her daughter and their cat in Asheville, North Carolina, walking in the woods, sipping tea, dancing in the living room, making art, reading books, meditating, or enjoying a delicious taco or two.

NOTES

Chapter 3: Working with the Inner Critic

1. Steven Pressfield. *The War of Art: Break Through the Blocks and Win your Inner Creative Battles.* Black Irish Books, 2002.
2. Sara Avant Stover. *The Book of She.* New World Library, 2015.
3. Hal and Sidra Stone. *Embracing Your Inner Critic: Turning Self-Criticism into a Creative Asset.* HarperOne, 1993.
4. Jaime Fleres. *Soma: Online Somatic Healing Course.* At SacredHeartHealingArts.com/soma/

FURTHER RESOURCES

- Read: Steven Pressfield's *The War of Art*, *Do the Work*, or *Turning Pro*
- Read: Tara Mohr's *Playing Big.* Avery, 2015.
- Read: Anne Lamott's *Bird by Bird.* Vintage, 1995.
- Watch: Brené Brown's talk "Why the Critics Aren't the Ones Who Count," https://vimeo.com/78769611
- Watch: "Your Inner Critic Is a Big Jerk" by Danielle Krysa (YouTube), https://www.youtube.com/watch?v=-3dEkLpeSZc
- Watch: "This Talk Isn't Very Good. Dancing with My Inner Critic" by Steve Chapman, https://www.youtube.com/watch?v=lnf-Ka3ZmOM
- Watch: "Understanding Our Inner Critic - Esther Perel & Dick Schwartz" on YouTube, https://www.youtube.com/watch?v=-NUKMNgJB_kw&list=PL-vH9r-QDUXMDm6O_XLu9_GnDmW7FgSH7&index=4

Chapter 4: Activating your Inner Genius

1. Elizabeth Gilbert. *Big Magic: Creative Living Beyond Fear.* Penguin, 2016.
2. *Creative Cross Training* is another form of creative expression you

might engage in as an author that helps you get into the flow and energetic current of what wants to move through you and into expression. It can help you keep the energy going for your book project to engage in other forms of creativity, and can also help you get unstuck. Examples include painting, dancing, pottery, drawing, gardening, and so on.

Chapter 10: Frameworks for Nonfiction

1. Cissi Williams. *Your Heart Knows How to Heal You: The Sacred Medicine of the Four Chambers of the Heart*. Findhorn Press, 2025.
2. John Gottman and Nan Silver. *The Seven Principles for Making Marriage Work: A Practical Guide from the Country's Foremost Relationship Expert*. Harmony, 2015.
3. Barbara Stanny. *The Secrets of Six-Figure Women: Surprising Strategies to Up Your Earnings and Change Your Life*. HarperCollins, 2004.
4. Hilary Hart. *The Unknown She: Eight Faces of an Emerging Consciousness*. The Golden Sufi Center, 2003.
5. Eleanor Henderson and Anna Solomon. *Labor Day: True Birth Stories by Today's Best Women Writers*. Farrar, Straus and Giroux. 2014.

Chapter 11: Frameworks for Memoir

1. Glennon Doyle Melton. *Love Warrior*. Flatiron, 2017.
2. Cheryl Strayed. *Wild: From Lost to Found on the Pacific Coast Trail*. Vintage, 2013.
3. Elizabeth Gilbert. *Eat, Pray, Love: One Woman's Search for Everything Across Italy, India and Indonesia*. Riverhead Books, 2007.
4. Sophie Strand. *The Body is a Doorway: A Memoir: A Journey Beyond Healing, Hope, and the Human*. Running Press, 2025.
- See also Marion Roach Smith's work, including her book *The Memoir Project: A Thoroughly Non-Standardized Text for Writing and Life*. Grand Central Publishing, 2011. As well as this article: https://marionroach.com/2018/01/how-to-choose-your-memoirs-structure/

Chapter 12: Story-Based Frameworks

1. Aristotle. *Poetics*. https://classics.mit.edu/Aristotle/poetics.1.1.html
2. Quintus Horatius Flaccus. *Ars Poetic*. https://www.poetryfoundation.org/articles/69381/ars-poetica
3. Maureen Murdock. *The Heroine's Journey: Woman's Quest for Wholeness*. Shambhala, 1990.
4. Sara Avant Stover. *The Book of She: Your Heroine's Journey into the Heart of Feminine Power*. New World Library, 2015.
5. LiYana Silver. *Feminine Genius: The Provocative Path to Waking Up and Turning On the Wisdom of Being a Woman*. Sounds True, 2017.
6. Heather Jo Flores. "How to Write a Heroine's Journey: Toward an Ecofeminist Storycraft." heatherjoflores.com, 2014.
7. Joseph Campbell. *The Hero with a Thousand Faces*. New World Library, 2008. (originally published in 1949).
8. Catherine Bailey. "The Heroine's Journey," *The Hilltop Review*: Vol. 5: Iss. 2, Article 8. 2012. https://scholarworks.wmich.edu/hilltopreview/vol5/iss2/8

Chapter 15: Fitting a Book Into Your Life

- Read about Elizabeth Gilbert's writing life: https://www.thedailybeast.com/elizabeth-gilbert-how-i-write
- Watch Cheryl Strayed talk about her writing life: https://www.marieforleo.com/2017/02/cheryl-strayed/
- Watch Robin Sharma talk about the practices of world-class creatives: https://www.marieforleo.com/2020/04/robin-sharma-5am-club/?uid=c9534879df48a6be21523358876328b7
- Read books like James Clear's *Atomic Habits: An Easy & Proven Way to Build Good Habits & Break Bad Ones*. Avery, 2018.

Chapter 19: Chapter Structure

1. Sophie Strand. *The Body is a Doorway: A Memoir: A Journey Beyond Healing, Hope, and the Human*. Running Press, 2025.

Chapter 23: Summarizing, Quoting, and Transitions

- All scripts in this chapter come from this book: Gerald Graff and Cathy Birkenstein. *They Say, I Say: The Moves that Matter in Academic Writing*. 2nd Editing. W.W. Norton & Company, 2010.
1. Nicolas Kristoff and Sheryl WuDunn. *Half the Sky: Turning Oppression into Opportunity for Women*. Vintage, 2010.

Chapter 24: Scenes and Summaries in Stories

1. Michael Crichton. *Travels*. Vintage, 2014.

Chapter 25: Layers of a Story

1. Clarisa Pinkola Estés. *Women Who Run with Wolves: Myths and Stories of the Wild Woman Archetype*. Ballantine, 1996.

Chapter 26: Dialogue and Beats

1. Anne Lamott. *Bird by Bird: Some Instructions on Writing and Life*. Random House, 1994.
2. Sarah J. Maas. *A Court of Silver Flames*. Bloomsbury, 2021.

Chapter 28: Self-Editing Best Practices

1. Adam Grant. *Originals: How Non-Conformists Change the World*. Penguin, 2017.

Chapter 30: Revision

1. This article explores commonly used redundant phrases in writing: https://www.thoughtco.com/common-redundancies-in-english-1692776

Chapter 32: Refinement

1. Surely AI tools exist to help you with editing and any number of other things. I personally don't use AI, and have concerns about its impact on human creatives, so I am not mentioning any AI tools purposefully here.

Chapter 33: Final Polishing

1. William Strunk Jr. and E.B. White. *The Elements of Style. Ed 4.* Pearson, 1999.
- The *Chicago Manual of Style. Ed 18* University of Chicago Press, 2024.
- Gerald Graff and Cathy Birkenstein. *They Say, I Say: The Moves that Matter in Academic Writing.* 2nd Editing. W.W. Norton & Company, 2010.
- Renni Browne and Dave King. *Self-Editing for Fiction Writers: How to Edit Yourself Into Print.* William Morrow Paperbacks, 2004.

Chapter 37: Exploring Your Publishing Options

1. https://publishdrive.com/what-is-the-typical-royalty-rate-for-an-author.html

Chapter 38: Publishing: Key Factors to Consider

1. Grammar Factory, "Will a book really boost your business? The cold, hard stats," https://grammarfactory.com/self-publishing/boost-your-business-cold-hard-stats/. Accessed June 2025.

Chapter 39: Traditional Publishing Path

1. Consult any of the following to find an agent:
   - Books such as *Guide to Literary Agents* or *Writer's Market*, or the like
   - Agent directory websites, such as Agent Query, Publishing Marketplace, PW, Query Tracker, and Duo Trope (best for poetry, short stories, essays, and literary novels)

Appendix D: Fair Use and Permissions

1. Further information: http://www.copylaw.org/2013/12/12-copyright-permission-myths.html, https://www.janefriedman.com/the-fair-use-doctrine/, and https://www.morse.law/news/writers-guide-to-fair-use
2. Some consider fair use to be less than 10 percent of the total word count of a source document, or less than 250 words for a full-length book reference. Again (and again), clear percentages and word counts are not written into law; it's much more complex. Some legal rulings have declared that less than 1 percent use is unlawful, while others have upheld fair use for nearly 100 percent of a source used.

Other Recommended Books

- Julia Cameron. *The Artist's Way: A Spiritual Path to Higher Creativity*. Penguin, 1992.
- Louise DeSalvo. *Writing as a Way of Healing: How Telling Our Stories Transforms our Lives*. Beacon Press, 1999.
- Carl Greer. *Change your Story, Change your Life*. Findhorn Press, 2014.
- Kelly Notaras. *The Book You Were Born to Write*. Hay House, 2018.
- Steven Pressfield. *The War of Art*, *Do the Work*, and *Turning Pro*. Black Irish Entertainment, 2002, 2011, 2012.
- Jody Rein and Michael Larsen. *How to Write a Book Proposal, 5th edition*. Writer's Digest, 2017.
- Marion Roach Smith. *The Memoir Project: A Thoroughly Non-Standardized Text for Writing & Life*. Grand Central Publishing, 2019.
- For more, please visit our website at JaimeFleres.com.

INVITATION FOR WRITING SUPPORT

If you are seeking additional support in your writing, editing, and publishing adventures, please visit Whale Song Creative at JaimeFleres.com for further information. There you can find a list of our services, a blog full of additional articles, free resources, and much more. We offer book coaching, all levels of editing, book proposal writing and editing support, self-publishing partnership, and marketing support, not to mention courses, group programs, and retreats too!

About Whale Song

Whale Song is a high-touch boutique creative agency specializing in helping visionary change agents write transformational nonfiction books. We show creative professionals on a mission how to write the book that can only be born through them. We help people express themselves—authentically, creatively, and powerfully—through writing to make a meaningful contribution to themselves and the world.

As a company, we are champions of soulful artists and transformational change agents.

We are the team to come to if you want real, deep, human-to-human support, stellar professional book support services, and devoted partners on the path to further your own soul calling. Our attention to detail and client experience is unparalleled. We are blessed by the relationships we build with our clients and community.

We are client advocates who value healthy relationships, strive for clear communication, and act in alignment with our integrity. We build trust and provide exceptional client experiences. We want people to feel relieved and overjoyed that they found us.

HERE ARE SOME OF OUR CLIENTS' WORDS ABOUT OUR WORK TOGETHER:

"I started writing my book ten years ago but was never able to finish it. Then I found Jaime. The biggest benefit I received from working with her was her ability to hold space for me as I talked through my challenges. So many coaches want you to "cut to the chase" and say what you need to say as succinctly as possible, but I don't actually know what's in my head unless I talk it out.

The biggest breakthrough came when I finally realized that the book I thought I was supposed to write wasn't the book that wanted to be written. I would never have gotten to that awareness without Jaime's gentle guidance and encouragement. I swim in pretty deep water, and Jaime was totally able to meet me there."

—SHANNON PRESSON

"Working with Jaime was hands-down THE best decision I ever made for my book. My manuscript is exponentially better since Jaime edited it. Her gifts of clarity, insight, wisdom, & compassion made the editing process a celebration. Her support and encouragement allowed me to fully embrace and deeply step into my gifts as a storyteller and writer. I would without hesitation recommend her to any author looking for an editor and guide. I am already excited to write my next book just so I can hire Jaime again."

—KYLE NICOLAIDES

author of *Thank God for Depression* and *Thank God for Anxiety*

"From the outset, Jaime became 100 percent invested in my project and coached me from my raw manuscript to a polished, published book. I am a first-time author with ZERO experience in editing, formatting, or publishing. She is an expert on every aspect of the process required to guide you through to success, and she has the connections to get it done quickly. Look no further, you have found in Jaime a caring, brilliant partner. She's a true professional. I will not write another book without having Jaime on my team."

—JAY ADAMS

coauthor of *Lions of Wall Street*

www.ingramcontent.com/pod-product-compliance
Lightning Source LLC
Chambersburg PA
CBHW060539010526
44119CB00053B/761